W9-CKG-946

WITHDRAWN

ACCIDENTAL ENCOUNTERS

ACCIDENTAL ENCOUNTERS

GEORGE FRIESEN

Copyright © 2018 by George Friesen.

Library of Congress Control Number: 2018904938
ISBN: Hardcover 978-1-9845-2263-4
Softcover 978-1-9845-2262-7
eBook 978-1-9845-2264-1

All rights reserved. No part of this book may be reproduced or transmitted in any form or by any means, electronic or mechanical, including photocopying, recording, or by any information storage and retrieval system, without permission in writing from the copyright owner.

This is a work of fiction. Names, characters, places and incidents either are the product of the author's imagination or are used fictitiously, and any resemblance to any actual persons, living or dead, events, or locales is entirely coincidental.

Any people depicted in stock imagery provided by Getty Images are models, and such images are being used for illustrative purposes only.
Certain stock imagery © Getty Images.

Print information available on the last page.

Rev. date: 05/31/2018

To order additional copies of this book, contact:
Xlibris
1-888-795-4274
www.Xlibris.com
Orders@Xlibris.com
777778

CONTENTS

To Connie

Hell isn't merely paved with good intentions; it's walled and roofed with them. Yes, and furnished too.

---ALDOUS HUXLEY, *The Collected Works (1953)*

All things to be truly wicked must start from an innocence.

--ERNEST HEMINGWAY, *A Moveable Feast: The Restored Edition (2010)*

Acknowledgements

The initial idea for this novel occurred to me during an Aegean Sea cruise with my family. Syrian refugees huddling on the docks in Rhodes, a tramp steamer boarded by the Greek Coast Guard, furtive drug sales on the streets of Istanbul and a slide toward authoritarianism in Turkey stirred my imagination. After my return home, new perspectives were added by my attendance at a lecture on the violent drug scene in Mexico; the indictment by the US Department of Justice of a major European bank for money laundering; a revelation by a friend of his troubled relationship with a brother which was impeding settlement of an inheritance; and the death of a television celebrity from an overdose of drugs. These separate strands began to weave themselves into a story.

While real events provided the impetus for this novel, it is a work of fiction. The main characters in this novel are products of my imagination and any resemblance to real individuals is coincidental. In my research on the international drug trade, I did not find evidence of an attempt to create a trans-Atlantic alliance of drug gangs. That too is fictional. However, that does not mean such an alliance is impossible or will never be attempted.

Many individuals have contributed to the successful completion of this novel and not all of them can be listed here. Andrew, Bryan, Jill and Emily have read all or part of this book and made constructive comments but I bear sole responsibility for how their advice was applied. I appreciate the dedicated efforts of the staff at Xlibris, including Fatimah, Cheryl and Shane, in helping me to achieve my goal. Special thanks, of course, go to my wife, Connie, whose encouragement and support for this project has never wavered.

Introduction

The Road to Hell

Chapter One

Appearances can deceive. A bright sun in a cloudless sky had ushered in a perfect day for a wedding at the cathedral in Morelia. The cream of Mexican society was assembled to witness the marriage of the governor's niece to the handsome scion of a wealthy businessman. The chords of a wedding march soared joyfully from the massive pipe organ, the largest of its kind in Mexico, as the father of the bride escorted his daughter—dressed in an elegant white dress that accentuated her slender figure and long dark hair—down the aisle to the altar, where the groom was waiting.

Every detail of the celebration was flawless except for the timing. Right place but wrong time. Ten minutes into the service, the voice of the officiating priest was interrupted by a loud shout.

"Sit down if you want to live!" The harsh and powerful voice echoed in the vast stillness of the cathedral. Pushing aside the priest and the wedding couple in front of the altar, the masked man aimed his gun at the man in the front pew. The visibly shaken governor of the Mexican state of Michoacán complied hastily.

"You asked who we are. We are Los Zetas. No one trifles with us. We do not believe in an eye for an eye, a tooth for a tooth. For every eye that we lose, we take ten."

A collective shudder passed through the wedding guests who, only minutes before, had chatted happily about how the young couple seemed ideally matched for each other.

"But why?" gasped the totally bewildered governor. He could not understand why a drug cartel whose stronghold was on the Gulf coast should have launched a daring raid on the west coast of the country—and not against a rival gang but against members of high society. This outrage was unprecedented in the drug wars that were devastating parts of Mexico.

Brandishing his gun for emphasis, the terrorist shouted, "Listen to me! We have seized the cathedral in Morelia to retaliate for the recent kidnapping of a Turkish businessman and the murder of his associate in Veracruz. The criminals—the Knights Templar, who hail from this state—still go unpunished because you are protecting them!"

He jabbed the index finger of his left hand accusingly at the governor.

El Verdugo ("The Executioner," for that was how Heriberto Lazcano was known within his cartel) glanced at the television crew, which had initially gathered outside the cathedral to record the arrival of the state governor and other leading citizens. Now they had been admitted into the cathedral to record a more dramatic event.

He gazed directly into the television cameras. "We have a message for the Mexican government and the nation. Until Demir Ozmen is released, hostages chosen at random will be shot daily and thrown outside onto the steps of the cathedral. If the federal or state governments attempt to take the cathedral by force, we will use explosives to destroy this building and everyone in it."

An incredulous murmur rippled over the congregation.

"Please, young man, reconsider your action!" The elderly priest, Father Antonio Cardozo, moved cautiously toward the gunman, speaking so softly that it was almost a whisper. "This is the house of God. Do not commit sacrilege. Whatever your quarrel with the governor may be, do not harm this innocent young couple and the people who have come here to celebrate their marriage. In God's name, let them go!"

The gang leader bared his teeth and snarled, "Do not provoke me, priest! One more word out of you and you will be the first to die!"

The sobbing of the bride became uncontrollable. She collapsed into the arms of the bridegroom.

The gang leader glared at the governor. "We do not want to destroy the happiness of this young couple. If you use your phone to persuade your cronies in the Knights Templar to release the Turk, all of you will be free."

The ashen-faced governor whispered, "I will do what I can." But he did not feel confident. Being called the protector of the Knights Templar was wildly inaccurate. At worst, he had ignored their criminal activities because he was powerless to break their organization. Where was this madman getting his information? Yet he had to do something. He was friendly with some local businessmen who were alleged to have contacts in the Knights Templar organization, but would these indirect contacts suffice? He turned toward the weeping bride, his eyes begging for forgiveness.

Lazcano's eyes swept over the elaborate baroque and neoclassical interior of the cathedral, including the sculpture of Christ. He was not overawed by his surroundings. Religion had never been a part of his life, even as a boy. He had no religious scruples. For him, all power flowed from the barrel of a gun. He spat into the chalice on the altar and placed his weapon next to it, smiling with satisfaction as he heard the shocked exclamations of the wedding guests.

Despite the potential risks, he and his men had managed to seize the cathedral without firing a shot or incurring casualties. Because the bride was the niece of the governor of the state of Michoacán, it had been widely reported in the media that he, accompanied by senior government officials, would be attending. The governor had presented an irresistible target. The curious spectators and well-wishers had been oblivious to a dozen young men—grim, tense, and armed—who blended into the crowd.

Suddenly, Lazcano stiffened. He heard the plaintive cry of a child. Out of the corner of his eye, he noticed movement in the shadows. One of the hostages was disobeying his order to remain seated. He saw the priest holding a young girl by the hand, advancing toward him. He reached for his gun.

Father Cardozo knew that it would be dangerous to ignore this hothead's commands, but even in a crisis, children had to go to the toilet. The child's mother had appealed to him. Surely, the gunman would be reasonable. He saw the gunman pick up the weapon that he had placed on the altar.

"Stop where you are!" shouted Lazcano. "Look, priest. I have warned you before. Do I have to put a bullet in your head to make my point?" He fired over the heads of the wedding guests, the bullet embedding itself in the rear wall of the cathedral. The sound of the shot reverberated.

Shrieking with terror and holding her hands over her ears, the girl ran back to her mother. The priest did not move. "Please. This girl needs to go to the toilet."

"She can wait."

"Only if you expect this crisis to be over in the next hour. If God is willing, it can happen. But perhaps we should plan for a longer duration." The priest spoke firmly. In his experience, miracles were rare, even if one prayed long and hard.

Lazcano considered the request. Under his most optimistic assumptions, the crisis would be over in hours. He shouted to the governor, who had been on his phone continuously for the last hour. "How much longer will this take?"

The governor called back, "The head of the state security administration is calling everyone who might know about the kidnapped Turk. This could take a long time."

Lazcano looked at the priest and then at the wedding guests huddled near the front of the cathedral. Hundreds of them. What if the hostage crisis dragged on for one day, even two? His plans to seize the cathedral had not taken into account the mundane details of how to care for the hostages. Grudgingly, he conceded the priest's request that hostages in groups of four would be permitted to use the toilets under escort. Five minutes, no more.

As the hours crawled by, the hostages coped as best they could—by sleeping, engaging in whispered conversations, and keeping their heads down. None of them wanted to be the first hostage selected at random to be shot if the crisis dragged on.

Except for one. Fernando Velasquez was willing to risk his life in attempting to escape. He was troubled by thoughts of his very sick wife and the two small children who would totally depend on him if she died. He also needed to get back to Mexico City to protect his job as general counsel at Europa Bank. Earlier in the week, the branch manager and he had met with an American lawyer, David Bigelow, who had been hired by the US Department of Justice to investigate serious lapses in anti–money laundering practices at the bank. He knew that the branch manager would be looking for a scapegoat, and he feared that it would be him.

As the late afternoon light inside the cathedral began to fade, the priest noticed that the tall businessman, with whom he had exchanged a few words, had not returned from his toilet break.

Lazcano had also noticed the absence of Velasquez. He beckoned one of his lieutenants who, after a brief consultation, walked quickly in the direction of the toilets. Moments later, there was a flurry of activity. Guards who had previously stayed in the background now paced up and down the aisles, their guns ready to fire. Other guards began to inspect the nave for the missing hostage, then widened their search to the towers and the crypt below the nave.

The missing hostage was found hiding in a closet behind the vestments of the cathedral choir. Two husky guards dumped Velasquez at the feet of Lazcano. Blood flowed from his nose and from gashes on his forehead. His suit coat was ripped and soiled. His eyes were closed, and his mouth gaped open.

Lazcano turned toward the hostages, who watched wide-eyed with fear. "We have treated you leniently, and this is our reward. Now let this be a lesson to you. Anyone who tries to escape will be shot like a dog." He pointed his gun at Velasquez.

"Wait!" pleaded the priest as he moved toward Lazcano. "I beg you to have mercy. This man tried to escape because he loved his family."

"The time for mercy is past."

"In God's name, no quarrel is worth the life of this man. Take my life and spare his. I am an old man nearing the end of my life. He still has reason to live."

Lazcano sneered at the priest, "So you want to be a martyr?" Turning to his guards, he ordered, "Take this meddlesome priest away. I will deal with him tomorrow."

He pointed his gun once more at the head of Velasquez and pulled the trigger.

Chapter Two

Dave Bigelow was unaware of the hostage crisis until he strode into the lobby of the Four Seasons Hotel in Mexico City. He had been tied up with meetings at Europa Bank all afternoon, investigating breaches of US anti–money laundering laws. The lobby would normally have been filled with guests or visitors sitting at tables and enjoying afternoon tea or cocktails in the hushed grandeur of its lobby. He looked in the direction of the concierge desk. He needed a reservation at an authentic Mexican restaurant tonight, but no one was there. Instead a crowd had gathered in a corner of the lobby in front of a flat-screen television.

He did not need to wait long. The concierge returned to her desk, apologizing for her absence. There had been a horrifying development—the seizure of the cathedral in Morelia by a terrorist gang—that had caught the attention of guests and staff alike. Many lives were at risk. The terrorists wanted the release of a Turk kidnapped by a drug gang. She shook her head as if mystified by this madness.

Within minutes, she had come up with a recommendation—a restaurant not far from the hotel, which was very popular with locals and tourists alike. She would call to make the reservation for five people at seven o'clock. She wrote the address on a piece of paper and handed it to him.

A wave of gasps from the crowd assembled in front of the television rolled across the lobby. Dave walked over to see what was happening. The doors of the cathedral had opened. Two hooded men appeared, brandishing guns, and were followed by gang members carrying the body of a tall man dressed in a business suit, whom they dumped onto the front steps of the cathedral.

The hostage crisis had claimed its first victim, but Dave felt emotionally detached from what he was seeing on the screen. Terrorist violence was common fare on television and the internet. He had also witnessed the collapse of the twin towers from his office in downtown Manhattan on that fateful September 11. Nothing could compare to that horror. He returned to the concierge's desk and asked if she would please confirm his flight back to New York the next morning.

As he walked toward the hotel elevators, he automatically checked his emails. Still no response from his brother. Whatever Bob was up to, he could surely take a few seconds to reply to his query. That would be simple courtesy. But then Dave brushed away the mild irritation that he felt. Why should he expect more from his ungrateful brother?

Before he could get on the elevator, an outcry from the crowd in front of the television set rekindled his curiosity. He retraced his steps.

A woman standing next to him spoke to him in English. "The victim has been identified. He is Fernando Velasquez, an executive at Europa Bank."

Dave was shocked. He stammered, "You-you mean the general counsel at Europa Bank?" He had met with the man only two days ago.

Chapter Three

At midday, Bob Bigelow, sitting in his room at the W Hotel in Mexico City, was flicking through the channels on his television set to relieve his boredom. He stopped at Channel Five. He was fluent enough in Spanish to understand what was being reported—the anxious faces of relatives and spectators gathered in the plaza in front of the cathedral in Morelia and the strutting masked spokesman for the terrorists who demanded the release of a Demir Ozmen in return for the safety of the hostages.

He pursed his lips in surprise. Had he heard the name "Demir Ozmen" correctly? What in the hell was going on? He listened intently. Again he heard the name: Demir Ozmen. The man whom he had come to Mexico City to ransom was now the cause of a mass hostage-taking in Morelia? He could not believe his ears. He eased back in his chair and muted the television. What had he gotten himself into?

He waited tensely for the call, which had not come as expected precisely at twelve noon. As the minutes slipped by, he checked his emails for new messages, once again ignoring the query from his brother Dave. Was Dave right in thinking that he had seen him near the entrance to Europa Bank on the Paseo de la Reforma in Mexico City on Wednesday? He had just arrived from the airport and could have sworn that he had seen Bob exiting the bank. Responding to that question would only raise more awkward questions, for which he had no time. He had enough troubles to deal with.

He paced the floor nervously. Several times he pulled his briefcase from underneath the bed to check whether the ransom money was still there and had not disappeared mysteriously while the maid had cleaned his room. A poor night's sleep and now these new developments in Morelia had rattled him. Was his mission beginning to spin out of control?

The call, when it finally came, was thirty minutes late. It was from an unidentified caller. At first, there was no response to his greeting, but after a pause of ten seconds came the question: "Are you alone?"

"Yes," answered Bob. He waited for the caller—who spoke English with an unmistakable Mexican accent—to introduce himself.

"I am Pedro Guerra. We have Demir Ozmen."

Bob breathed a sigh of relief. This was the man that his boss in New York, Recep Murat, had said would be calling him. "How is he?"

"He is okay. He is worth something to us only if he is alive."

"To which group do you belong—Knights Templar or Los Matas Zetas?" Bob wanted to clear up the confusion over which gang had actually kidnapped Ozmen.

"It is not necessary for you to know that."

"But how do I know that you really have Ozmen?"

"I have a message for the president of your company. If the exchange of five million dollars in cash for the prisoner goes smoothly, El Chapo will be contacting him directly, as he requested, about a long-term business relationship."

That reassured Bob. He recalled the recent teleconference in Murat's office shortly before his departure for Mexico City. Emir and Omer Tilki, the owners of the company in Istanbul, had expressed an interest in using the ransom negotiations to explore working with a different Mexican cartel than the one they had linked up with.

"What's your connection to what is going on in Morelia?"

"You mean the seizure of the cathedral? None whatsoever. I have only news reports of who is responsible, but they do not belong to us."

"So what do you want me to do?"

"The police and military are on high alert in Mexico City. If you are under observation, they may try to follow you and spring a trap. Therefore, we must take precautions."

"But I have been very careful," protested Bob.

The caller cut him off. "Do as I say. Tonight you will eat dinner at a nearby Mexican restaurant, Villa Maria. A table has been reserved for you on the second floor for 6:30 p.m. At precisely 8:00 p.m., get up and walk to the back of the dining room as if you are going to the men's room. Instead, take the back stairs to ground level and go through the exit door to the back alley, where a black BMW will be waiting. Ask the driver for directions to the Sanatorio Español because you are not feeling well. His reply should be 'I will take you there.' You get into the car, and he will take you to a destination where you will turn over the agreed ransom."

"You will be releasing Demir Ozmen to me at that time?"

"You will be dealing with my men. I will be watching you, but you will not see me. The Turk will be freed as soon as we have confirmed that the conditions for his release have been met."

Bob did not like the sound of those words. "But how can I be sure that you are keeping your end of the bargain?"

"What choice do you have? Do as I say or you will never see Ozmen again." The caller hung up abruptly.

Bob walked to the window of his hotel room to peer out, wondering what he should do next. There was no unusual police activity in the busy street scene below, but appearances could be deceptive. Were his movements being watched? Growing up in an affluent Connecticut suburb had not prepared him for dealing with murderous Mexican kidnappers or scheming Turkish drug dealers. What guarantee did he have that he would not be mugged and shot by the driver who picked him up behind Villa Maria? He thought about calling Recep Murat, but that would be pointless. He was on his own.

Except that he was not entirely on his own. There was Miguel Rodriguez, the DEA agent in Mexico City. He picked up his phone and called the number that he had memorized.

"I have been waiting for your call," said Rodriguez. "Have the kidnappers contacted you?"

"Yes, a few minutes ago. But I don't like the plans for tonight. I need some backup." Bob described the instructions that he had been given. "Can you provide me with some protection in case I need help?"

"I can arrange to have two police cars parked near the exit from the back alley behind the Villa Maria. They will follow the BMW after you have been picked up. Do you have a locator app on your mobile phone?"

"What do you mean?"

"It is an app that you download so that your movements can be traced. Parents like to use it to keep track of their children. Try Mama Bear. Google discontinued support for its Latitude app last month. Take care of it this afternoon and keep your phone on at all times tonight."

"Did the man who called you this afternoon identify himself or his organization?"

"He introduced himself as Pedro Guerra, but he was vague about which gang he belongs to. He referred to El Chapo—whoever in the hell he is—contacting the president of Ottoman Trading Company if the Ozmen deal went through."

Rodriguez seemed surprised. "You do not know who El Chapo is? That's the nickname of Joaquin Guzman, the head of the Sinaloa Cartel."

"So who carried out the kidnapping?"

"The Los Zetas gang that has seized control of the cathedral seems to think it was the Knights Templar. But my sources indicate that it could have been Los Matas Zetas, rivals of the Knights Templar. It is complicated, but both are allies of the Sinaloa Cartel, which uses them as violent enforcers against Los Zetas."

These arcane references to Mexican drug gangs bewildered Bob. "You mean the seizure of the cathedral could be a big mistake, directed against the wrong party?"

"Possible, even likely," answered Rodriguez. "Those hostages in Morelia are depending on you, even if they do not know it. If you can free Ozmen and show his face in public, the hostage crisis should be over, and you will be a hero."

"And if I screw up?" asked Bob.

"Los Zetas has no scruples about killing civilians. A lot of innocent lives could be lost."

Chapter Four

When Bob Bigelow arrived at Villa Maria, the restaurant was already boisterous with mariachi music and a large clientele, even though the dinner hour was early by Mexican standards. He waited at the reception desk for the jefe de sala to arrive.

"Senor, you have a reservation?"

"Yes, at 6:30 p.m., for a party of one on the second floor. My name is Bigelow." Bob spelled his name.

"I have a reservation here for a party of five at 7:00 p.m. under the name of Bigelow. The Four Seasons Hotel called an hour ago to make the reservation."

"No, there must be a mistake. I did not make the reservation personally. My . . . uh . . . secretary called this morning to reserve the table."

"Ah, pardon my confusion, senor. I see it now. Please follow me. I will introduce you to your waiter. Would you like to check your briefcase?"

"No, thank you. I prefer to keep it with me," said Bob, clutching the handle of his briefcase more tightly.

"As you wish."

At the foot of the stairs, a smiling waiter was ready to take him to his table on the second floor. Soon he was seated and poring over the menu. His stomach was churning nervously, and he considered not ordering a main course but ultimately decided in favor of a margarita and grilled red snapper served on a bed of rice. He remembered to tell the waiter that he had to leave at 8:00 p.m. and was assured that he would get his food and the bill promptly.

Within minutes, a cocktail waitress in a short body-clinging dress approached his table carrying his margarita. Despite her bleached blond hair, she was strikingly attractive. "My name is Marizol," she spoke softly, her eyes dwelling on him. "Enjoy your evening, senor."

Normally, Bob would have given her an appreciative response. But tonight, he was tense and focused. The stakes were too high. He recalled one of his father's favorite sayings: "The road to hell is paved with good intentions and well-laid plans that go awry."

Knock on wood, he thought as he tapped his knuckles against the table.

He removed his phone from the inside of his suit jacket for an incoming call. It was Rodriguez again. By now, the noise of the music and the voices of many diners speaking at the same time had become a roar. He bent over his table, trying to make out what Rodriguez was saying. He heard snatches of sentences: "Hostage in Morelia killed . . . Cars waiting outside to follow you . . . Any change in your plans?"

Looking up to make sure that the waitress was no longer standing by his table, Bob raised his voice to make himself heard. "Hostage killed?" He had not checked on the hostage crisis before leaving his hotel. "Who was it?"

"Fernando Velasquez. A prominent Mexican businessman."

Bob sucked in his breath and remained silent, then remembered he had not answered Rodriguez's question. "No, no change in plans. Pedro Guerra has not called again."

"Bueno. Call me if he does."

When the call ended, Bob placed his phone on the table. He wanted to make sure that he would be able to pick it up quickly if necessary. Unfortunately for Bob, he was unaware that while he was talking to Rodriguez, a waiter had ushered a group of five men to their table only twenty feet away. If his food had not arrived at that point, he might usefully have spent a few minutes surveying the diners at nearby tables so that he would have been able to choose his escape route.

Instead he was eating his grilled red snapper with renewed gusto. Despite the jarring news about the hostage, his stomach had settled, and he had not eaten much since breakfast. As fate would have it, the path that led from the adjacent tables to the men's washroom passed by Bob.

"Well, I'll be damned!" exclaimed Dave Bigelow. "Bob, what are you doing in Mexico City? I could have sworn I saw you on Wednesday afternoon. Now I know I wasn't hallucinating after all."

Bob swallowed his food carefully to avoid choking. His heart sank as he mustered a smile for his brother. "Hello, Dave. Fancy meeting you here. Small world, isn't it?"

"Didn't you get my email? I sent you an email the day before yesterday asking whether you were in Mexico City. When you didn't respond, I concluded that I was imagining things. You've been on my mind a lot lately."

Bob shook his head in denial. "I didn't get it. Maybe it went into spam. You know how unreliable email can be sometimes."

"You're here on business? I can't help noticing your large briefcase. What business can be important enough to keep you on a Friday night in Mexico City? Nobody does important business this late."

Bob evaded the second question but answered the first. "Yes, I'm here on business. And you?"

"The same. I am involved in a major project monitoring a European bank. They were fined by the Department of Justice for laundering money on behalf of Mexican drug cartels, among other things."

"No kidding." Bob tried to keep his voice as bland as possible. It was so like Dave to puff up his feathers about some damn project of his.

"Would you like to join us?" asked Dave, pointing in the direction of his table. "My buddies—Jeff Braunstein and three auditors on our team—and I are enjoying our last night here before we fly home tomorrow. We wanted an authentic Mexican night out, and this is the restaurant that our hotel recommended. Strange coincidence that we should choose the same restaurant."

"Another of life's ironies," said Bob mockingly. "You were always the philosopher, trying to figure out whether our lives are predetermined or shaped by random events. But let's not get into that. The short answer to your question is that I can't because I have to leave at 8:00 p.m."

"When the evening is still young? Well, let me at least buy you a drink. What are you having tonight? Margaritas? Okay, waiter, bring us two margaritas at this table," Dave called out to the waiter who was standing unobtrusively a few feet away.

Moments later, the same blond waitress who had served Bob his first drink arrived with the margaritas.

Dave looked at his brother curiously. "A lot going on in your life?"

"You could say that."

"How's Andrea?"

"We broke up."

"I am sorry to hear that," said Dave sympathetically. He saw that the subject was sensitive and dropped it. "A lot of strange things happening in Mexico today."

Bob nodded. "You mean the hostage crisis in Morelia?"

"I know the man who was shot—Fernando Velasquez. I met with him only two days ago, right after my arrival in Mexico City. He is . . . was the general counsel at Europa Bank."

Bob muttered his sympathies then retreated into silence. Dave made a final attempt to keep the conversation going. "They make fabulous margaritas here, don't they?"

"Yes, they do." Bob sipped dutifully at his drink but then stopped. He could feel the alcohol going to his head. He looked at his watch. It was 7:50 p.m. "Sorry, but I have to go. Waiter, my check please!"

Chapter Five

After signing for the bill, Bob grabbed his briefcase and headed downstairs. A black BMW was parked in the back alley near the exit, just as Pedro Guerra had said. He tapped on the passenger window, which the driver lowered.

"Can you give me directions to the Sanatorio Español? I am not feeling well."

"Hop in. I will take you there."

Bob opened the back door of the car and sank into the seat. He was not alone. There was another passenger sitting in the back seat who, despite the late hour, was wearing dark sunglasses. His curly black hair was slicked back, and his teeth flashed white against his brown skin.

"*Buenas noches!* We are glad to be of assistance, Senor. . .?"

"Bigelow."

"Ah, yes, Senor Bigelow. We have been expecting you." The man did not introduce himself—which, in normal circumstances, would have been odd. But this evening was anything but ordinary. Instead he looked intently through the side windows and then craned his neck to look back as the car exited the alley onto Galileo. He could see a man running after them, waving something that he held in his hand.

"Did you leave someone behind, Senor Bigelow? There is someone in the alley running after us."

"No, I am alone."

The activity in the back alley had not gone unnoticed by Pedro Guerra. He was a meticulous planner, which is why he had advanced so far in the Sinaloa Cartel. He was sitting by a window in the building across the alley from the Villa Maria watching a man running down the alley in pursuit of the BMW.

One can never be too careful, he thought as he picked up his phone and called one of his men parked in a minivan on Galileo.

"Did you see that man come running out of the alley?"

"Yes, he just got into a taxi heading down Galileo."

"Follow him!"

Then Guerra called the driver of the black BMW. "Pablo, make sure you are not being followed. A gray Ford Explorer parked in the back of the restaurant started up just as you were pulling away. It could be an unmarked police vehicle."

Pablo looked in his rearview mirror. "I see him. He is fifty meters behind us." He whistled between his teeth. "There are two of them. The second Explorer is in the other lane, twenty meters behind the first. I will lose them," he promised Guerra.

As Pablo turned the BMW onto Avenida Horacio, he accelerated in the direction of Parque America. "Ernesto," he called out to the man in the back seat, "Policia*!*"

Ernesto twisted his body to look through the back window. Bob, on hearing the word policia, was about to do likewise; but he arrested his motion and felt the inside of his suit jacket. Empty! Where was his phone? He remembered leaving it on the table in the restaurant. Had he forgotten it? His dismay as he realized his mistake only increased when he turned around because he was staring into the barrel of Ernesto's gun.

"Looking for your gun, Senor Bigelow?" He reached over and patted Bob's suit jacket.

"I don't have a gun," insisted Bob. "I was looking for my phone. I think I forgot it in the restaurant."

Ernesto seemed unconvinced. "Who are those people following us? We do not like to be double-crossed."

"I have no idea who they are." Bob was terrified.

"Hand me your briefcase," ordered Ernesto, pointing with his gun. "I want to see what other surprises you have for us."

Bob reluctantly complied. "It's not locked," he said.

Ernesto opened the briefcase and squealed in delight over the crisp Cleveland bills neatly bundled. *"Magnifico!"* While continuing to point his gun at Bob, he called Guerra on his phone.

"I have the money. Do you want me to count it?"

"Later," Guerra replied curtly. "There is no rush."

"What do you want me to do with Bigelow? Shoot him?"

Bob understood enough Spanish to know that his life was hanging on a thread. He was sweating with fear.

"Tell him the deal is off. Police were not part of the bargain. We keep the money and Ozmen. When you have lost the police, return to base. We will figure out what to do with Bigelow and Ozmen later."

Chapter Six

For Dave Bigelow, the day had started out well. His business meetings at Europa Bank had gone smoothly, and he had toyed with the idea of leaving early on Friday afternoon to fly back to New York for the weekend. He and his wife, Melanie, had not had a weekend alone together for what seemed like months.

But some of his business associates had suggested that he stay around because they might need his advice for meetings that they had scheduled for late afternoon. That meant he would miss the last flight to New York. He had agreed, provided that they wound up their business trip with a festive dinner at a Mexican restaurant before flying home on Saturday morning. He had called his wife and justified his delay in coming home as an exercise in team building. Melanie had been understanding.

That was when things had started going wrong. First, there was that totally unexpected meeting with his estranged brother, Bob, in a restaurant in a city far from home. He was in the Mexican capital for a legitimate reason. But his brother? He worked in New York City for a trading firm and, as far as he knew, had no reason to be in Mexico. After the initial confusion at their chance encounter, his brother had seemed reticent and distracted, volunteering no explanation.

When Dave had steered the conversation toward Bob's upcoming marriage, his only response had been that the engagement to Andrea was broken off. Again there was no explanation. Dave felt sorry for his brother, who was recently divorced and, he suspected, desperately trying to restore stability to his life. They had not touched on the other matter—the loan that Dave had recently obtained for Bob to help him out of his financial difficulties. Dave had expected at least some expression of gratitude, but he had waited in vain.

After Dave had returned to his own table to explain to his curious companions that he had been having a drink with his brother, whom he had discovered sitting at a table nearby, the waiter had come up.

"Pardon, senor, do you know the gentleman who was sitting at the table over there? He appears to have forgotten his phone. It was underneath his napkin."

"Thank you, waiter. Give it to me and I will take it to him."

Dave grabbed the phone out of the waiter's hand and hurried to the men's washroom, sticking his head through the door. "Bob?" he called out. There was no answer. If his brother had taken the main stairs to the first level, he would have seen him. Bob must have taken the back stairs.

At ground level, Dave made a second decision. Would Bob have walked through the crowded dining room to the front entrance, or would he have taken the back exit, readily accessible and marked by a bright sign? Again he made the right choice, exiting to the back alley only to glimpse a passenger (who could have been Bob) in the back seat of a black BMW that was pulling away.

"Bob!" he cried out, running after the car and waving the mobile phone in his hand. But he could not keep up. He saw the BMW turn onto Galileo. If reason had prevailed, he would have given up the chase at this point and decided to return the phone to Bob in New York. However, Dave did not give up easily once he was engaged in pursuit of a goal. Loitering on the curb on Galileo was a yellow Volkswagen beetle taxi, the kind of gypsy cab that the concierge at the Four Seasons Hotel had warned him against using. Jumping into the taxi, Dave ordered the driver to follow the black BMW.

"Si, senor," said the driver, not believing his good fortune that a gringo businessman had so easily fallen into his trap.

Unaware of the attention he had attracted, Dave fumed in the back seat of his taxi, which had followed the black BMW but then had lost it in the traffic. It was now dark, and the chances of finding it were slim. But the driver seemed nonchalant.

"Don't worry, amigo. I know a shortcut." He turned off the Avenida Horacio, and for the next ten minutes, Dave was taken through a maze of side streets and back alleys until the taxi came to rest at a Banamex location with a drive-up ATM at an office building that had been emptied of its workers hours before. The location was deserted—no pedestrians and no cars.

"Why are you stopping here?" asked Dave. His unease of the last few minutes had now turned into alarm.

When the driver turned to answer, he was no longer smiling. There was a gun in his hand. "I hope that you brought your ATM card with you, senor. Go over to that machine and withdraw the maximum that you can take out in a day. Believe me, I will not hurt you. All I want is your cash."

Dave slowly got out of the car, silently cursing himself for his stupidity. The driver walked two paces behind him. He inserted the card, punched in his pass code, and withdrew his daily maximum of a thousand dollars, denominated in pesos. He handed the cash to the driver.

"Gracias, senor. Your wallet as well."

"Look, leave me at least one credit card," pleaded Dave. "I need to get back to my hotel."

"Sorry, amigo. I am treating you generously. You still have your life. Eventually, you will find help." The driver clambered back into his Volkswagen beetle and began backing away from the ATM location toward the street.

Mugged in Mexico City! Dave struggled to contain his panic and his fury as he watched the receding headlights of the taxi. But then cool reason began to return. He realized how lucky he had been. The driver had not frisked him. He still had his phone and Bob's as well.

Before Dave could place a call to his hotel to explain his predicament, unexpected help came from a minivan, which blocked the exit of the taxi onto the street. Dave could see two men questioning the taxi driver, and their gestures seemed threatening. Light from a streetlamp glinted on the guns they held in their hands. Perhaps they were plainclothes police officers.

Dave began walking toward the taxi until he could see the terrified expression on the driver's face. One of the men interrogating him stepped away from the taxi to watch Dave's approach, his gun held ready. The other waited calmly for the driver to surrender his ill-gotten gains of the night—the wallet and the cash. He turned toward Dave and asked, "These are yours, senor?"

"Yes. Thank you for coming to my rescue. This man robbed me at gunpoint," he said, pointing toward the taxi driver.

"You were at the Villa Maria earlier tonight, were you not?"

"Yes, I was. How did you know?"

He did not receive an answer, only another question. "And your name is . . .?"

"Bigelow."

This seemed to arouse the interest of his questioner. He spoke rapidly in Spanish to the second man, who placed a call to Pedro Guerra. Brief consultations followed. The first man motioned Dave toward the minivan.

"Get in the van. You will need to come with us for further questioning."

It soon became obvious to Dave that his captors were not plainclothes police officers. They had not arrested the man who had robbed him. His wallet and cash were not returned to him. Instead, he was thoroughly frisked before he got into the minivan, and he gave up his passport and the two phones. They did not take him to a nearby precinct for questioning, as would have happened in New York. They drove for what seemed like hours, frequently reversing direction, until they arrived at a motel on the outskirts of Mexico City. During that entire ride, one of the two men sat beside him, pointing a gun at him as if he were a dangerous criminal.

If Dave had known about the app on Bob's mobile phone, which enabled his location to be traced, he would have felt less desperate over his situation. The police officers in the two Ford Explorers pursuing the black BMW had been informed about the app by Miguel

Rodriguez, the agent at the US Drug Enforcement Agency who had contacted them. At first, the BMW and the signal emitted by the phone had headed consistently in the same direction. Then they had diverged, confusing the drivers of the two police vehicles. They had prudently decided to split, one following the BMW and the other tracing the signal. The BMW had eventually evaded its pursuer on the Bulevard Manuel Avila Camacho, but the signal had been a reliable guide, leading, after three hours, to the Guadalajara Motel on the western outskirts of Mexico City.

Dave braced himself for an interrogation when they arrived—for what purpose, he did not know. It was already late, and he felt exhausted. But Pedro Guerra had decided to visit his mistress that night, so Dave was spared.

The two units occupied by his captors were at the back of the motel, secluded and screened from the view of other guests by trees. The two men in the minivan escorted him to one of the units, where they were greeted by an armed guard who rose sleepily from a sofa bed in the sitting area. Beside him were empty cans of beer, an unfinished takeout dinner, and an ashtray filled with cigarette stubs. The room reeked of sweat, stale cigarette smoke, and rotting food.

"We have another guest for you, Hernando."

The guard grunted, pulled out his key, and unlocked the bedroom door. Dave was pushed into the darkened room and saw, huddled against the wall, the figure of his brother. The light from the sitting room also showed a second man lying on a single cot in the corner. Then the door was shut, and Dave heard a key turning the lock. The room was completely dark again.

Chapter Seven

Dave's relief at being reunited with his brother lasted only seconds. Bob's whisper broke the silence.

"Dave, is that you? What are you doing here?"

"I might ask the same of you. All I wanted to do was return the phone you forgot in the restaurant. As a result, I have been mugged and taken captive by some Mexican thugs. Why is it that no good deed ever goes unpunished?"

"I have wondered that myself sometimes."

"What kind of business are you in, if you don't mind me asking? You hurried off to a meeting after dinner and now you are a prisoner of these criminals."

"Have you been following the local news? I was delivering the ransom for Demir Ozmen, an employee of my company kidnapped while on a business trip to Veracruz. The police found out about the plan and tried to get involved. The kidnappers think I tried to double-cross them. That's why I'm a prisoner."

"This guy Ozmen is the one the terrorists in Morelia want to rescue?"

"Yeah. The same Ozmen, by the way, is sleeping on the cot over there. When I arrived, I explained to him what had happened. Do you think he showed gratitude? No, he just started swearing at me in Turkish."

A roar from Ozmen's cot interrupted Dave before he could snap that Bob was receiving some of his own treatment.

"Will the two of you shut up? I am trying to get a few hours of sleep before I am executed, thanks to your screw-up."

Bob ignored him. "You said, Dave, that our bandido friends confiscated my phone?"

"Yes. Why?"

"Just asking." *Would that Mama Bear app come to our rescue?* he wondered.

"Bob, after I heard about the seizure of the cathedral in Morelia by some gang, I wondered to myself, why does a Mexican drug cartel care about an employee of your company? Got any answers?"

"Dave, what are you getting at?"

Bob's evasive response was only too typical of him. Dave's patience snapped.

"Bob, if we ever get out of here alive, would you do me a favor? Get as far out of my life as possible. Go to some remote location—Tahiti or even Antarctica. Will you promise me that?"

"Dave, the thought has crossed my mind too. Imagine saying 'to hell' to the Ottoman Trading Company, Andrea, you, and some other unnamed individuals that I would like to forget about!"

With that final outburst, the two brothers declared a temporary truce. The room became silent—for which Ozmen, at least, was grateful.

Chapter Eight

Dave regretted his angry words as soon as they left his mouth. He and his younger brother rarely saw each other, yet when they did, they quarreled. They always seemed to bring out the worst in each other. He would try to make amends in the morning, which he guessed was still hours away. The small shaft of light streaming through the crack underneath the door suddenly faded. Their captors must have turned in for the night.

He leaned back against the wall and tried to doze but could not. His mind drifted to his wife, Melanie, secure in their home in Greenwich, Connecticut, and to his daughter, Helen, a sophomore at Dartmouth College in New Hampshire. Had they been informed by Jerry Braunstein—the head of the bank monitoring team with whom he had been having dinner at the Villa Maria—about his unexplained disappearance? Surely Jerry would have suspected that something was wrong when Dave failed to return to either the restaurant or their hotel and would have contacted the Mexico City police. Then he would have called Melanie. She was probably frantic with worry now, and maybe Helen too, unless his wife had decided not to call until she had better information.

A few weeks ago, Melanie, Helen, and he had returned from an Aegean Sea cruise. Melanie and Helen had been so excited about going. As a child, Melanie had heard stories about the Greek countryside from her grandmother, who had emigrated from there to the United States. The cruise had lived up to their expectations, even exceeded them—the Acropolis in Athens illuminated at night, the excursion to mountainous Delphi, the spectacular island of Santorini, the ruins of Ephesus, and the breathtaking *Hagia Sophia* in Istanbul. At least the two people he loved most would have happy memories of their time together if he never saw them again.

He wrinkled his brow over that grim thought. Wasn't he being too pessimistic? His capture and that of his brother were the result of a complete misunderstanding. That would become obvious once they had explained their actions to their captors' boss, the one to whom they referred as Pedro, and they would be released. Yet doubts gnawed at his certainty. What had the Turk said—that he now expected to be executed because of the botched ransom attempt? If he were right, why should Bob and he expect a better fate? Their captors were killers, not reasonable men.

Dave cursed his stupidity. He could so easily have returned his brother's phone to him when they were both back in New York City, or even left it with the management of the restaurant so that his brother could reclaim it when he realized that he had forgotten it at his table. What had possessed him to rush into the back alley behind the restaurant and then jump into an unlicensed taxi in a vain attempt to return the phone? It was a shocking lapse of judgment, which could cost him dearly.

He knew why he had done it. He had a sense of obligation to his brother—and to his father. Dave thought about the last conversation that he had had with his father. Sitting beside his hospital bed, he had watched the man whom he revered, now reduced by cancer to a frail skeleton, breathing shallowly and apparently asleep. Then his eyes had flickered open.

"David, take care of Robert. Will you promise me that?" he had whispered.

Bending over his father to hear, Dave had promised that he would, not wanting to upset his father by asking the obvious question. How could he be his brother's keeper if they were hardly on speaking terms?

"The two of you turned out so differently. I feel that I am to blame . . ." His father's whisper had trailed off until it was no longer audible. A tear had rolled down his wasted cheek.

But it was more than his father's dying request. There was also a sense of guilt. Because of Dave's negligence, Bob could have died years ago when they were still boys. They had spent a summer vacation in Vermont with their parents, who had rented a house in the country far away from a town of any size. One warm afternoon, Dave had decided to go fishing at a nearby creek by himself, but his much younger brother, separated from him by eight years in age, had insisted on tagging along.

Absorbed in learning how to use his new fishing rod, Dave had, for the most part, ignored Bob, who, left to his own devices, had wandered off into the woods by himself. Only hours later, when he was ready to return to the house, did Dave discover that Bob was missing. After a futile hour of looking and dreading that Bob had drowned in the creek, he had raced back to the house to report to his horrified parents. A massive search had been launched involving neighbors, county police, state troopers, and dogs. Hours later, just before nightfall, after what had seemed an eternity, Bob had been discovered. He was covered with insect bites but otherwise unharmed.

Chapter Nine

In the darkness, Bob Bigelow also retreated into his own small world. How many hostages in Morelia would lose their lives because of tonight's fiasco? His pride smarted from his failure to carry out the Turk's ransom successfully. That had been the pattern of his life—reaching high to grasp the brass ring but failing to achieve victory.

He began to brood about his past, those seemingly innocent high school parties in Greenwich years ago when he had first begun to experiment with drugs and alcohol and the brushes with the local police that had not stained his record because his father had had friends in powerful places. He had disappointed his parents, especially his father, who had once shouted at him that he would never amount to anything because of his lack of discipline. Why couldn't he be more like his brother, Dave?

The unfavorable comparison with his brother had bedeviled his youth. Dave had always been a class act—an excellent student, a star athlete on the high school football team, president of the student council, a well-spoken young man with whom mothers would entrust their daughters. Even when he messed up, as he had years ago on that summer vacation in Vermont, he was readily forgiven by their parents for his uncharacteristic lapse. Dave was the sort of person who could fall into a sewer hole and come up smelling like roses.

Bob had sought to emerge from his shadow by being his opposite—taking daring risks, acting rakishly with the girls, and showing only rare flashes of brilliance in his studies in high school. What had his father called him when he had driven home from a party after drinking too much and sideswiping another car? A feckless youth who deserved to be taken to the woodshed and whipped. Except his father had never laid a hand on him. Instead, he had punished Bob by becoming aloof. The competition for his father's affections had been over before the race started. Dave had won hands down.

Bob had been determined to prove his father wrong when he left for college, excelling at his studies in his first year. But then had come that semester abroad in Mexico City when his roommate, Tony Santelli, had invited him to a number of parties where pot had been smoked. He had slipped back into his old ways, and by the end of his second year, his grades had deteriorated to the point where he had been asked by the college administration to leave.

His mother had been forgiving, even overly protective, sparing him from his father's wrath. Somehow he had managed to pull himself together, surviving in a tough job market because of his good looks and quick wit. But success at a major company or investment bank in New York had eluded him. He had ended up working for the Ottoman Trading Company and peddling drugs on the side to support his expensive lifestyle.

Then he had fallen into a police trap. Only a few weeks ago, although it seemed like eons now. Right around the time his friend Tony Santelli had been killed. His boss, Murat, was the guilty party—if his FBI handler, John Shafer, was to be believed. But that was the thing about Shafer. You could never be certain that he was telling the truth.

Tony had been on the run from the police when he had called him at the office and left a voice-mail message. He had sounded desperate—out of money, needed his help, thinking about surrendering to the police. Could they meet? He would call back later. Except that he had never called back. His body had been found in the Hudson River. Bob had failed Tony by not being at his desk when he called.

Tonight his botched mission to ransom Ozmen had left the hostages in the cathedral in Morelia at the mercy of a Mexican drug gang. If he and his fellow prisoners were not rescued soon, many innocent people could die. His only dealings with Los Zetas so far had been with Diego Alvarez, but maybe he wasn't representative. Rodriguez, who worked for the DEA, should know what he was talking about. How had he described Los Zetas—brutal and murderous?

God, he hoped that Mama Bear app worked.

Chapter Ten

The three men ate their breakfast of fried beans and bitter black coffee in silence. Their outbursts of the previous night cast a pall over the room, inhibiting conversation beyond a curt morning greeting. Dave had requested (in English) to see Pedro Guerra when the two armed men had delivered their food, but they had spun on their heels and left without saying a word. He realized that he should have asked Bob to make the request in Spanish.

In the gray morning light filtering through the overhead skylight, Dave could make out the morose features of the tall, thin man whom Bob had introduced last night as Demir Ozmen. He sat on his cot, chewing methodically, his eyes fixed on the floor. Dave had seen him before somewhere, and it had been recently. In Mexico? No, that was not possible. Apart from hotel staff at the Four Seasons Hotel in Mexico City and the waiter at the restaurant last night, he had met only with members of his own bank regulatory team and with managers at the local headquarters of Europa Bank. New York was also unlikely.

Then it had to be Europe. Istanbul? Ozmen was an employee of the Ottoman Trading Company headquartered in Istanbul. But he could not recall their paths crossing on his recent business trip to Istanbul to meet with the general manager of Europa Bank's Turkish subsidiary.

Except that they had. The realization jolted him. He could feel his pulse quickening. Dave had not made the connection last night when

Bob had revealed the name of the third occupant of their room, the Turkish businessman who had been kidnapped and whom Bob had intended to ransom. After all, there could be a hundred Turks with the name Demir Ozmen.

But this morning, there was no mistaking that their fellow prisoner, bearded and balding, resembled the clean-shaven, smiling young man whom Dave had seen in a photo in a meeting at the home of Hayat Yilmaz, a university professor who had been brutally attacked and was now a patient in an Istanbul hospital. Two decades had taken their toll, adding wrinkles and gray hairs, but the tall, thin build was the same, and a week's stubble could not disguise the resemblance in facial features.

The parents of Hayat had identified the youth as the man to whom their daughter had once been betrothed, but their engagement had been broken off when she had discovered that he was dealing in drugs. The Istanbul police were still puzzled over who her attacker could be but suspected a lovers' quarrel. Could this man be implicated in her savage beating? Dave had suggested to the Istanbul police that it was certainly worth an inquiry, even if Ozmen was a lover from the distant past. But that proposal appeared to have been lost in the Istanbul police bureaucracy.

Other memories came flooding back. There had been another encounter with Demir Ozmen in London four weeks ago, before the meeting with Hayat Yilmaz's parents in Istanbul.

He had been forced to interrupt his Aegean Sea cruise by flying from Athens to London to attend a meeting at Europa Bank's headquarters at Canary Wharf. He had been standing in line, waiting to check into his hotel after the taxi ride from Heathrow, when a tall man ahead of him, taking an incoming call on his mobile phone from someone he had greeted as Mehmet, had suddenly turned and bumped into him before rushing off to the hotel entrance. He remembered the incident now, not because of the man's perfunctory apology but because of the anxious (even shocked) expression on his face as he hurried away from the reception desk.

When the tall man was joined a few minutes later by a business associate—a short rotund man who had been trying to ingratiate himself with the pretty receptionist as he checked in—their excited voices initially echoed across the lobby. Dave understood only the first few words they exchanged in English. "Not again!" They then started speaking in more guarded tones in a language he did not understand.

What chain of events had brought this Turkish businessman in a matter of weeks from the luxury of a London hotel to this squalid motel, the captive of a Mexican drug gang? Could there be a link to what he had witnessed in the taxi ride from Heathrow to his hotel?

As they were about to enter the highway on the final approach to Canary Wharf, the driver narrowly avoided colliding with a white truck that was pursued by several police cars. Dave had no time to prepare himself. Despite his seat belt, he crashed against the window, and his overnight bag, placed on the floor beside him, was hurled against his leg. The driver was very apologetic, but Dave assured him that he was fine—only a few small bruises—and a trip to a hospital was not necessary.

The driver then maneuvered the taxi onto the entrance ramp of the highway but almost immediately came to a stop. Police blocked the road where the truck had been pulled over to the side of the highway. Two men leaning against the side of the truck were being frisked, their arms extended upward. A third man, who tried to escape when the truck had been forced to stop, was being wrestled to the ground by police. Oncoming traffic on the other side of the highway slowed to a crawl as motorists gawked at the evening's unexpected entertainment.

The driver explained, "The police have arrested some criminals. It looks like a bad business. See that registration plate on the back of the lorry?"

Dave squinted in the fading daylight and shook his head. "No."

"It's Bulgarian. You know what that means? Drugs."

"Why drugs?"

"The *Evening Standard* has had a number of stories in the last week or so about the drug trade in Britain and the rest of Europe. See, most of it is controlled by Turkish gangs."

The gist of the articles was that despite NATO's efforts to stabilize Afghanistan, the heroin business there is bigger than ever. The drug flows through Iran, Iraq, and Syria into Turkey. There the middlemen break up shipments into smaller packages that are put on vehicles bound for Bulgaria and Romania. The drugs are often hidden in shipments of goods like vegetables, shoes, cement, and bales of cotton before they are transferred to other trucks headed for Holland, Germany, or Britain.

"The police haven't been able to put a stop to this trade?"

"The *Standard* says the Turkish government is cooperating. Someone must have tipped off our police about this shipment. Imagine driving all the way from Bulgaria to be welcomed into the open arms of the police!" The driver chortled.

Then he became sober again. "Still there's plenty of heroin on the streets in London. Turkish officials may be trying their best, but there are so many ways that heroin can be smuggled into or out of their country. Same with Britain. Not everything comes by lorry via the Chunnel into Britain. Some of it comes by air or by sea."

"These Turkish gangs in London—the British police have been unable to break them?"

"It's not easy to get into these gangs, you see. The drug business is a family affair."

The driver provided Dave with some background information. Some Turks, especially those who came from Cyprus when it was part of the British Empire, have lived in Great Britain for generations. Others came more recently, in the seventies or eighties—Turks and Kurds from the southeastern part of the country. Most may be law-abiding, but those who are criminals use family connections (brothers, cousins, uncles) here and in Turkey to get supplies of heroin and distribute it.

A police officer walked over to their taxi to apologize for the delay. The driver then returned to his story, showing a surprising memory for detail.

"When I was in the police force in the nineties—I retired ten years ago and now drive cab to top up my pension—the Baybasin clan was the most prominent drug family. They were originally Kurdish. There were four brothers. The organization they ran was closely associated with two gangs in north London, the Kurdish Bulldogs and the Bombers. Not only did they smuggle drugs into Britain, they also ran a protection racket."

"Wasn't there a horrendous murder recently in north London?" asked Dave. "The police found a dismembered body."

"You must have read about it, right? The gangs extort money from Kurdish businessmen, claiming they support the cause of Kurdish secession from Turkey. But really, they are only lining their pockets. If businessmen resist, they can be very persuasive—killings, torture, kidnappings, that sort of thing."

"What's happened to the Baybasin clan?"

"The oldest brother, Huseyin, known as the Emperor—the one who got the business going by starting a travel agency with a fleet of buses to smuggle drugs throughout Europe—ended up in prison in England under a false name. While there, he spilled the beans to interrogators, how he had been aided in his business by corrupt government officials in Turkey. The Turkish authorities, knowing who he was, got him released through an exchange for a British citizen held in a Turkish prison. Soon he returned to his old ways, got caught, and was jailed for life in Holland."

"End of story?"

"Not quite. His three brothers had, by this time, established themselves in London. One of them, Abdullah, who was arrested shortly after I retired from the force, revealed during his trial how the clan laundered money through Scottish and Cypriot banks and then invested the money in real estate. They owned office and apartment buildings in some of the most posh parts of London—even a retirement home for police officers, if you can believe that!"

By this time, the police roadblock had been lifted and traffic had begun to move again. As the driver merged his cab into the flow of traffic, he twisted his head back to look at Dave and grinned.

"Want to hear a funny one? Although Abdullah was convicted at his trial, he was given refugee status in Britain because his life would be in danger if he were deported to Turkey. The judge was sympathetic because he had been crippled in a gunfight in Amsterdam years before. Then in a retrial, Abdullah was acquitted because the judge found that prosecution evidence was insufficient. That's British justice for you."

If that was British justice, thought Dave, what chance was there of getting justice for Hayat Yilmaz in Turkey, especially when there was so little concrete evidence to work with? Still, his shared captivity with a potential suspect in the attack on his friend was an opportunity that he did not intend to let pass.

Chapter Eleven

Dave thought carefully about how he could best extract the information that he wanted from the Turk. If this man had anything to fear, a direct approach might cause him to clam up. He decided on an indirect strategy—getting the Turk to talk so that he would relax and possibly divulge some personal details relevant to the attack on Hayat Yilmaz.

"Demir, we were never properly introduced last night, and I apologize for disturbing your sleep. I am Dave Bigelow, Bob's brother."

Ozmen seemed startled when Dave called out his name. He did not smile but acknowledged Dave's apology with a nod of his head. "Please understand the reason why I cursed yesterday. Being a prisoner for nearly a week has been a terrible ordeal."

Dave was sympathetic. "I can well imagine. Your story has been all over the media, especially the last twenty-four hours with the seizure of the cathedral in Morelia."

"What seizure? What are you talking about? Remember I have not seen a newspaper since I was made a prisoner. Your brother did not mention it last night."

"Yesterday, terrorists claiming to represent Los Zetas, a drug cartel, took control of the cathedral and threatened to kill members of a wedding party inside unless you are released immediately."

Ozmen grimaced. "That is unfortunate. I do not welcome publicity of any kind, nor does my company." Almost as an afterthought, he asked, "Has anyone been killed?"

"Yes, one hostage was executed last night, and who knows what has happened since? This crisis could put pressure on the Mexican government to get you released."

Bob joined the conversation. "Omer Tilki does not want governments to get involved. When I was asked to come to Mexico City to deliver the ransom, Tilki was going to contact the kidnappers directly to arrange how to drop off the money."

"How would he do that?" asked Ozmen. "I was going to ask you this morning how the kidnappers knew to call you."

"Simple. Your kidnappers allowed you to use your phone to call Omer Tilki. He called them back on your phone."

"Ah, I see, and the kidnappers picked up," murmured Ozmen. Something still puzzled him. "Did you coordinate with Diego Alvarez on this plan?"

"No, we are doing this on our own," Bob replied quickly. "Omer Tilki felt that bringing a third party into the negotiations would only hinder communications."

He wished Ozmen had not brought up Alvarez's name. He could be straightforward with Dave about Tilki but had to be circumspect about Alvarez. He could not tell Ozmen in front of his brother that Alvarez's links to the Los Zetas cartel would destroy any chance of reaching an agreement with the Sinaloa Cartel, the suspected captors. Dave had to be kept ignorant about the kind of company he worked for, even if his evasive answers ran the risk of irritating Ozmen.

"Who are these people?" Dave's curiosity was piqued.

Bob interjected before Ozmen could respond. "Alvarez is our business contact in Mexico. He came to New York in early September to meet with Demir and Murat to discuss future trade deals between Ottoman Trading Company and his firm, Veracruz Sugar. Demir and Batur Comooglou were invited to Veracruz for further discussions after the New York meeting."

Ozmen frowned at Bob. He expected this junior employee to be more deferential to him, especially after bungling his ransom mission. Another score to be settled if they survived their captivity, but he decided to let it pass for now.

"That is correct," said Ozmen. "We were pleased with the success of our business trip to Mexico as guests of Diego Alvarez in Veracruz. He was a gracious host."

"But security must have been lax," protested Dave. "How did you get kidnapped?"

"Security was very good, or so it seemed. Our villa was heavily guarded. Each morning, Comooglou and I were picked up by a chauffeur-driven limousine with bodyguard and taken to the docklands. We were greeted there by Alvarez's assistant, a young man working in the shipping department of Veracruz Sugar. He ushered us past friendly security guards and customs officials at the docklands with ease. We were impressed."

"What about the police? Were they visible in the streets?" asked Bob.

"The police?" Ozmen snorted contemptuously. "Two years ago, the central government of Mexico dismissed the entire local police force of Veracruz because it was considered to be in the pocket of Los Zetas."

"Los Zetas is . . .?" Dave had heard the name in reference to the seizure of the cathedral in Morelia.

"A drug gang which—by reputation at least—controls much of the Gulf coast of Mexico," responded Ozmen. He glanced at Bob, whose gaze wavered uneasily. He understood the signal. That was all Dave Bigelow needed to know.

"On our last day in Veracruz, Batur and I were sitting in a sidewalk café in the center of the city at the Plaza de las Armas. I was on my phone reporting to Omer Tilki in Istanbul. Our bodyguard sat at a separate table nearby."

He could recall that morning in perfect detail—the square lined by palm trees, shops, and restaurants; the Municipal Palace of the city council with soldiers standing guard outside; a cathedral; Comooglou flirting with the pretty waitress who was bringing them coffee.

"The attack occurred in the square?" Bob was incredulous.

"No, too many soldiers in the square. When I finished my call, Comooglou and I walked, our bodyguard a few paces behind, to a side street where our driver and car were waiting. I was about to open the back door of the car when I heard the bodyguard swear. A shot rang out. He collapsed in a pool of blood, a bullet in his head. I heard the sound of feet running toward the car. I did not see the man who knocked me down from behind and then pinned me to the ground. The rest is a jumble."

Ozmen closed his eyes and gingerly fingered the bruise on his head. It had all happened so quickly—the shattering glass, more shots ringing out, screeching brakes as a van pulled up beside the car, the grunts of scuffling men followed by the sound of someone running away from the car, more shots, and then complete silence.

"All this happened a short distance from the Municipal Palace guarded by Mexican soldiers?" Dave was aghast.

"Oh yes. As I was dragged into the back of the van by two armed men, I looked back. Our driver was slumped over the wheel, and about a hundred feet from the car, the body of Comooglou was lying very still on the pavement."

"Why were the military so slow to react?" Dave exclaimed in amazement.

Ozmen shrugged his shoulders. "Who knows? The van sped away at high speed. I was gagged, handcuffed, and blindfolded by two men who sat on either side of me on the middle seat. A third in the back seat held a gun to my head. Two men sat in the front of the van—the driver and a big shot, who was giving instructions. They spoke among themselves in Spanish but otherwise ignored me."

Ozmen leaned back on his cot, reclining against the wall. Talking about his ordeal seemed to have fatigued him, or perhaps he did not want to talk anymore. Gazing at him in the brightening room, Dave was convinced that Ozmen was the man he had seen at his London hotel. Was now the right time to ask? He did not want the conversation to end. He had other more important questions about Hayat, which were begging for an answer.

"Demir, let me compliment you on your English. You speak it very well!"

Ozmen opened his eyes and acknowledged the compliment. "I was head of the London office of the Ottoman Trading Company for several years before I assumed my current position."

"Tell me, were you a guest at the Four Seasons Hotel at Canary Wharf in London a few weeks ago? I think I was standing in line at the reception desk, waiting to check in, and you were immediately ahead of me."

Ozmen looked more closely at him. "I do not recall seeing you, but yes, I was a guest there. It must be a quirk of fate that our paths should cross again."

He closed his eyes again and then muttered, "Do you remember the man who was with me on that trip? That was Comooglou. He is dead now."

Chapter Twelve

Dave did not allow Ozmen to drift off to sleep. He wanted to keep the dialogue going. "Where did your captors take you?"

The Turk pretended not to hear. He kept his eyes closed. That was the part that he wanted to forget. It came back to him now. After a while, the van had pulled off the highway and jounced at low speed down a rutted dirt road, finally coming to a stop. He heard shouts, then the voices of men talking, before they pulled him out of the van and pushed him into a small hut. A door slammed, and a key turned a lock. He was now alone.

He opened his eyes reluctantly. "I was taken to an abandoned farm, where they locked me up in a room. My arms were handcuffed in front of me rather than in back, so I was able to remove my gag and blindfold. When my eyes adjusted to the darkness, I could make out a room very much like this one—a cot in one corner, a washbasin, a chamber pot, light filtering through a small barred window near the ceiling."

His voice faltered then trailed off into silence. He was not a man prone to show weakness. Death was not a stranger to him. He had killed several men and perhaps a woman himself, but only with great effort was he able to resume.

"The smell—I will never forget that smell. Sweat, piss, and something else that I did not immediately recognize. It was the smell of dried blood and rotting flesh!"

The Bigelow brothers stirred uneasily. "How did you know . . . that . . . it was the smell of death?" The words stumbled out of Dave's mouth.

Ozmen brushed away the question. "I will tell you in a minute. I was in a room where others had been shot. I am certain of that. I could feel it. But I was certain that they would not kill me immediately. After all, they had gone to the trouble of dragging me to this hut in the middle of nowhere. One good sign was that they fed me."

Ozmen's nostrils flared in disdain. The food had nauseated him, but he had been thirsty enough to drink the beer.

"Then the interrogation began. Three masked men with symbols of the cross tattooed on their bare arms entered my cell. Two pointed guns at me while the third barked questions in Spanish."

Fear flickered across Ozmen's face. "Although I am not an observant Muslim, I felt like a prisoner of the crusaders, to be burned at the stake like an infidel if I did not convert. I could only shake my head. I could not understand a word. My interrogator spat at me and then stalked out."

Darkness fell before the next round of questioning resumed. "My inquisitor, a different man who spoke English, finally identified his gang. He said they are . . . Los Matas Zetas, whatever that means." Ozmen hesitated over the unfamiliar Spanish words.

Bob translated, "That means killers of Los Zetas."

"Did he give a motive for your kidnapping? Was there a misunderstanding? Were you a random victim?"

Dave did not see Bob shaking his head slightly, warning Ozmen to be careful how he answered his brother's questions.

Ozmen did not need to be prompted. He would not repeat the inquisitor's threat. *We know all about you—you are trying to forge an alliance between Los Zetas and the drug cartels in Turkey. We will foil your scheme before it can take shape. We would like to rid Mexico of scum like you and them. That is why you have been kidnapped.*

His face froze into a grim mask. "He said only that I had a choice. I must convince the Ottoman Trading Company to pay a ransom of five million dollars or they would cut off my head."

"Cut off your head!" exclaimed Dave. "They must have been bluffing!" Murderous blackmail and threats were rare in the social and legal circles to which he was accustomed.

"Oh no!" rebutted Ozmen. "They were serious! They took me from my cell down a dimly lit path toward a shed on the other side of the abandoned farmhouse. The strange odor in my cell now became an overwhelming stench. One of the guards pulled open a door and shone his flashlight into the darkness of the shed, revealing its contents. It was like a war zone—dismembered bodies, torsos without heads lying in pools of blood, swarming with flies."

Ozmen remembered gagging, holding his handcuffed hands to his retching mouth. His inquisitor had pointed to the interior of the shed. *These are former members of Los Zetas. This is how they fight us, without mercy, and we respond in kind. We fight fire with fire. Now you know what your fate will be if you fail to deliver your ransom.*

"Then they marched me back to my cell, gave me my phone, and ordered me to call Omer Tilki in Istanbul. I was to tell him that he had one week to pay the ransom."

The Turk's face looked pale and resigned. Nearly a week had passed since his ordeal had begun. "After that first day, we never stayed two nights in the same place. They drove mostly at night. During the day, I was kept confined in a room, sometimes with a guard present but mostly alone. Every day, I was moved to a different location—a farmhouse or cheap motel in a rural area.

"Two days ago, there was a change in my routine. I ended up here. I knew from the steady roar of traffic outside that we were by a major highway near a large city. At sunset, I was not forced after supper into a van to begin a night of wandering over the back roads of Mexico. Instead, my jailer allowed me a full hour to eat my supper.

"But the most important sign of change was that my captors from Veracruz disappeared without explanation. The jailer who returned to pick up my plate and utensils was accompanied by a guard I had never seen before. For the first time since Veracruz, I spent the night on a cot. A second night followed in this place. I began to hope that I would soon be released. Then the two of you joined me in captivity last night!"

His voice trailed off in disgust. He glared malevolently at Bob, then at Dave.

Chapter Thirteen

Dave felt the tension building—three men confined in a small room, resentful of each other, withholding secrets, but bound together by their common predicament. He had gotten Ozmen to talk but still did not have the information he wanted. Pushing him further with more questions at this point could provoke him into another outburst of profanity or, even worse, sullen silence. He directed his next question at Bob.

"The hostage-takers in the cathedral in Morelia want Demir released by a gang with a different name. Not Los Matas Zetas. You must have watched the news reports on television, Bob. Help me out."

"You mean the Knights Templar. They are based in Michoacán, of which Morelia is the capital."

"So Los Zetas is targeting the wrong enemy?"

"Apparently so," agreed Bob. "That is bad news for the hostages in the cathedral." *For me too*, he thought. He felt responsible.

"Then who are our captors if they are not the same people who kidnapped Demir in Veracruz?"

"They could just be allies of the original gang, but I am only guessing."

"Like who? What did you hear in in New York?"

"Diego Alvarez, when he called Omer Tilki, thought that the kidnappers were the Knights Templar. But Tilki had learned from a different source, probably Demir, that they were Los Matas Zetas."

"Did he pass that information back to Alvarez?"

"I don't know for sure, but I suspect not."

"Tilki does not trust Alvarez?"

Bob knew perfectly well but shrugged his shoulders. "Beats me."

"Our situation is getting murkier by the minute. Then who did you think you were dealing with when you came to Mexico City to deliver the ransom?"

"The guy who called me in my hotel room introduced himself as Pedro Guerra and said that he had Ozmen in his custody. I asked him point-blank to which group he belonged."

"His response?"

"It was not necessary for me to know that."

Guerra had given him a hint. His group was led by someone named El Chapo, whom Miguel Rodriguez had identified as the leader of the Sinaloa Cartel, but Bob could not reveal that he had talked to a DEA agent. Instead he recounted the details of the instructions that he had been given by Guerra for the delivery of the ransom.

"What guarantee did you have that he would keep his word?" queried Ozmen, whose frown had deepened as he heard Bob's story.

"None, but what choice did I have? He told me to do as instructed or you would be dead."

"And then I showed up, and you forgot your phone at the restaurant," Dave added. "And I chased after you, and here we are."

"Now you understand why I acted strangely last night."

"I am glad to know that it was not all about me, your unwanted big brother, showing up unexpectedly. What a coincidence that I was eating at the same restaurant as you last night. The concierge at my hotel recommended it as an authentic Mexican experience!"

The irony of that comment was not lost on the two brothers, who grinned at each other until Ozmen snapped at them, "Your comedy of errors could have tragic consequences!"

"You are right about that," Dave conceded lamely. "Sorry, Demir."

He looked at Bob, who avoided his gaze. That made him more uneasy than Ozmen's angry words did. His brother was a mystery to him in some ways, but he sensed that Bob was not telling the whole truth. Either that or he was feeling guilty about the possible massacre of the hostages in the cathedral. Maybe both.

"So what exactly happened after you left the restaurant last night?" he asked Bob.

"I was picked up by a driver and passenger in a black BMW, just as Guerra had said. As the car pulled out of the alley, the passenger looked back and saw someone running after the car. He asked me if I had left someone behind, and I said that I hadn't."

"My apologies," muttered Dave. He would have to share responsibility for this fiasco.

"Then the driver of the BMW received a call from Guerra, alerting him that two unmarked police vehicles were following us. To make a long story short, the driver and Ernesto, the guy in the back seat, concluded that I had double-crossed them. Before I knew what was happening, Ernesto was holding a gun to my head. They had the money, but the deal was off. Ernesto asked Guerra if he should shoot me on the spot. It was not a good feeling, knowing that my life depended on someone's whim."

Bob's nervous high-pitched laugh startled Ozmen and Dave. "You know why I am laughing? When Murat, my boss, and Tilki asked me to deliver the ransom money, they said there would be no risk to me. Everything would go like clockwork!"

Ozmen failed to see the humor of the situation. "This is not a laughing matter. Are you sure no one overheard you talking to Guerra?"

"No, he called me when I was in my room."

"In the restaurant, I mean."

"He didn't call me again in the restaurant. The only explanation I can think of for the police trap is that his call was intercepted by the police, or that the police were already trailing some of his men and accidentally stumbled onto the plan to pick up the ransom money."

The lie flowed glibly from Bob's lips, but Ozmen was unconvinced. If the bungling Bigelow brothers had deliberately plotted to destroy any chance of his release, they could not have done better. He held his tongue, but the scowl on his face betrayed his feeling.

Dave's professional curiosity prompted him to ask a different kind of question. "Do you mean to tell me, Bob, that when I sat at your table at the restaurant last night, your briefcase contained five million dollars in cash?"

"Yep." Bob grinned. "That briefcase and I did not part company for two days. It was always with me, day and night."

"Did you bring the money with you from New York and smuggle it past customs?"

"No, I withdrew it from an Ottoman Trading Company account at a bank in Mexico City."

"Was it, by any chance, the Europa Bank branch on the Paseo de la Reforma?"

"Why, yes." He again averted his gaze. He knew what was coming next.

"On Wednesday, when I arrived at the bank to meet with its executives after my flight from New York, I could swear that I saw you leaving the building. You had just finished picking up the money?"

"Possibly, although if we were there at the same time, I did not see you," Bob said with as much conviction as he could muster. But of course, he had seen his brother and had plunged into the crowd on the Paseo de la Reforma to avoid being seen.

Dave smiled but he knew Bob was lying. "Did you have any difficulty withdrawing such a large sum in cash from the bank?"

"Not really. The first time I arrived, the bank had not yet received the transfer from an offshore account in the Cayman Islands. But later that day, the money was waiting for me, in neatly bundled Grover Cleveland denominations."

"No questions asked?"

"None."

"Who did you deal with?"

"I am a little vague with names. Gomez in private banking, I think."

"If I ever get to resume my former life, I will follow up on that lead," said Dave grimly. "I mentioned last night at the restaurant that my firm, Marshall Steiner & Watkins, has been retained by the US Department of Justice to implement compliance with an anti–money laundering system at Europa Bank. They were indicted and convicted for transferring more than nine billion dollars on behalf of Mexican drug gangs into the United States."

Ozmen, who had been listening quietly, now spoke what was on his mind. "Bigelow, why did Omer Tilki choose you to deliver the ransom when someone more experienced, like Recep Murat, would have been available?"

Bob resented the inference that he was inexperienced but did not challenge it. Ozmen had enough reason to be ticked off with him as it was. "Tilki suggested Murat but left the choice up to him. Murat said that he was too busy to go to Mexico City and recommended me. I can't recall much was going on in New York. You will have to ask him the reason if we ever get out of here. Maybe he thought the risk was too high."

Ozmen snorted sardonically. "That would be like Murat not to put his skin on the line, especially for me. We have known each other a long time at the company. He was passed over when I was promoted to my current job. It must still rankle."

So they were business rivals, thought Bob. That did not surprise him, although as someone who had been with Ottoman Trading Company for only nine months, he was not yet familiar with the executive intrigue and maneuvering for personal advancement at corporate headquarters.

Ozmen was not finished. "The interesting question is who tipped off the police. It is possible that Murat did because he wanted me to disappear. But what kind of contacts does he have with the Mexican police? None would be my guess, so we can forget that idea. You may have tipped off the police—accidentally, as you suggest. It could also be that you are a police informer."

Dave glanced sideways at Ozmen. *He must be an abrasive son of a bitch for making the accusation so boldly.* He looked at Bob, whose face was flushing with anger. His brother's reply was predictable.

"Like hell I am! That is a load of bullshit!" retorted Bob hotly. This was one insult that he could not ignore because its implications for his safety were dangerous, here in Mexico City or back in New York. He glared at Ozmen, who returned his gaze coolly. They would have some grudges to settle when this was over.

Amid rising tension, the three prisoners fell silent. Dave was disappointed because he had more questions to direct at Ozmen, but he sensed that any small spark could ignite an angry explosion. He decided to bide his time.

Chapter Fourteen

Ozmen dozed fitfully on his cot. A scornful and accusing woman hovered on the edge of his consciousness. As her image receded, the thin-lipped, contemptuous face of Omer Tilki appeared. Then two dark figures appeared from behind, seizing him by the arms and dragging him away. Was it to his execution? He could not tell. He was grateful when the sound of a key turning in the door woke him from his nightmare.

Two guards entered the room and silently placed the prisoners' food by the door before leaving. Once more, the door was locked. Ozmen breathed a sigh of relief. A simple lunch of tacos and beer was better than nothing, which would be a sign their captors had decided to kill them.

The three men bolted down their food and drank their beer without conversation until Ozmen sensed that someone was staring at him. Self-consciously, he brushed away a fleck of food at the corner of his mouth and looked up. But he was mistaken in thinking that Dave was about to comment on his eating manners.

"Demir," he said with a smile, "while you were sleeping, I was thinking that the president of your company—what's his name again?"

"Omer Tilki."

"Thank you. Omer Tilki must have a very high opinion of you if he is willing to pay a ransom of five million dollars for your release."

Ozmen's lips twitched in a slight smile as if he was too modest to acknowledge the compliment. The reality was so different. On his first day of captivity, when his kidnappers had insisted that he call his boss in Istanbul to relay their demands using his own phone, Tilki's response to his plea had been chilling. *You are not worth that much!* This was after Ozmen had explained to him the consequences of a failure to deliver the ransom. *They will cut off my head!* If Tilki had decided to pay the ransom, it was for reasons other than loyalty to him. He was certain of that.

Dave did not dwell on the ransom, which he had used only to lead to a different objective. Ozmen was not prepared for Dave's question when it came.

"Do you know someone named Hayat Yilmaz?"

Ozmen's eyes narrowed as he held his breath, struggling to remain calm. Even in this Mexican hellhole, he could not escape. He managed to keep his voice steady when he replied, "No. Why do you ask?"

"I met her recently through a mutual friend when my family and I were on a cruise in the Aegean Sea. She showed us around Istanbul, including the Grand Bazaar, which is not that far from where your company is headquartered."

"Istanbul, as you must know, is a very large city with millions of people. Most people remain strangers without ever meeting each other." There was a touch of condescension in Ozmen's voice.

Dave protested, "But she was quite prominent—a university professor who appeared frequently on television during the Taksim Gezi Park demonstrations."

"I may have seen her on television a few times, but I cannot recall what she looks like." Ozmen's face remained impassive, not betraying his inner turmoil.

Dave knew he was lying. The man had something to hide. He thought quickly about what he should do next—confront Ozmen with his former betrothal to Hayat Yilmaz? But if this man was the person who had attacked Hayat, he was potentially dangerous and could turn violent if pressed too hard. Could he rely on Bob, who was listening curiously, to come to his defense? He decided to test his brother's loyalty.

"My question was not as naive as it might seem, Demir. I visited her parents' home recently when I returned to Istanbul on business. They showed me a photo of her and a young man to whom she was betrothed twenty years ago. The man looked very much like you."

"Perhaps he was my doppelgänger." Ozmen shrugged derisively.

"If he was your doppelgänger, why would he also go by the name of Demir Ozmen?"

"Ozmen is a common name in Turkey. It seems to me to be a remarkable case of coincidence, nothing more. Why are you so interested in this woman who is only a casual acquaintance, if I may ask?"

"She was badly beaten on the last night of my family's vacation in Istanbul. I was questioned by the police, who are looking for clues."

"Well, I am sorry. I cannot help you there."

Dave decided to switch to a different subject. "Hayat mentioned that she has a cousin, Husayin Yilmaz, who is captain of a Golden Horn Shipping vessel owned by your company. Ever come across him?"

Ozmen answered without hesitation. "Ottoman Trading Company is very large, and shipping is a relatively small part of its operations. I am vaguely familiar with the name Golden Horn Shipping but have no direct knowledge of its activities or this captain Yilmaz." He shrugged his shoulders as if to say *Why are you bothering me with these silly questions?*

"Pardon my ignorance, but what is your current position in the company?" asked Dave.

"I am the vice president for special operations, which means that I am responsible for opening up new markets, such as Mexico, or developing lines of business outside of our traditional areas of banking, real estate development, and trading in chemicals, automotive parts, footwear, and commodities. If you will excuse me, I would like to get some sleep."

Ozmen lolled back on the cot and rolled over to face the wall. His message was clear. He would ignore any further questions.

Chapter Fifteen

Father Cardozo kneeled in the sacristy of the cathedral in Morelia. He was praying for the quick release of the kidnapped Turk and the peaceful resolution of the hostage crisis. He had no access to a television or radio or computer but suspected that, by now, the cathedral would be surrounded by police, armored vehicles, and military personnel. With the governor of the state among the hostages, the federal government would be responsible for a resolution of the crisis.

There would be a breaking point. If the terrorists proceeded with their plan to execute a hostage each day, the pressure on the Mexican president to act would be overwhelming. What then? The outcome of a military assault on the cathedral could not be in doubt, but the cost in innocent lives and the destruction of the church building he loved horrified him.

The priest was grateful that he had been allowed to spend the night here, in the company of church vestments and the archdiocese records, familiar objects that gave him comfort. He had done what he could to save the businessman's life, and the rest was in God's hands. He rose from his kneeling position and sat down at his desk, his head bowed in reflection and remorse.

Was he the one who was responsible for the breakdown in security? The cathedral should have been cleared of tourists—of anyone who did not have an invitation to the wedding—an hour before the service began. Anyone attending the wedding had to enter through the front doors. So how had these terrorists managed to elude detection by the security guards?

The plazas surrounding the Cathedral of the Divine Savior had buzzed with activity this Friday morning. Businessmen, shoppers, tourists, and government officials entering or leaving the State Palace immediately in front of the cathedral had filled the historic center of this old colonial city with the sounds of life. As noon approached, wedding guests had congregated at the front entrance to the pink-stoned cathedral as they waited for the arrival of the bride and bridegroom. Strolling musicians especially hired for the event entertained them while vendors hawked flowers and flasks of champagne.

He should have been in his office by eleven o'clock, preparing for the wedding ceremony, but he had been running late. He had been visiting a travel agency across the plaza to plan a trip to Italy and Spain upon his retirement in six months. Loaded down with travel books and pamphlets, he had pushed his way through the crowded plaza to a side door of the cathedral, to which he had a key. It was only a short distance from the side door to the sacristy, where his vestments were stored. Perspiring in the late morning heat, he had fumbled for his keys, relaxing his grip on the travel material, which had tumbled to the ground. Before he could stoop to pick up the books and pamphlets, a young man who had been standing nearby had rushed to his aid.

"May I help you, Father?" he had asked in a pleasant voice. Father Cardozo remembered that the young man had quickly picked up the scattered material and then had held the door open for the priest after he had unlocked it. The priest had thanked the young man for his kindness and hurried to his office, assuming that the door would close and lock behind him. But it had not. The young man must have held the door slightly ajar and then slipped into the dark interior of the cathedral unobserved, waiting for an opportunity to admit his comrades.

Ten minutes into the wedding service, masked men—their guns at the ready and grenades held aloft—had rushed to the altar and taken up position at the doors, blocking any attempt to escape. The outnumbered security guards had no choice but to surrender their weapons.

Hours later had come the execution of the businessman. He had protested to no avail, only incurring the wrath of the terrorist leader. The guards had beaten him as they dragged him away before throwing him into the sacristy. One of his assailants resembled the young man who had helped him earlier in the day to retrieve his scattered brochures and unlock the cathedral door. His formerly pleasant features were now hardened into a savage mask.

"I will pray for your soul," he had promised before the door was slammed shut.

Hours passed before the sound of footsteps outside the door alerted him that his fate had been decided. The door opened and three men entered—El Verdugo flanked by two guards. No word was spoken. The guards seized him by his arms and led him out of the sacristy into the nave of the cathedral. He shrugged off their hands and walked slowly down the corridor toward the massive doors at the front of the church. It was a desolate scene—women weeping, men sitting in stone-faced silence. Which among them would be the next victim?

The guards threw open the doors. The priest was blinded by the midday light. He felt the cold metal of a gun pressed against the back of his head. His last thought was *Father, protect the innocent victims of my mistakes!*

The Police Informer

Chapter Sixteen

Bob glanced warily at the Turk, who had once again stretched out on his cot but with his eyes open. Occasionally his eyes flicked toward Bob. Ozmen's suspicions were well-founded although Bob had denied his accusation. He was a police informer, but not a willing one. He had been forced into it. In retrospect, he was certain the evening in Greenwich six weeks ago, when he had gone to plead for Dave's help in getting a loan, had been the opening move by the FBI to entrap him.

That night, John Shafer, Bob's FBI handler, had invited himself and his wife over to Dave's house for dinner. "Just passing through town and would love to reminisce about our college days at Princeton"—or so the pretext went. Dave was too trusting and honorable to suspect Shafer's real motive, which was to ferret out information about Bob's activities. Bob had known Shafer for only a few weeks, but he judged him to be a man cynical enough to use old friendships, even to employ blackmail against his friend's brother, in pursuit of his professional goals, which included the shutdown of the Ottoman Trading Company operations in the United States.

Of course, Shafer would not have known that Bob would drop in unexpectedly. Shafer's curiosity would have been aroused when Dave excused himself from the dinner table because he had to meet with his brother. Was that why Shafer had come in from the patio just as Bob was about to leave Dave's house—to catch a glimpse of him?

Bob's meeting with Dave that evening was awkward. It was their first meeting since Bob's divorce from his wife, Jennifer. To break the ice, he brought along his Boston terrier, Jack, who succeeded at making friends wherever he went. He dreaded this meeting, requesting it only as a last resort because he hated to admit that he had made a mistake after their father's death two years ago.

At that time, Dave had proposed to divide the estate equally with Bob after the sale of the family home in Greenwich and the auction of their father's valuable art collection at Sotheby's in New York. The proposal had been reasonable, but Dave's patronizing manner in offering to overlook Bob's unpaid debts to their father had grated. What had he called it—an offer too good to refuse! Left unsaid but implicit was Bob's need for money.

Impetuously, Bob had objected to Dave's plan—not to the sale of the house but to the sale of the art collection. He had never shown much interest in art in general and their father's collection in particular. It was too traditional to suit his tastes. His arguments that the art collection should be kept within the family or at least not broken up had been insincere, deliberately contrived to annoy Dave. He still remembered his satisfaction at seeing the shocked expression on his brother's face. Their dispute over the art collection had now simmered for two years.

Seated in his cherry-paneled library lined with books, Dave asked, "Why the sudden urgency? Why do you want to sell the paintings now?"

Bob said tersely, "I need the money."

"So what else is new?" The sarcastic tone of Dave's voice stung.

Bob suppressed the urge to shoot back with *You are a smug son of a bitch, aren't you?* But his discomfort was evident.

Dave laughingly apologized, "Don't take offense, Bob. I meant that as a joke. Besides, we could both use the money! Anything happening in your life that I should know about?"

Bob improvised what he hoped would be a plausible story—that he was falling behind on alimony payments and was also getting remarried to Andrea, a young lady from Philadelphia who worked in New York as a producer for one of the major television networks.

He did not mention the real reason for his financial woes: the police seizure of drugs that he had stashed in the apartment of his friend, Tony Santelli. They planned to go fifty-fifty on the deal, but Tony had not paid him yet for his share. Until he did, Bob could not pay their supplier, Murat. Now Tony was on the run trying to avoid arrest. His chances of being paid were slim. Tony had not tried to contact him yet, which was a relief because any communication—a telephone call, a letter—might lead the police to his door.

"Could you get a bank loan for me using the paintings as collateral? I am okay with selling the paintings at a Sotheby auction, but that would take too long. I need money now."

"Couldn't you get the loan yourself?"

Bob felt humiliated admitting to his brother, "It would be better if you did it. My credit is kind of shaky now."

Dave's face betrayed his feelings. He did not like the proposal. "How much would you need?"

"One million. It would be an advance on my share of the paintings."

The paintings had been appraised at $10 million, but the proposal stunned Dave, who stammered, "I'd like to think about it over the weekend and discuss it further over lunch next week. How about the Harvard Club?"

Bob shook his head. He needed no reminders of how he had disappointed his father. Dave, realizing his miscue, hastily agreed to meet at a restaurant instead.

Then Bob's phone rang, a fateful call which changed the direction of his life. Jack trotted after him into the hallway, where he talked softly so that Dave would not be able to overhear. He concluded the call with words that he wished now had never been spoken: "Don't worry, buddy. I'll take care of you. See you in two hours at the same place we met last time!"

The faint scent that the FBI hounds had been sniffing at now became overpowering.

Chapter Seventeen

Bob selected a steak-and-seafood establishment in midtown Manhattan, which had been one of their father's favorites. Photographs of celebrities (movie stars, athletes, politicians) and iconic buildings in New York lined the walls. The lunchtime crowd was thinning. The tables next to them were already empty, and a waiter anxiously glanced in their direction to determine whether they wanted their check. But Dave remained unconvinced.

"Bob, your story does not hang together. Melanie spoke to Jennifer, your ex-wife, on Sunday afternoon. This may not be news to you, but Jennifer will be marrying a wealthy hedge fund manager in Greenwich in a few weeks. So why should she be beating on you for missed alimony payments? Soon she will have more money than she knows what to do with. You don't have children to support. So what's the deal?"

"Look, I need the money. I don't need to give you any further explanation. I am a big boy now. I don't have to answer to big brother. You don't trust me, do you? You never have, always looking down your nose at me, the little brother who could never quite get his act together."

Bob's face flushed, his voice rising. The waiter turned to look at them.

"Bob, I am sorry if I pissed you off, but don't blame me. You would have had the money from the paintings a long time ago if you had only agreed to put them up for auction at Sotheby's."

"I am agreeing now."

"Putting the paintings up for auction will take two months. Sotheby's will want to appraise the paintings again to make sure that everything is in order. Will that be soon enough?"

"No, I need the money now. It's rightfully mine. If you get a loan on my behalf, your skin will be on the line for only a few months. We know what the paintings are worth. You're covered. So why are you stalling?"

"If I am to get a loan on your behalf, I need some background information." Dave could not help showing his exasperation.

"Like what?"

"For starters, what have you done with the money that you inherited from the sale of Dad's house and your share of his financial assets? Frittered it away?"

"Okay, if you want to know," Bob said through clenched teeth, "I made some bad investments in a biotech company that went bust, using a margin account. My broker is demanding that I pony up the money fast."

Dave sighed in relief. At least Bob's explanation seemed plausible. But he still felt uneasy. "Is that all? You aren't in some kind of trouble, are you?"

"Isn't that enough trouble?"

"Are you still employed?"

"Yes, with an import-export trading firm."

"Which one?"

"Ottoman Trading Company. We import mostly Turkish textiles, but also carpets, dates, sunflower seeds, shoes . . . whatever into the United States."

"And you export?"

"Whatever there is a market for—electronics, pharmaceuticals, you name it."

"Where are they based?"

"In Istanbul, with offices in New York and elsewhere around the world."

Dave pondered in silence. He did not want to risk an irrevocable breach with his kid brother. “Okay, Bob. I’ll do it. We’re family. I will call my banker this afternoon. I may have to offer my own investments as collateral, but I should have the money before we leave on our cruise, toward the end of next week.”

“Thanks, Dave. I knew you’d come through.” Bob’s face relaxed in a grin, his forehead glistening with perspiration.

Good old reliable Dave got that loan for Bob. But the difficulties which it was intended to solve were quickly overtaken by a chain of events leading to this rendezvous with death in Mexico City. It was strange how his former differences with his brother now seemed trivial.

Chapter Eighteen

Bob Bigelow rang the doorbell of the brownstone at 400 West Eighty-Fourth Street; he was juggling two bags of takeout food that he had picked up at a nearby Italian restaurant. The setting sun was already casting long shadows, offering relief from what had been a warm and humid day. He squinted in the fading sunlight, searching for signs of the two men in a car who had been following him for several days. They had parked on the curb by the restaurant earlier today, when he had lunch with his brother, and he was certain that he had seen them outside the offices of the Ottoman Trading Company yesterday.

Hearing the light tread of a woman's heels on the carpeting inside the brownstone, he turned, his heart beating faster, to greet Andrea Williams as she opened the door. She looked stunning framed against the doorway, her light dress hugging her trim figure and accentuating her shoulder-length dark hair. Normally, she would have kissed his lips and clung to him; but tonight, she gave him only a small peck on the cheek. She seemed tense, a small frown furrowing her forehead.

"Dinner is served, my love," he joked, holding up the two bags of takeout food. "Sautéed calamari, beet salad with goat cheese, and trout filet—"

She motioned him inside and shut the door. "I am not in the mood to eat tonight." She sighed. "I've had an absolutely awful day. I'm sorry, sweetie."

He was puzzled, but before he could ask what had happened, she turned on the television, clicking through several channels before she came to one offering the evening news.

"Look!"

The news anchor finished a report on the latest bloody fighting in the Syrian civil war. Then, gazing somberly into the cameras, he continued gravely, "The entertainment world and Fred Sanford's many admirers were shocked to learn today of the untimely death of the actor, an Emmy Award winner whose comic talents catapulted the television show *West Side Follies* to the top of the Nielsen ratings in prime time three years in a row. He was discovered dead in the bedroom of his Manhattan apartment. An investigation is being carried out, but it would appear that he died from an overdose of heroin. He was known to have been suffering from severe back pain due to a skiing injury last year. He is survived by his wife and two children."

Andrea shivered as she muted the television set. "I don't know what I will do. He was the star of my show, and I don't have an obvious replacement. It could take months to find someone, and I can do reruns of old shows for only so long. Our Nielsen ratings could plummet!"

Bob hastened to reassure her, "Don't worry, sweetheart. You'll find someone soon. There are plenty of actors looking for jobs now, and your show would be a plum assignment." He had never before seen Andrea—a thoroughly professional, self-possessed woman—as distraught as she was tonight. His words seemed to calm her. She even attempted a smile and squeezed his hand.

"Let's have dinner," she said. "We will overcome together."

Bob was less confident than Andrea. He took a deep breath to steady himself. The news shocked him, but for reasons unknown to her. He was relieved that his hands were not trembling as he spread the plates, utensils, and food on the dining table and poured the wine.

Andrea bravely sipped her wine and nibbled at her food but then slumped in her chair and wailed, "How could he be that stupid! I talked to him last Friday. He seemed in good spirits. What could have happened over the weekend? If he needed a fix, I could have provided him with some stuff. So could you for that matter. There is so much good coke out there right now. Instead, he picked up some weird heroin capable of killing him."

Bob shook his head, not looking at her. "You maybe, but not me. You are forgetting. My supplies are drying up. Two weeks ago, the police raided Tony Santelli's apartment, where I had most of my stuff stashed. You've met Tony, right? He's been on the run ever since the police raided his place. He wasn't home at the time. He still hasn't paid me for his share. Maybe he never will. He left a voice-mail message at my office today when I was out for lunch with Dave. He sounded like he was at the end of his rope, ready to turn himself in to the police."

"Did you talk to him later?"

"No. He didn't leave a number, and he didn't call back."

"So where does that leave you?"

"If I don't pay Murat for the last deal, he won't give me any more, for starters. He said so at a meeting this afternoon when I got back from lunch with my brother."

"You told him that you were getting the money?"

"Yes. At first, he was a real bastard, almost threatening me physically. He said that if I knew what was good for me, I would pay my bills. I was only a small-time peddler, and there were dozens eager to take my place. He had only cut me into a deal because you and he are friends."

Andrea sighed. "I regret introducing the two of you at that New Year's party. But you needed a job. He did me a favor. Do you want me to talk to him again? I already called him yesterday."

"No, that won't be necessary. He seemed to chill out when I told him that my brother would be providing me with the money. We then got to talking about the latest venture that he is working on. He implied that there could be a big payoff for me if I played by the rules."

Andrea raised her eyebrows. "What could that be?"

"A lot of heroin, cocaine, and amphetamines from Colombia and Mexico are flowing into the United States. He wants to get a bigger slice of the business. Murat is talking with Istanbul about a bilateral deal—exchanging US machinery for Mexican cement—that could open up some interesting possibilities. After the free trade agreement is signed between Turkey and Mexico later this year, he can also foresee getting some of that Colombian cocaine and heroin into the European market as well."

Andrea pursed her lips disapprovingly. "Do me a favor. Be very careful. Murat is a clever man, but he scares me. There is safety in being a small fish. If you get too big, you will be busted. I love you and don't want you to get in trouble, okay?"

They cleared the table of dishes, rinsed them, and put them into the dishwasher. It was a very domestic scene, almost as if the death of Fred Sanford had never occurred, as they chattered about the other events of the day.

"Dave mentioned a couple of times he would very much like to meet you."

"I would love to meet him and his wife, Melanie, too. But not this week. Okay?"

He caressed her cheek. "Would you like me to stay the night?"

She smiled weakly. "That's sweet of you, but not tonight. I am feeling tired. I still need to talk to Fred's wife. I tried to call her this afternoon, but she was not taking calls. I will try again now. It will be tough." Her eyes glistened with tears.

"Okay." He tried to look disappointed but felt relieved. He had a call to make.

Walking along the darkened streets in the direction of Columbus Avenue, he relived the sickening details of Saturday evening. The call he received while he was sitting in his brother's library in Greenwich had been from Fred Sanford. They had met at one of Andrea's dinner parties, where guests had openly smoked pot. In this permissive setting, Bob had revealed to Fred that he could provide him with recreational drugs whenever he wanted.

Fred seemed in genuine pain. "Look, Bob, my back is killing me, but my doctor won't renew my prescription for a painkiller. He fears that I am becoming addicted. Can you help me out?"

Bob made his fateful promise to help. Most of his supplies had been seized by the police, but he had one last pouch available. They agreed to meet at a bar near Lincoln Center, where the transfer was made. Fred was grateful. He trusted Bob.

Now Bob had a man's death on his conscience. To make matters worse, if the police traced the last telephone call Fred made to him, he would be brought in for questioning. If Andrea found out, would she ever forgive him?

Bob struggled to contain his anger, which had been building all evening. Stopping when there were no pedestrians nearby to overhear, he phoned an unlisted number. A man with a foreign accent answered, and his voice chilled when he recognized Bob.

"I have told you never to disturb me at home."

"You gave me bad stuff!" Bob shouted into the receiver.

"If you had paid your bills in a timely manner, I would have given you better stuff."

"Murat, you killed Fred Sanford!"

"Watch what you say, my friend. Your words could come back to haunt you. I have had enough for tonight." The menace in the man's voice was unmistakable before he hung up.

Chapter Nineteen

Later that week, on Friday night, the FBI pounced, although they had the good taste to wait until Bob and Andrea had eaten dinner at *Per Se*, the highly acclaimed French restaurant on Columbus Circle, to put the final touches on plans for their wedding and honeymoon. They were waiting for their dessert and coffee when Andrea shifted the conversation away from their nuptial plans. It was the first ominous storm cloud on the horizon.

"I had a visitor today. An investigator from the City police department. He was accompanied by someone from the FBI."

"No kidding."

"They wanted information about Fred Sanford—how long I had known him, whether he had any professional or personal problems that would have driven him to suicide. I told them what I knew. We were friends for a long time. We met and dated at college. Our lives thereafter went in different directions, but eventually, he became the star of my television show. By that time, he had married and lived with his wife and two small children in Westport, Connecticut. After he started working for me, he got a small apartment in New York, where he could stay on nights when he had to work late."

"I didn't know there was a personal side to your relationship."

She smiled reassuringly. "Don't worry. That part of our relationship died a long time ago. More important is that they asked about you—what connection you had to Fred Sanford."

"Why me?"

"They said telephone records showed that Fred called you on the night of his death."

Bob shrugged nonchalantly. "So he called me. I can't even remember what he called me about. Oh yeah. It was about our wedding date. He had travel plans in October and wanted to make sure that he was here for the wedding."

"Well, if that was what he wanted to know, why didn't he call me? He's known me for a long time. He only met you at one of my dinner parties."

"Look, the police are on a wild fishing expedition for leads as to the cause of Fred's death. It was probably an accidental overdose, not a suicide. It doesn't surprise me that they asked you. They called my office today when I was out for lunch. The call was referred by the secretary to Murat."

"What did Murat say?"

"He only confirmed that I am an employee of Ottoman Trading Company. For further information, they would need to talk to me."

"Murat and you are still on speaking terms?"

"Oh yes. I told him that my brother would have the money to me by Monday or Tuesday of next week."

"You really seem to burn through money. You have a salary and you make extra by selling . . . you know what." She looked over her shoulder and lowered her voice as she said it, to make sure no one was within hearing distance. "Now here you are, borrowing money from your brother."

"I have some debt hanging over from my marriage and divorce, some bad investments, an expensive lifestyle . . ." His voice trailed off.

His words made him sound like a loser, which was definitely not the impression he wanted to give to Andrea. He was a little afraid of her. She was a very successful professional, dedicated to her career twenty-hours of the day, forever checking her emails, even when they were having dinner. How could he have been so lucky as to win this beautiful woman? What had she seen in him? A handsome man down on his luck, someone she felt sorry for? He knew that the affair she had been having with the president of her company, a married man, had broken up shortly before they met. Was he merely the most eligible available male that she could find on the rebound?

She looked hard at him then smiled. "Bob, I hope you are not hiding anything from me about Fred. When we marry, I have to have complete confidence that you will never withhold the truth from me. Is that understood?"

"Of course. I will expect the same of you." He returned her gaze and grasped her hand, which he raised to his lips. The coffee and dessert arrived conveniently at this point, and the conversation reverted to their wedding plans.

It was a pleasant evening in late August, still warm but with a hint of fall in the air. They considered walking to Andrea's brownstone but decided to take a taxi instead.

When they were inside, Andrea embraced him and apologized. "I'm sorry, Bob. I didn't mean to sound as if I doubted you."

They whispered mutual forgiveness and then made love passionately. For a few moments, it was possible to believe that nothing was changing, that their relationship still had a solid foundation. Around midnight, he left her brownstone, not expecting two figures to emerge from the shadows.

Chapter Twenty

"Mr. Bigelow? We are police officers." They flashed their badges. "We would like to talk to you."

"About what?"

"I think you know. Did Ms. Williams tell you that we visited her earlier today? We also called your office, but you were apparently unavailable."

The taller of the two, a black officer who identified himself as Leroy Brown, motioned him toward a waiting police car, its engine idling.

"Look, Officer, this is very unusual, interrogating me at midnight."

"We will only take a few minutes of your time. Get in the car."

The two officers, one on either side, grabbed his arms and pushed him into the back seat of the car. Then they were beside him, one on either side. The doors slammed, and the car pulled away from the curb. It happened so quickly that only an observer standing nearby would have noticed anything unusual.

Bob was both frightened and furious. "Where are you taking me? If you are going to arrest me, I want to see my lawyer."

"We are only taking you to the Eighty-Second Street West precinct for questioning. Then you will be free to go."

Soon they were sitting in a small conference room—bare gray walls, a flickering fluorescent light, a shabby table, and hard wooden chairs.

"Coffee?" Brown asked.

Bob declined. The smell of stale cigarette smoke and coffee turned his stomach.

Brown began the questioning. “Mr. Bigelow, telephone records indicate that Fred Sanford, the television actor, called you the night of his death. You are aware that he died on Saturday night and that his body was discovered on Monday morning?”

Bob nodded.

“Why did he call you?”

“We were acquaintances. I met him at a dinner party given by my fiancée, Andrea Williams. He wanted to know our wedding date. He had travel plans in October and wanted to make sure that he would be here for the wedding.”

“I think you are lying.”

Bob did not respond. *Keep your cool*, he told himself.

“We have talked to the doorman of Sanford’s apartment building on Riverside Boulevard. He went out the night of his death and was gone for an hour. Your apartment building is near Lincoln Center, a few blocks away. Did you meet?”

“I am not answering any more questions unless my lawyer is present.”

“Look, the police are asking the public for information about Sanford’s whereabouts on the night he died. A doorman, a bartender, a pedestrian on the street might have noticed. His face was known to millions of television viewers. Sooner or later, the information will come out.”

Bob remained silent, looking past Brown at the wall.

“At least, you can give us some basic facts. You are employed by Ottoman Trading Company?”

“You know that already, so why bother asking?”

“What kind of work do you do?”

“I keep the financial records for the New York office of Ottoman Trading Company.”

“And you report to whom?”

“Recep Murat, the chief operating officer.”

“That’s all?”

"I also send regular reports to the head office in Istanbul."

"How long have you worked there?"

"Since January."

Bob recognized the second officer, white and dressed in a business suit, who now intervened. He had been his brother's dinner guest less than a week before on Saturday. He said, "Allow me to introduce myself. I am John Shafer of the FBI. I have been asked to assist in this case."

Shafer took charge. "You have been under surveillance for some time, well before the death of Fred Sanford. Do you know an investment banker named Edward Sutton? He was admitted into hospital on April 3 after injecting heroin. He identified you as the supplier who sold him the drug at a charity ball. Two months later, a retail executive, Alfred Draper, was stopped for reckless driving. Tests indicated that he was under the influence of a drug, cocaine. In his car, police discovered a pouch of heroin. He said he had met the vendor of the drugs at a political fund-raiser at the Waldorf-Astoria. He did not know the vendor's name, but his description fits you."

Bob began to have difficulty breathing. His sweaty palms told him that he was in deep trouble.

"Our labs have analyzed the heroin in the Sutton, Draper, and Sanford cases. They have the same source—Middle Eastern. Perhaps you could shed some light on the origin of the drug and how it is getting into this country."

"I have nothing to say."

"Do you know Tony Santelli?"

"We were roommates during a college semester in Mexico City."

"The police raided his apartment a few weeks ago. He evaded arrest at the time. They discovered a stash of drugs—also Middle Eastern in origin—and combed the place for fingerprints. Yours were among them."

"Look, I can explain. Tony threw a birthday party some weeks back. He invited a whole bunch of people, me included. I don't know much about his personal life or why he would be in trouble with the police."

Shafer snorted in disbelief and then looked quizzically at Brown. Brown nodded his head in agreement.

"When did you last see or hear from Tony Santelli?"

"At his party."

"Not more recently since his apartment was raided?"

"No."

"Where were you on Monday night of this week?"

"With my girlfriend, having dinner at her place."

"That squares with what we know about your whereabouts. You have an alibi. Tony Santelli's body was found floating in the Hudson River on Tuesday, inside a garbage bag, a gunshot to the head. The coroner estimates the time of his death as Monday night. Do you know who would want to kill Santelli?"

Bob was so shocked by the news of Santelli's death that he could barely whisper, "No."

"He called the police last Saturday, offering to turn himself in, but he never showed up at the bar where he wanted to be picked up. An informant claims to have last seen him on Monday in the company of a big burly guy—someone who looks like a nightclub bouncer. Does the name Buzz Malone mean anything to you?"

"He works at Ottoman Trading Company as the driver and personal bodyguard of Recep Murat."

"Any idea why Murat would need a bodyguard?"

Bob remained silent.

"At least you can confirm some personal details. Dropped out of a business program at New York University after two years of college? Divorced? The brother of David Bigelow, a partner at a prominent New York law firm?"

Suddenly, Bob became agitated, his numbness fading. "You leave him out of this!" he snapped.

"For his sake, I will do my best." Shafer smiled. "Dave was my college roommate at Princeton."

"If you are going to lock me up, I demand to see my lawyer."

"We have a better idea." Shafer looked over at Brown, who again nodded his head. "You are free to go, even though we have enough evidence to arrest you and put you behind bars for some time. The reason is that we would like you to work with us. You are a small fry in the big pond. We would like to catch the big fish. You could be very helpful."

"How?"

"We have our suspicions about Ottoman Trading Company but no proof. You have access to the financial records of the New York office of OTC and contact with head office in Istanbul. Over time, if you gain their trust, you should be able to gather useful information about their operations."

"If I cooperate, what do I get in return?"

"Leniency. We might even drop all charges."

Bob was tempted. What other option did he have? He could try to escape to a country that did not have an extradition treaty with the United States, like Brazil, but what kind of life would he have? Andrea would not follow him if she found out why he was fleeing.

He swallowed hard. "Let me think about it. Where can I reach you if I decide to work with you?" he asked, looking at Shafer.

"My office is in the Federal Building in downtown Manhattan."

"Okay." He looked at both Brown and Shafer then walked out of the conference room and through the front doors of the police precinct, a drowning man gasping for air.

Chapter Twenty-One

Several days after Shafer's offer, Bob was summoned to Murat's office. He was nervous when asked to close the door and sit down. What did Murat know about the death of Tony Santelli? Had Murat ordered Buzz Malone to meet with Tony Santelli to prevent him from turning himself in to the police?

For a moment, Murat said nothing while he fidgeted with the drawer of his desk. As the seconds ticked by, Bob's panic heightened. Did Murat have a gun in the drawer? Was he next on Murat's hit list? When Murat finally spoke, his large eyes focusing on Bob, he made a proposal that nearly bowled him over.

"My visitors from Istanbul and I discussed your future yesterday. You have done a good job taking care of the financial records of the New York office to make sure that nothing will seem irregular to our auditors. Our public image must be that of an ordinary trading company and nothing more. That is very important to the owners of this company. But as you know, we have a sideline business."

He paused to let the words, spoken with a thick Turkish accent, sink in. His intonations were not harsh, but he substituted the sounds of "v" and "w" for each other and had difficulty with the diphthong so that "th" sounded like "t." He also struggled with the sounds of "er" and "or," which came out sounding like "oor."

He continued, "You received drugs from me to peddle to your wealthy and glamorous friends. They belonged to the company, not to me. There was some risk to me in trusting you, but you have an expensive lifestyle. I calculated correctly, did I not—that you could use extra income? Unfortunately, I had to mention to my visitors that your failure to pay for these drugs is a stumbling block to the further advancement of your career in this company."

"No longer!" Bob interrupted as, with shaking hands, he extracted a check from his wallet and placed it on the desk in front of Murat. He had received the expected money transfer from his brother that morning, and as previously instructed by Murat, he had made the check for a million dollars payable to GH Holdings rather than Ottoman Trading Company.

Murat's somber face was suddenly wreathed in smiles. "We have had a few tense moments when it appeared that you might be unable to pay for the merchandise."

"I made some bad investment decisions. I am not a spendthrift," Bob had said defensively.

"Ah yes, the stock market can be fickle at times. I prefer real estate myself. But let us put that behind us. I apologize if I seemed unpleasant at times."

Bob prudently disguised his anger, shrugging his shoulders. "No problem."

"There have been some recent police enquiries about you. I was always confident that you would be discreet in your sale of drugs. Should I be concerned? We would not want a repetition of the police raid on Tony Santelli's apartment. He was, fortunately, not an employee of Ottoman Trading Company so that he cannot be directly traced back to us."

"No need to worry," Bob lied smoothly, steadily meeting Murat's gaze. "The police only wanted to talk to me about a call Fred Sanford made to me about my upcoming wedding."

Then, casually, almost as an afterthought, he asked, "Have you heard from Tony Santelli since the police raid?" Bob's curiosity about Murat's role in Santelli's murder had finally overcome his caution.

Murat picked up Bob's check from his desk, examining it as if he wanted to verify its authenticity. His face was impassive and his eyes hooded when he looked up. "Yes, he called me at home and left a voice-mail message that he needed to talk to me. He said that he was using a prepaid disposable phone because he did not want the police to be able to trace his call. He angered me because, as you know, I do not like to be called at home."

"When was that?"

Murat frowned before answering, "I cannot remember exactly. It was on the weekend. Then on Monday of last week, he called my office—something he had never done before. It showed bad judgment. I was in a meeting and my secretary was away from her desk so that Buzz Malone took the call. Santelli sounded very upset. Buzz offered to help him. They agreed to meet at a Starbucks in Chelsea, but Santelli never showed up, and we have not heard from him again."

Neither met nor heard from him again? Bob thought, his heart pounding. That contradicted what John Shafer had said about Santelli last being seen in the company of Malone.

Murat's face now relaxed into a smile. "But that's enough about Santelli. He was a talented but unreliable man. Not right for our organization. Unlike you. Demir, Batur, and I concluded yesterday that you could be very helpful to us in setting up a new business in Mexico. I looked at your file. You studied Spanish in high school, and you spent a semester at the National Autonomous University of Mexico before you dropped out of college."

Bob nodded, not wanting to arouse Murat's suspicions by probing further about Santelli, his roommate that semester. "Yes, that's right. What kind of business would this be? Are you talking about transferring me to Mexico City?"

"No, you can be more useful to us here. You would continue as you are now but would make occasional trips to Mexico, acting as liaison with our trading partners. It would be a typical trading operation, exchanging electrical equipment for tomatoes and avocadoes or whatever else we can come up with." He winked at Bob. "Would this interest you?"

"Why, that sounds great!" Bob's voice cracked. The proposal was risky, and he was nervous, but what choice did he have? He had to play along if he wanted to keep his job and not provoke Murat. "Would there be any danger to me? I mean, the drug gangs in Mexico have become increasingly violent in recent years."

Murat hastened to reassure him. "No risk at all. You would be an American businessman visiting Mexico. The Mexican drug gangs only attack each other. You have lived there and, since then, have visited Mexico a couple of times. A very pleasant country."

No risk at all. Murat's words echoed in Bob's mind as he hurried into Penn Station on a late lunch break, stopping at a shop to buy a throwaway phone. After getting the FBI telephone number from information, he waited anxiously for John Shafer to answer.

Turning back was no longer an option. His mouth dry, a bead of sweat rolling down his brow, Bob awkwardly introduced himself.

Shafer did not seem surprised by his call. "Have you thought over my offer?"

"Yes. I-I need to see you," Bob stammered.

"Where are you now?"

"Penn Station, using one of those disposable cell phones. I don't want this call to be traceable or to be seen anywhere near the Federal Building. Where can we meet?"

"I can't come to Penn Station now. Let me think for a moment." There had been a long pause. "Okay. Let's meet at six at a bar in the Edison Hotel on Forty-Seventh Street West between Seventh and Eighth Avenues. I think it's called Rum House. I will be sitting at the bar with someone I would like you to meet. We will save a seat between us. When you get there, walk over to join us."

That evening, Bob walked from his office to the meeting with Shafer, stopping several times to survey other pedestrians. He felt paranoid about being followed by Buzz Malone or any of Murat's other henchmen.

Tour groups milled around the ornate Art Deco lobby of the historic hotel as he entered. It was not a businessmen's hotel. The Rum House, just off the lobby, was already lively. Most of the clientele were casually dressed. Shafer, sitting at one end of the curving bar, stood out because he was in a business suit. The seat next to him was empty.

Bob walked over to claim the empty seat. Only after he placed his order with the bartender did Shafer speak to him, but as if they were casual strangers.

"Nice evening, isn't it?"

Shafer looked around to make sure that no one was close enough to overhear, but there was no danger. The happy hour chatter in a crowded barroom provided safe cover. "I'd like you to meet a friend of mine," he said, nodding his head in the direction of the man sitting to Bob's right.

Bob took the man on his right to be a tourist, casually dressed in denims and open knit shirt, sneakers, a baseball cap on his head, a camera slung over his shoulder. His eyes were intently fixed on the television screen over the bar, watching a baseball game between the New York Yankees and the Boston Red Sox. But now, as if on cue, he turned toward Bob and introduced himself.

"Hi. I am Jim Connors of the Drug Enforcement Agency." He did not shake Bob's hand but rather pushed a cocktail napkin in his direction. Protruding from underneath was the corner of a card with his contact information.

"Jim and I work closely together. He will be your alternate contact if I am not available," Shafer added. "Jim has written my direct telephone number on the back of his card. To be safe, memorize the contact information and destroy the card."

"By the way," Shafer whispered, "the bartender at the Bar Boulud positively identified you as the man who drank with Fred Sanford the night he died."

Bob knew instantly that Shafer was bluffing. It had not been the Bar Boulud. But Bob felt trapped. His world was spinning out of control. He wanted to run out of the bar and escape, hail a taxi on the street to take him to Kennedy Airport. But where could he go? Running would be futile. They would eventually find him. Somehow he had expected this first meeting to be different. A few welcoming words from Shafer, for instance. Instead, Shafer was making clear who was in charge. He would be their informant, not a colleague—someone to be used until he was no longer needed.

Connors broke the silence. "John tells me you might have something interesting to tell us."

Bob took a deep breath. "There was a new development today. Murat called me into his office today. I have been asked to help OTC set up a trading operation in Mexico. Murat wants to get a slice of the illegal drugs flowing into the United States."

"This will be a drug operation only?"

"No, a legitimate trading operation—with a sideline. Murat discussed this proposal with two Turks who visited him yesterday."

"What are their names?"

"I know only their first names, Demir and Batur. I can get their last names if you want. They weren't around today, so they may have flown back to Istanbul last night."

"Don't arouse suspicion by asking too many questions. We can check the departing passenger lists. So when do you go to Mexico?"

"Next week. Mexico City. I do not have detailed instructions yet."

"Anything else?"

"Murat admitted to me that Santelli had called him at home and at his office just before he was killed. Malone had agreed to meet him, but Murat claims that Santelli never showed up."

Shafer grimaced. "We will follow up on that lead. By the way, a report crossed my desk late this afternoon. We have been monitoring your checking account. There was a very large deposit and almost simultaneous withdrawal this morning. Anything you want to tell us?"

Bob gulped. Didn't he have a right to privacy? "I owed Murat money for some uh . . . merchandise that he had given me."

"How much was the check?"

"A million dollars."

Connors whistled softly. "Nice. And the merchandise was . . .?"

"Cocaine and heroin."

"To whom did you make out the check?"

"GH Holdings, an affiliate of Ottoman Trading Company in the Cayman Islands."

"A typical daisy chain. Multiple stops before it gets back to headquarters," Shafer said.

"Do you know any of the other people who have been peddling drugs for OTC, apart from the late Tony Santelli?" Connors asked.

"No."

"Interesting," Connors murmured as he got up from his chair and walked closer to the television screen to get a better view. The Red Sox had just hit a home run.

Shafer motioned to the bartender to get him another drink. "Let's keep in touch. Keep feeding us information. But don't take any crazy risks, understood?"

The meeting was over, but Bob's career as an informer for the FBI and DEA had just begun.

Chapter Twenty-Two

Murat gave Bob careful instructions before he departed for Mexico City. The host for the lunch at the Olivier—a French bistro on the fashionable Avenida Presidente Mazaryk—would be the commercial attaché at the Turkish embassy in Mexico City, Kemal Balbay. He had worked tirelessly to bring about the free trade agreement between Mexico and Turkey, which would be signed and ratified in December. Also attending would be Aslan Celik—chairman of the Turkish Federation of International Trade and a good friend of Emir Tilki and the Ottoman Trading Company—who was visiting the Mexican capital from Istanbul.

These worthy gentlemen would provide cover for his meeting with the most important person there: Diego Alvarez, an executive with Veracruz Sugar. The ostensible object of the luncheon was to discuss the import of Mexican refined sugar into Turkey and to explore similar opportunities in the United States. If an opportunity presented itself, he could deliver a sealed envelope to Alvarez during lunch. Otherwise, Alvarez would call him and invite him to a second meeting at a place of his choosing, where the delivery could be made without attracting notice.

Their Turkish host was at the point of despairing when Alvarez finally arrived, apologizing for being delayed by heavy traffic. He spoke rapidly in flawless English delivered in a soft Mexican accent, his white teeth flashing against his tanned brown skin. Unlike the other men, he wore a light summer suit, tieless, with an open-necked shirt. When he gestured with his hands, Bob noticed three rings on his fingers, one of which was set with a sparkling diamond. Alvarez was not your typical businessman.

Within two hours, the business luncheon ended with handshakes all around. Alvarez promised that he or a representative of his company would visit Istanbul in the fall to discuss possible deals with his Turkish counterparts. Celik and Balbay offered their assistance in setting up meetings.

To Bob, he said, "I will be visiting New York in early September. Could you schedule a meeting for me with your firm so that I can learn more about your market expertise and trading capabilities? Perhaps we can explore sales opportunities in both the United States and Turkey." Again he smiled, but his opaque eyes did not reveal a hidden meaning.

When Bob walked back to his room at the W Hotel on Campos Eliseos in the Polanco business district, he reported to Murat on his phone. "The lunch went as planned. Alvarez indicated that he is coming to New York in early September and would like to meet you."

"Excellent. My schedule is open the week after Labor Day."

"I will mention that to him tonight. I am in my room waiting for his call."

"You still have the instructions with you?"

"Yes. I took the envelope to lunch with me, in case he could not meet tonight."

"Smart. One can never be too careful."

After Murat hung up, Bob decided to change into casual clothes. Opening his suitcase, he had the first surprise of the day. The contents of his suitcase had been disturbed. He always packed his underwear and socks beneath his folded shirts. Now the order had been reversed. Had the hotel maid searched his suitcase, looking for something valuable like gold cuff links or a watch? He had been the victim of petty theft on a vacation in Rio de Janeiro years ago, so that was a possible explanation. Yet nothing was missing.

But perhaps the maid (or whoever it was) had been looking for something that was not there—the instructions, for instance. But who knew about the instructions? Only Murat, who gave him the sealed envelope; Alvarez, who was expecting it; and Shafer, whom he called from the airport to alert him that he was leaving for Mexico City. Murat and Alvarez were unlikely suspects. That left only Shafer. But did his reach extend to Mexico City?

Bob settled back on the bed and dozed off, waking with a start when his phone rang. He heard the voice of Alvarez. "I will see you in the bar downstairs at 7:30 p.m."

At 7:25 p.m., Bob left his room and headed toward the elevators. He heard a door close and footsteps following him down the hallway. On reaching the elevator, he was joined by a tall young man neatly attired in a business suit and wearing dark sunglasses. After exchanging greetings, they stared straight ahead, taking the elevator to the lobby in silence. The young man exited from the lobby to the street. Bob headed toward the Red Lounge, whose neon tube lighting could be seen from the lobby.

After ordering a whiskey, he sank into one of the lounge chairs easily visible from the entrance and observed the parade of elegantly dressed women and their escorts, who entered or sipped cocktails at nearby tables. Music pulsated softly in the background. After a half hour passed, he surveyed the occupants of the bar more closely, in case Alvarez was sitting unobtrusively away from the entrance. He did not see Alvarez, but sitting several tables away was the man who accompanied him down the elevator, still wearing sunglasses even though the lighting in the bar was dim.

Arriving late apparently was a characteristic of Alvarez. Bob checked his watch. Already 8:30 p.m. He was getting tired of people watching. He considered ordering a second drink but decided against it. Looking at the business card Alvarez had handed him at lunch, Bob was about to call him on his phone when he heard a pleasant female voice.

"Buenas noches!"

Standing in front of his chair was a chic young woman whom he had noticed, some time ago, sitting by herself at a nearby table. "You seem to be alone tonight. May I join you?" Without waiting for his response, she sat down in the chair next to him.

"I am actually expecting someone. He seems to be running late."

She smiled. "Ah, that is a trait of us Mexicans. Being punctual is less important to us than to Americans. You are from the United States, yes?"

He nodded. "Yes."

"Would you like to buy me a drink?" she asked as she leaned toward him.

Bob thought quickly about how to extricate himself without creating a scene. Linking up with an expensive hooker was not part of the plan. What had happened to Diego? How could he be so careless about keeping appointments?

"I need to make a telephone call," he said.

Then came the day's second surprise. She pouted and leaned even closer to him, whispering softly, "I have a message for you from Diego. You are to meet him in front of the Pied de Cochon, a restaurant located in the Presidente InterContinental Hotel, not far from here, at 9:00 p.m. He will be waiting for you in a car. Now do you want to order me a drink?"

Bob looked closely at her pretty face. "Okay. What would you like?"

"Champagne, of course."

He motioned to the waiter and ordered two drinks.

After signing the bill, Bob asked her, "What is your name?"

She shrugged her bare shoulders. "It does not matter. But if you like, you can call me Juanita." That amused her. Her laughter tinkled over the sound of the music.

"How did you get to know Diego?"

She arched her eyebrows, pausing briefly before replying, "We met at a party and became friends. That's all." She lit a cigarette and exhaled before asking, "Do you mind?"

"No. Go right ahead."

She swiveled in her chair to gaze around the lounge before whispering to him, "We are being watched. I do not mean ordinary people watching. The young man sitting a few tables behind us is Miguel Rodriguez, who works for the Drug Enforcement Agency in the United States."

He whistled under his breath. "Interesting," he said but caught himself before revealing that the young man was staying at the hotel and had a room on his floor. Could he be the person who had searched his suitcase?

She tossed her head in the opposite direction. "You see that middle-aged man over there sitting with his bleached-blond lady friend and two bodyguards?"

Bob's eyes moved around the lounge until they came to rest on a table only thirty feet away.

"That is Vicente Garcia, who is a competitor in our business. Normally, he stays on the west coast of Mexico, in the state of Sinaloa, close to where his boss, Guzman, is thought to be hiding out. Mexico City should be neutral territory, but I think it favors their cartel more than Diego's."

"And his cartel is?"

She looked genuinely surprised. "Diego did not tell you? He is Los Zetas. But you had better go. Diego is waiting."

Bob glanced at his watch and excused himself, walking in the direction of the men's washroom. Pausing to look back, he observed her still sitting at the table; and on either side of her, several tables removed, were Rodriguez and Garcia. It occurred to him that he might be heading into a trap and that his life could even be in danger, but he resolved that he could not leave Mexico City without delivering Murat's instructions.

A small group of people straggling by provided him with the screen that he needed to make a sharp turn away from the washroom toward an exit door leading onto a side street. Within minutes, he was in front of the Pied de Cochon, where Alvarez was waiting for him in his Mercedes-Benz. By the time the men watching Juanita saw her get up from her chair to walk out of the Red Lounge, Bob and Alvarez were speeding along the Campos Eliseos.

Chapter Twenty-Three

"Buenas Noches, amigo*!* I am sorry about the confusion tonight. Let me explain. My girlfriend and I were about to enter the lobby of your hotel when I spied some people in the vicinity whom I would rather not meet. So I asked Maria Elena to go alone to the Red Lounge to make contact with you."

"Maria Elena? I met a Juanita."

Alvarez chuckled. "That is Maria's joke. She likes to play cloak and dagger sometimes. It amuses her to use different names. But let me make amends." He gave some quick instructions to the driver. "I have asked the driver to take us to the Bulldog Café. It is a popular nightclub south of here—three big dance floors and a decent bar. Perhaps you will meet some of our local girls." He winked.

Soon they had been driving along the Calzada Chivatito. Alvarez became more serious. "Tell me about yourself. Lunch did not provide us with the opportunity to talk much."

Bob provided a brief sketch of his life.

"So you joined Ottoman Trading Company only at the beginning of this year? Recep Murat must trust you by asking you to deliver important instructions. You have them with you?"

"Yes, right here." Bob pulled the sealed envelope from the inside of his suit pocket and handed it over.

Alvarez tucked it away in his jacket. "I will read it later. I do not know Murat, your boss, personally. But I did know the man who once reported to Emir Tilki, the chairman of Ottoman Trading Company.

But that was many years ago. Does the name Abdullah Catli mean anything to you?"

"No." Bob shook his head. "Should it?"

"I was a young clerk starting out in the shipping department of another sugar exporting company. The name does not matter, but it was the one I worked for before I joined Veracruz Sugar. I became involved with an organization that was smuggling Colombian cocaine into the American and European markets. That is how I met Abdullah. He was a genius. He had contacts everywhere, but especially in Europe. Working with him, we succeeded in making big shipments into the Italian and British markets. Then it suddenly ended. Abdullah was killed in a car accident in Turkey, wiped out by a rival gang."

"When did that happen?" Bob asked curiously.

"In 1996. There was a big investigation in Turkey, and Ottoman Trading Company decided to lay low. Our European business dwindled, so my organization focused on the US market. We gained control of the supply routes to the United States passing through the eastern half of Mexico. You may have heard of it—the Gulf Cartel. For a while, everything went well. We hired a private army to enforce our control. Then the troubles came. Our leader, Osiel Cardenas Guillen, was arrested in 2007, and a big fight broke out over who would succeed him. Many people were killed. I became aligned with the Los Zetas group when it broke off from the Gulf Cartel in 2010."

"That is what Maria Elena told me tonight—that you belong to Los Zetas."

"Yes, that is correct. During the day, I am a businessman having lunch with Turkish diplomats and businessmen. But at night, I have a different identity." Alvarez smiled, looking pleased with his double life. "Did Maria also tell you who our worst enemies are?"

"She pointed out two men in the Red Lounge tonight—one who belongs to the Sinaloa Cartel and the other who works for the Drug Enforcement Agency in the United States."

Alvarez's face hardened. "Exactly. We have been at war with Sinaloa in recent years. But let us not forget the Mexican and US governments. One of our leaders, Miguel Morales, was arrested last year by the Mexican Navy."

He became pensive for a moment and then continued, "That is enough of the past. Let us get back to the present. I received a call ten days ago from New York—from Demir Ozmen who, like Abdullah before him, reports to Emir Tilki, although he mentioned that most operational responsibilities are now in the hands of his son, Omer. He said that he wanted to renew old ties. Cocaine prices in Europe are twice what they are in Mexico. He said that a business proposal would be delivered by a personal messenger from New York. That must be you."

"Yes, I'm the man."

As the Mercedes-Benz pulled up to the entrance of the Bulldog Café, two burly men emerged from the shadows and opened the rear doors. As Bob stepped out of the car, Alvarez advised the driver to stay in the car because he would be back shortly. They walked into the club together, flanked on either side by the two bodyguards.

The dance floor at ground level was crowded with young people gyrating to the rhythm of the music. The two bodyguards plowed a channel through this mass of humanity so that Alvarez and Bob could make their way to the bar, where two empty stools were conveniently waiting.

"Let me show you a little Mexican hospitality. What would you like to drink?" When the orders had been placed, he spoke to one of the bodyguards, who walked onto the dance floor and returned in a few minutes with a lovely young woman in tow.

With a flourish, Alvarez introduced Teresa. "She will be your hostess tonight."

Teresa was beautiful. She was tall and slim, dressed in a short, clinging low-cut dress that revealed the swell of her breasts and her shapely legs. Her shoulder-length black hair framed her large eyes and red lips.

"Your name is Bob, right?" Her voice was melodious and warm. "Would you like to dance?"

Before he could protest that he was not a good dancer, she pulled him to the dance floor, and they began moving in time to the throb of the music. She pressed her body against his, and as they whirled around, he glanced back at the bar. Alvarez and his bodyguards had disappeared, leaving him on his own.

Suddenly, there was a commotion at the entrance to the nightclub. A disc jockey blared over the loudspeakers that a celebrity rock band had arrived and would be performing that night. Dancers on three floors roared their approval as disco lights flashed and the beat of the music became deafening. Trailing behind the rock band were the paparazzi, pointing their cameras at the entertainers and then at the dancers. Bob did not realize that within twenty-four hours, a photo of him dancing with the lovely Teresa would be on YouTube—irrefutable evidence of his infidelity to his betrothed, Andrea.

Bob had no memory of how the evening progressed thereafter except that he woke up in his hotel room with the lovely Teresa beside him in bed.

Chapter Twenty-Four

The punishment for his indiscretion was swift. Several days after his return to New York, he was getting out of the shower with the intention of going over to Andrea's for dinner, as they had agreed the previous evening, when the telephone rang.

"Andrea, I was just about to come over."

"Don't bother!" The fury in her voice startled him.

"What's the matter?"

"I was having drinks earlier today with Derek Taylor, a former flame of mine who's been helping me to find a replacement for Fred Sanford on my television show. We got to talking. He's been doing a special television program about the career of Bruce Cockburn, the Canadian songwriter and guitarist. He did a little research for the program on YouTube."

"So what does that have to do with me?" Bob asked apprehensively.

"Everything. Last week, a Mexican rock band, Luge Mx, performed at the Bulldog Café in Mexico City and sang one of Cockburn's songs, "Love in a Dangerous Time." He pulled out his iPad and showed me the clip he intends to use. Of course, the clip included more than just the rock band's rendition of that song. It also showed the people on the dance floor, cheering them on. Who do you think I saw hugging and dancing with some slut?"

"Andrea, I can explain! She was introduced to me by the businessman I flew to Mexico City to see. We went to this nightclub after our meeting. We danced, that's all. Nothing to be concerned about."

"She didn't look to me like your typical businessman's wife or girlfriend. Her dress was so skimpy she might as well have been wearing nothing!"

"Sweetheart, please be reasonable. Can you trust a video clip made by Derek Taylor? He's an old flame of yours, and he's jealous of me. He probably altered it to make me look bad."

"Nice try, Bob. But that wasn't his clip. He got it from a vendor on YouTube, so he had no chance to doctor it." Her voice cracked. "You're rotten! You couldn't even wait until our wedding day to be unfaithful! Why are you men all the same? Do you even know what the word 'fidelity' means? Our engagement is off. I never want to see you again!" she cried, slamming down the receiver.

Bob tried calling her back but got only her voice mail. He poured himself a cocktail, downing it in one gulp, and then pulled out and lit up a joint, staring sadly into space. He was a born loser—a college dropout, a divorced man, a business failure, a prime suspect in the death of a television actor, and a police informer. Now he was a jilted lover as well. Nothing in his life had gone right or ever would. He was convinced of that. Suicide did not seem an attractive option, but fleeing to Rio de Janeiro was becoming ever more appealing.

Jack, lying on the floor by his chair, looked up at him with soulful eyes and whimpered sympathetically. His dog was the only friend he had.

Then the telephone rang again. Was it Andrea?

He picked it up without looking at the caller ID and answered, "Andrea?"

"Sorry to disappoint you, buddy. It's only me."

His heart sank. It was the unmistakable voice of John Shafer.

"Connors and I need to see you again to get a report on the fun you had in Mexico City. You've been back a few days and still haven't called us. We feel hurt and neglected. You've got to be more responsive if our friendship is to survive. Got the message, buddy? How would you like to get together tonight?"

Chapter Twenty-Five

Shafer and Connors decided at the debriefing session after Bob's trip to Mexico City that meeting casually in bars would no longer do. Too public, too visible, too much risk of being overheard. Their solution was to take a room at a hotel conveniently located close to his office to permit him to meet them there during the day, if necessary.

They also gave him a small video camera and listening device the size of his fingertip to plant in the conference room where Murat, Ozmen, Comooglou, and Alvarez would be meeting the day after Labor Day. A van would be parked outside the Ottoman Trading Company office building to monitor and record the meeting.

Connors seemed keenly interested when Bob told him about Alvarez's imminent arrival in New York. "Alvarez hasn't been in New York for years. He is not a Los Zetas kingpin, but he is a senior official in the cartel, a front man to set up deals. But we have never been able to pin anything on him."

Clearly, a big deal was brewing. Murat seemed nervously excited on Tuesday morning. He reserved the main conference room from 2:00 p.m. for the remainder of the afternoon. Bob overheard Murat's secretary making dinner reservations for that evening.

What drove Bob to despair was that the doors to the conference room were kept locked all morning so that he did not have an opportunity to plant the camera and listening device. A new bodyguard, Dimitri Rostov, stolidly sat outside the conference room to ensure that no unauthorized personnel entered. He had replaced

Buzz Malone, who had mysteriously disappeared. According to Murat, he had gone on a fishing vacation in Canada and then had announced that he would not be returning. Bob suspected that a police inquiry was the real reason, but in the short term, he had a more pressing problem: how to get into that conference room.

Murat, a meticulous planner, came to the rescue. He asked Bob to find the Best Shoes file and place it on the conference room table, in case Alvarez had any questions about how Middle Eastern heroin had entered the US market. Ten minutes before the meeting began, the doors to the conference room were unlocked, providing him the opportunity to slide the spyware underneath the speakerphone in the center of the table.

Bob sat at his desk for several hours, staring at the closed doors of the conference room until the participants in the meeting departed for dinner. After retrieving the spyware and making a photocopy of the Best Shoes file, which had been carelessly left on the conference table, Bob Bigelow walked past the Hilton Garden Inn on Thirty-Fifth Street West once, twice, three times before slipping through the front doors. Room 219 was on the second floor, away from the elevators, so that it would not be too obvious who was entering or leaving. He had one of three keys to the room.

Shafer and Connors were already waiting in the room when he arrived. "Want to see what happened at the meeting?" Connors asked, pointing to the screen of his laptop computer.

Bob pulled up a chair.

The meeting began on a disconcerting note. Murat explained to Alvarez the reason for Bob's exclusion. "He is relatively new to our organization, so I think it might be best to be careful. But we wanted you to meet him because we intend to use him as our courier with you."

Alvarez nodded his head in agreement. "I was surprised to learn last week that you had entrusted him with delivering important instructions from Demir Ozmen. But then when I opened the envelope, I understood. It was only a simple message: *Let us meet soon in Veracruz to renew old trading ties*. And it was signed *A*

Friend of Abdullah. It was not a message that would incriminate anyone, yet I understood its meaning."

"You received the envelope in good condition? No sign of tampering?" asked Ozmen.

"Everything has worked out perfectly. Tell me, Demir, how did you get to know Abdullah Catli?"

"He was my mentor who got me my job at Ottoman Trading Company when I graduated from university. Since then, I have worked my way up in the company and am now vice president of special operations."

"Ah yes, a good person to know in our business in the nineties. So what kind of new business are you suggesting now? I talked to Recep by telephone, but he said that you would provide the details." Alvarez's earlier smiles had faded. He was now looking steadily at the dour Ozmen, sizing him up.

"The Syrian civil war is causing some disruptions in our normal supplies of heroin from Afghanistan. Police action has also messed up our distribution network in northern Europe, notably in the Netherlands and the United Kingdom. We would like to establish an alternative source of supply from Mexico."

Alvarez nodded his head. "That should be possible. Heroin and cocaine fetch much better prices in Europe than in the United States. There is only one problem."

"What is that?" Ozmen looked apprehensive.

"Some Middle Eastern heroin has been getting into the New York-Philadelphia market in the United States. My sources have traced much of that heroin to Ottoman Trading Company."

Murat protested, "It was only a small shipment, hidden among an order of Turkish shoes destined for the French market. We got a tip that the French police had been alerted and were ready to seize the shipment in Marseille, so we redirected the shipment to New York. Once it got here, we had to sell it into the local market. It was no big deal, not part of a plan to make major inroads into the US market."

Pushing the Best Shoes file across the table toward Alvarez, Murat added, "See for yourself. Some of the invoices had to be doctored for the benefit of US Customs, but it should be obvious what the intended destination for the shipment was."

Alvarez flashed a smile. "Wonderful! If we are to do business, there should be no misunderstandings. Europe is for Ottoman Trading Company, North America is for us and our Mexican compatriots."

"Absolutely! We agree!" Slapping the table for emphasis, Ozmen looked meaningfully at Murat to squelch other ideas that he might have. "Any internal discussions that we have had about gaining a share of the US drug market were preliminary and will not be given further consideration."

"You can trust our word!" It was the voice of Omer Tilki, connected to the meeting via teleconference. This was the first of the two times he spoke during the entire meeting.

"Good! Let me give you a little history. Since 2000, heroin production in Mexico and exports to the United States have increased sixfold. Despite that growing pie, competition for market share among Los Zetas and our compatriots—Sinaloa, Gulf, La Familia, Tijuana, Knights Templar, and Beltran Leyva—has been savage. Deaths run into the tens of thousands. There is no room for a new competitor. Understood?"

"Understood!" echoed Ozmen and Comooglou. Murat nodded his head but without enthusiasm because conceding the American market to the Mexican gangs would mean a diminished role for him.

"Besides, the American market is saturated. Most of the drug trade used to be on the Atlantic and Pacific coasts and along the border with Mexico. In recent years, we have penetrated Chicago and the Midwest."

"Diego, we are familiar with some of this history," Ozmen said dismissively. "We have done our own research." Then he went on the offensive. "Tell me, how stable is Los Zetas? Was not your leader, Miguel Morales, arrested last summer? We want a long-term relationship with a stable organization."

Alvarez grinned, holding up his crossed fingers for all to see. "The successors to Morales are as close as this."

"At Ottoman Trading Company, I can assure you, we have no succession problems either. At the top, we are family-owned and operated." That was, again, the voice of Omer Tilki.

"Family ties are also very important in Mexico," Alvarez responded without further elaboration.

"Then let us get down to business," Ozmen urged, eager to move ahead. "How would you propose to ship heroin and cocaine to the British market?"

"That should not be a problem. My daytime company, Veracruz Sugar, frequently exports refined white sugar to the British market via Liverpool and Glasgow. It should not be difficult to hide some brown sugar—as we like to call it—in the hold of the cargo ship."

"Liverpool or Glasgow would suit us perfectly. The Port of London gets a disproportionate amount of police scrutiny. Our distribution network extends throughout the United Kingdom, and our agents could be present in either city to accept shipment."

"Of course, we would expect payment prior to the transfer of the shipment. How would you propose to make payment? Which banks do you use?"

"In the past, we have relied on Europa Bank because of their worldwide presence, but they are under investigation by the US Department of Justice. In future, we will rely more on smaller British or Cypriot banks and on Turkish banks as well. We also have an account with a Swiss bank in the Cayman Islands. It might be useful for you to establish an account there, if you do not already have one."

"I will check into what we have in the Cayman Islands," said Alvarez.

Comooglou, who had barely spoken until now, asked, "If, in future, a problem were to develop with sugar shipments, do you have alternative channels?"

Alvarez smiled confidently. "The possibilities are infinite. The only limit is your imagination. We have hidden our merchandise among boxes of tomatoes and avocadoes being trucked across the US-Mexican border."

"One possibility might be Turkish chemicals for the processing of amphetamines in exchange for the finished product hidden in a shipment of Mexican cement," Murat suggested. "We have some expertise in altering invoices to disguise transactions."

Ozmen then proceeded to discuss price. "Can we agree on price? We will split the difference between the American and European prices for heroin and cocaine, net of shipping costs? Does that sound reasonable to you?"

"It does," a beaming Alvarez replied. "That will create an incentive to make this joint venture successful."

"One more thing, Diego. Comooglou and I will be spending a few days in Mexico City to explore opportunities for our normal trading business. We intend to set up a regular trading office there, which should make contacts between our organizations easier in future."

"Excellent!"

"Would it be possible to use this opportunity to see what precautions you take when you are planning shipments to the United States? Maybe one of your smaller shipments. It would reassure us that proper security procedures will be followed with our big shipment to Liverpool. We do not want to risk our firm's reputation. Perhaps we could also learn some tricks that could be applied in our European distribution."

"Why, of course! We would be flattered. You will be my guests in Veracruz."

Ozmen seemed visibly relieved. He even smiled. "Well, that completes our business discussion for this afternoon, does it not? Murat, you have a dinner planned for us tonight?"

Everyone stood up to shake hands. Murat handed out typed directions to the restaurant where they would be meeting for dinner at 7:30 p.m. He extended his arm, ready to usher his guests out of the room, when Alvarez halted and moved back to the table.

"I almost forgot the Best Shoes file." He flipped through it casually and put it back on the table. "Everything seems to be as you said."

Turning off his laptop computer, Connors asked, “What was in that Best Shoes file?”

Bob pulled out the photocopy that he had made. “It shows how invoices were altered to disguise a shipment of Middle Eastern heroin into the United States. The shipment was originally heading for France.”

Connors smirked. “Middle Eastern heroin—probably some of the stuff that you were peddling. Some coincidence, wouldn’t you agree?”

Bob flinched. Shafer and Connors never missed an opportunity to remind him of the leverage they held over him. Someday he would get even and make them pay for their arrogance.

Chapter Twenty-Six

Bob arrived at the office expecting a routine day. He was called into a meeting with Murat to discuss the monthly financial report when the telephone rang. Murat answered brusquely, his voice betraying irritation over what he assumed would be an unnecessary interruption of the meeting.

The volume was loud enough for Bob to hear the voice of Murat's secretary. "It is Mr. Tilki, calling from Istanbul about an urgent matter."

Bob rose from his chair, prepared to leave, but Murat waved to him to sit down as he switched lines, his voice unctuous and eager to please. "Omer, what a pleasant surprise to hear from you!"

Bob could not decipher the agitated staccato of Tilki's voice—who was probably speaking in Turkish in any case—but he noticed Murat's face flush and his large eyes bulge in excitement. "No!" he exclaimed.

Then turning on the speakerphone, Murat interrupted Tilki. "Omer, could we speak in English? I have someone in my office—Bob Bigelow, the chief financial officer of the New York office—who should hear this."

Bob had never met Tilki before but had been introduced to him via telephone shortly after he joined the company. They had had little direct contact since then.

Tilki was fluent in English and readily complied. "We have a crisis in Mexico. Comooglou has been killed, and Ozmen has been kidnapped by a drug cartel."

"In Veracruz, of all places! What kind of country is Mexico?" Murat cried out, conveniently forgetting how recently he had described it as a wonderful country to visit.

"Murat, do not interrupt me when I am speaking," Tilki reprimanded him. Murat contritely apologized. Tilki continued, "Alvarez called me yesterday to alert me to this outrageous attack! Ozmen also called me from captivity—and this you must never tell Alvarez, who does not know. The kidnappers want a five-million-dollar ransom for Ozmen. Otherwise, they will cut off his head!"

Bob gaped in disbelief at Murat, who asked the question on the tip of his tongue. "But how could this happen? Didn't they have protection?"

"They had a bodyguard and driver. Both were killed. Alvarez was not with them when it happened."

"But who are these kidnappers? Do we know?"

"Alvarez thinks they are the Knights Templar retaliating for incursions by Los Zetas into their territory. They are allies of Sinaloa, the main rivals of Los Zetas in Mexico. From what Ozmen told me, I think differently—that they are Los Matas Zetas, who are also believed to be allies of Sinaloa."

Bob kept silent, deferring to Murat, who said, "So how do we contact the kidnappers if we are unsure who they are?"

"That is the problem. We are new to Mexico, and finding the right channels to communicate with Sinaloa and their allies will take more time than we have. The kidnappers want the money within a week."

"Can't we get the Mexican government involved, Mr. Tilki?" Bob finally spoke up. He neither liked nor disliked Ozmen but recoiled at the thought of his execution.

"Alvarez already has. He called the Turkish embassy, which has brought this matter to the attention of the highest levels of the Mexican foreign ministry, pointing out that this kidnapping could endanger approval of the Turkish-Mexican free trade agreement. The

Mexican military will try to find the kidnappers, but we cannot rely on the police. Alvarez complains that the police have been corrupted by informers beholden to the drug cartels, especially to Sinaloa."

"Then we have no plan, Omer?" Murat reasserted himself.

"That is what I would like to discuss with you. My father too. He has just joined us for this teleconference. One moment please and I will patch him in."

Emir Tilki was the chairman of the company, with whom Bob had no prior contact. After Murat had greeted him, the teleconference continued.

Omer spoke deferentially to his father. "I have a rather daring proposal to make, Father. Ozmen's kidnapping could be a godsend. Ozmen has angered us over his careless behavior with a woman. Murat does not know the details, and I will not repeat them now. However, if we do nothing and Los Matas Zetas kills Ozmen, then the police investigation in Istanbul will quite literally come to a dead end. There will be no awkward questions about the kind of business Ozmen and the Ottoman Trading Company are in. What do you think?"

"Give me a moment to consider," Emir Tilki intoned.

Bob stared aghast at Murat. The suggested disloyalty to a company employee—and not just any employee, Ozmen was the vice president for special operations—shocked him.

Trying to sound sincere, Murat rushed to Ozmen's defense. "Demir is a devoted and experienced employee of the company who could not easily be replaced."

Bob was tempted to laugh. Murat was an ambitious man who would eagerly replace Ozmen if he were sacrificed by his employer.

Having mustered his thoughts, Emir Tilki now cautioned against Omer's proposal. "A potential obstacle to a neat resolution of our problem is this woman. Do we know the status of her health or even where she is being kept?"

"I do not know, Father, but I will use our contacts in the Tilki Foundation to determine her status. I am furious over the publicity that Ozmen's kidnapping by a Mexican drug cartel is receiving in the Turkish media and do not want the crisis to blow up further, especially if this woman talks."

"Have you also considered that the involvement of the Mexican and Turkish governments reduces our chances of controlling the outcome?"

"I agree," Omer responded glumly.

"I think we should take the long-term view in deciding whether to ransom Ozmen. I have built up this business empire over several decades. Someday it will belong to you and your brother. The kidnapping of Ozmen should be viewed as a potential opportunity rather than a disaster. One of the guiding principles of my long business career is that alliances are temporary. Only the interests of our family are permanent. Thus today's enemy could be tomorrow's ally and vice versa."

"I do not follow your meaning, Father." Omer seemed genuinely puzzled.

"What impresses me about the kidnapping of Ozmen is the daring and skillful execution shown by Los Matas Zetas in the heart of Los Zetas territory. Their success and the confusion of Los Zetas about their true identity suggest that the grip of Los Zetas over the drug routes along the Gulf of Mexico to the United States is weakening. Some of their leaders have recently been arrested. Infighting and police arrests allow few Mexican cartels to remain on top for long, as you know.

"If the rumors are true that Los Matas Zetas is allied with the Sinaloa Cartel, then negotiations for the release of Ozmen might provide an opportunity for communicating with Joaquin Guzman, the reputed lord of the Sinaloa Cartel. That could be the start of a very profitable business relationship, if our venture with Los Zetas fails. Is that understood? I have to go now, Omer, and will leave you to work out the details of Ozmen's ransom."

Murat broke the brief silence that followed Emir Tilki's signing off. "What a brilliant man your father is, Omer! I like his plan. Now how can I help to get Ozmen released?"

"We need to send someone to Mexico City to establish liaison with the kidnappers. Because of the importance of this matter, perhaps you should go, Murat."

Murat protested immediately. "I would go except that I have too much business to take care of in New York. I have a better idea. Why don't we send Bigelow?"

"Can he be trusted?" Omer Tilki barked. "I do not want an amateur."

"He is totally reliable," Murat assured him smoothly.

Bob had no wriggle room. He did not want to go but could hardly voice his reluctance to the president of Ottoman Trading Company, not to mention the head of the New York office. He knew that Murat was making excuses. There was nothing that important going on in New York. He just did not want to put his own neck at risk. Bob avoided looking at Murat to disguise his growing dislike for the man.

Speaking directly to Omer Tilki, Bob asked an obvious money question, "How will I deliver the ransom?"

"We cannot send you to Mexico City with a suitcase filled with five million dollars in cash. That could create issues with customs. Therefore we will be transferring the money from our Cayman Islands account to our account with Europa Bank in Mexico City. The address is on the Paseo de la Reforma."

"When will I be leaving?"

Murat cut him off before he could finish. "My secretary will make the reservations for you. Assume that you will be flying to Mexico City tonight. You will be staying at the same hotel as before."

"Let's get the important details settled first." Tilki's voice left no doubt as to who was in charge. "Murat, I will confirm with you later, but I am confident that Wednesday morning Bigelow will be able to go to the Europa Bank branch to withdraw the money. Then he can go back to his hotel room and await further instructions."

"Okay, so that's the easy part. How does he make contact with the kidnappers?"

"We will do that for him."

"But how?"

"Simple. They allowed Ozmen to use his phone so that he could call me. We will call them back on his phone. We know his number. We will arrange a meeting for Bigelow, if that is necessary, or a place where he can drop off the money. He should not be at risk."

Let's hope, Bob thought before asking an important question. "Are you coordinating with Diego Alvarez on this plan, Mr. Tilki?"

"No, we are doing this on our own. Because of the enmity between Los Zetas and the other cartels, Diego Alvarez would only hinder communications. If you should accidentally meet him, he must not know about our plan. Understood?"

After Tilki hung up, Murat made a cutting motion with his hand against his throat. "There is a lot at stake here. Don't screw up!"

The warning was clear. Bob nodded his head uneasily. If the plan went awry, he would not be able to call Diego Alvarez. But he did not want to leave himself totally defenseless and dependent on the mercy of the Ottoman Trading Company. To protect himself, he knew what he needed to do.

As Bob walked toward the door, Murat mused aloud, "I wonder why Tilki is so annoyed by this woman. I will have to make a few calls to Istanbul to find out. When Ozmen was in New York for the meeting, he seemed distracted at dinner. Sometimes he can be a very good conversationalist, but not that night. Perhaps this woman is the reason." He snickered in anticipation of the incriminating affair that he expected to discover.

Chapter Twenty-Seven

Before leaving for lunch, Bob informed Murat's secretary that he would not be returning to the office that afternoon. He needed to go home to pack for the trip and to arrange for his neighbor to take care of his dog. However, as soon as he was out on the street, he called Shafer. "I need to see you and Connors this afternoon. I have something important."

"Can you meet now?"

"Yes. The earlier the better."

"Okay, we'll see you in an hour at the usual place."

Bob arrived at the Hilton Garden Inn before Shafer and Connor. After glancing nervously at his watch and checking his email messages, he daydreamed. In a few weeks, he would have his share of the money from the Sotheby art auction. He would not need a job at the Ottoman Trading Company any longer and would disappear without leaving a trace. He would say goodbye to Murat, Shafer, Connors, Andrea, and his brother, Dave. A new life far away from New York, a man without a history starting life afresh! Connors and Shafer entering the room quickly erased the smile from his lips.

"So what's up?" Connors asked. "I hope this is bigger stuff than the Best Shoes deal!"

"I think it could be. After that meeting last week, the two Turks, Ozmen and Comooglou, went to Veracruz to negotiate some business deals with Alvarez."

"Do you know what kind of deals?" Shafer asked.

"Murat didn't tell me. Look," Bob protested, "I didn't call you guys because I want to alert you to some drug deals that might be happening. Something bad happened to Ozmen and Comooglou when they visited Veracruz. Ozmen's been kidnapped, and Comooglou was killed!"

Shafer and Connors looked at each other. "This could be interesting. When did it happen?" Shafer asked.

"Two days ago, in broad daylight, in Veracruz!"

"Any idea who did it?"

Bob recounted what he had learned from Murat and Tilki about the attackers and then outlined the plan for ransoming Ozmen. "What scares me about this plan is that Alvarez does not know about it, and I'm not supposed to tell him! What if something goes wrong? I can't call him. Tilki says using him as liaison with the kidnappers would compromise the negotiations for Ozmen's release."

"Tilki is probably right. Alvarez would be suspect in the eyes of Los Matas Zetas or Knights Templar or Sinalo*a* or whoever is behind this kidnapping. But there could be more to this plan than meets the eye." Connors looked at Shafer.

"Such as?" Shafer queried, his eyebrows raised.

"I smell a double cross in the making," Connors said.

Bob nodded in agreement. "Emir Tilki, the chairman of the company and father of the president, implied as much when he joined the teleconference."

"Tilki may want to keep this rescue plan secret because he is thinking about changing sides. He wants a reliable business partner in Mexico, and this kidnapping has raised questions about whether Los Zetas will be around for the long haul. Sinaloa and their allies—whether Los Matas Zetas or the Knights Templar—might look like a better bet."

Bob did not like the helpless feeling of being a pawn in a triangular power struggle between one Turkish and two Mexican drug cartels. "Look, guys, I am desperate. The reason I asked to meet with you is that I need some protection. I could be killed in some Mexican standoff. Don't you have some agents in Mexico City to call if I have to?"

"Bob, don't you like our business? Getting a case of the nerves?" Shafer joked.

Connors was supportive. "I see your point, Bigelow. Which hotel are you staying at tonight?"

"The W Hotel on Campos Eliseos. The same place as last time."

"Ah yes, a very popular place with the highfliers of Mexican society. Even the drug lords like to go there. We have an agent who covers the scene at the W Hotel—a young man named Miguel Rodriguez. He knows who you are from your last visit. Here is his telephone number." Connors handed Bob a piece of paper on which he had written the number. "Memorize the number and then destroy this note. Don't add this number to the directory on your phone, and call him only if you absolutely need to, okay?"

"Thank you," Bob said. It was better than nothing.

But his relief was short-lived. When Shafer stood up to leave, he shook Bob's hand and gravely said, "Good luck, Bob!" Isn't that what commanding officers said to fighter pilots before they left on a suicide mission in wartime?

Fugitive from Justice

Chapter Twenty-Eight

If Ozmen conveyed an air of indifference while Dave Bigelow questioned him about the woman in Istanbul, his mind was far from settled. How had this man Bigelow—a complete stranger until less than twenty-four hours ago—been able to ask such probing, discomforting questions? Was he who he claimed to be—a lawyer from New York in Mexico on business? Maybe he was from the FBI working in cooperation with the Turkish police—a potentially dangerous man who should not be allowed to live.

But how could he get rid of him? He would find a way. Even in this hellhole, there must be a way. He was a resourceful man, a survivor with street smarts who had outwitted more clever rivals many times.

His mind flipped back to the morning of the day he had been kidnapped. Sitting at a sidewalk café in the Zocalo, the center of Veracruz, he had taken a call from Tilki on his phone. Tilki had wasted no time on pleasantries about their visit to Veracruz. He had gotten straight to the point. "How is business?" he barked.

Ozmen replied, almost smugly, "Everything is going as planned." He waited in vain for a rare word of praise.

"Good, but we still have a problem." Tilki's terse sentence, spoken in a soft voice but with a hint of menace, caused Ozmen to pull in his breath sharply. "I was visited this morning by Inspector Tosun of the Istanbul Police Department. That is the second police visit in ten days. We are not pleased."

Ozmen felt a shiver run down his spine. Why had Tilki used the pronoun *we*? Was he suffering from Ottoman delusions, using the royal *we* to refer to himself? Or perhaps, more ominously, he had consulted with the patriarch, Emir Tilki, about the matter which displeased him.

Suspecting what the answer would be, Ozmen nonetheless asked, "Why?"

"Hayat Yilmaz. She is still alive!"

Ozmen choked, as if someone had hit him in the stomach. "Alive?" he gasped. "But how could that be?"

"I claimed ignorance when Tosun asked me about your betrothal to her when you were university students many years ago. But something the police officer let slip implied that she is still alive. I had one of my assistants scan the newspapers for the last two weeks. There is no obituary reporting on her death. He called Istanbul Technical University, asking for her. The receptionist said that she was on temporary leave, having suffered a mishap. She is probably being kept under guard at one of the city hospitals. In what condition, we can only speculate. But she must not be allowed to talk. That would be bad for you and for the Ottoman Trading Company. *No scandal must be allowed to touch the company!*" Tilki stressed the last words.

Ozmen stood up from the table and walked a few steps away from Comooglou, whose eyes were fixed anxiously on him. Comooglou knew that something was wrong, but what? Ozmen felt a bead of sweat roll down his forehead, stinging his eye. "What do you want me to do?" he whispered into his phone.

"I would like to send you to hell!" Tilki exclaimed. Then, after a pause, he asked, "When are you planning to come back to Istanbul?"

"We plan to fly to Mexico City tomorrow and then take the next flight back to Istanbul."

"When you get to Mexico City, await further instructions. Do not come back to Istanbul until I tell you."

"What do I tell Comooglou?"

"Tell him whatever you want. That is the least of your worries." The call disconnected with a bang.

Ozmen's head was reeling as he and Comooglou walked across the Plaza des Armas to a side street where their driver and car were waiting. A momentary act of rage, when he had struck Hayat Yilmaz on the side of her head, now threatened to destroy him. Omer Tilki did not forgive mistakes easily, particularly when the reputation of Ottoman Trading Company was at stake. If Tilki had deliberately consorted with the powers of darkness to send Ozmen to hell, his abduction by a Mexican drug gang in Veracruz could not have been planned more successfully.

Chapter Twenty-Nine

Ozmen remembered the day when he got out of his car in front of the office building of Ottoman Trading Company, his mind preoccupied with police disruptions of drug shipments into the British market, and he spied Hayat across the street. Their eyes locked for the first time in decades, and then she looked away. He was not able to read the expression on her face. Was it disgust, anger, or simply embarrassment?

That evening, he found out. He was working late, after office hours. The main receptionist had already gone home, and the night guards were on duty. She came to the front entrance, and one of the guards had called him with a suggestive leer in his voice. "There is a young lady to see you. Should I send her up?" It would not be unprecedented for harried, overworked executives to avail themselves of the services of ladies of the street.

On impulse, he agreed to see her. He regretted the way their betrothal had been terminated—with stormy words followed by icy silence. Their families no longer socialized with each other. He had lost track of her over the years, focusing on his business career. He was now married with children, but he had to confess that his matronly wife no longer excited him. Then Hayat resurfaced during the Taksim Gezi Park demonstrations, appearing on television and looking poised, slim, and attractive. She was introduced by television interviewers as a university professor and a former member of the Turkish delegation to the United Nations.

Their meeting began awkwardly, as if they had never been childhood friends or once betrothed at university. To put her at ease, he remarked, "You have been very visible lately in public."

"You mean the Taksim Gezi Park demonstrations?" Then she added with a wry smile, "We were aligned against you, as you must know. Galata Heights Realty has a significant interest in the development of Gezi Park."

"That we are on opposite sides is regrettable. How can I help you tonight? Have you come to make a peace offering?"

"I will not sacrifice my principles. You know me too well."

"You have not changed over the years?" It was a question more than a statement.

"No, but I think you have, unfortunately."

"You must be referring to my thinning hair?" he countered, trying to take the sting out of her rebuke, but he felt his anger rising. Why had she come if she wanted to insult him?

"I think you know what I mean, but I did not come here to discuss that tonight. I do not want to revive the past."

"Then why have you come?"

"To request your help in getting the release of my cousin, Husayin Yilmaz, who is now in a Greek prison after his ship was seized by the Greek Coast Guard near Rhodes. He was the captain of a ship belonging to the Golden Horn Shipping Company, a subsidiary of the Ottoman Trading Company."

"Your cousin means nothing to me. Ottoman Trading Company has many employees, and I do not know him."

She winced, a blush rising to her cheeks. "Does it mean nothing to you that we were once friends and were even betrothed to be married?"

"Aha, so you do want to bring up the past after all," he said mockingly. "On what charge is your cousin being held?"

"My sources tell me his ship was carrying an illegal shipment of arms to rebels in Syria."

"Then he must have taken this action on his own, without authorization from Golden Horn Shipping. Our businesses are completely legitimate."

Her lips compressed in anger. "Do not take me for a fool! That assertion is a complete lie, and no one should know that better than you. My cousin has told me about the illegal drug business of Ottoman Shipping Company. If he was taking arms to the Syrian rebels, it was with full knowledge of the company, who expected to be paid in heroin."

"Your cousin is playing a dangerous game by spreading those false rumors. He should be punished. Maybe we should let him rot in that Greek prison!"

His derision put her on the defensive. With trembling voice, she pleaded, "Do not hold what I have said against my cousin. He swore me to secrecy when he told me. He has never told anyone else, believe me!"

"But you did not keep your vow with me! You told me!" he replied, his voice rising.

"That is because of who you are. I would never tell anyone else, nor would I try to blackmail you with the public authorities."

"And who am I?" he shouted sarcastically.

"An idealistic young man who I once knew and loved, who has become coarsened and corrupted over time—first by supplementing his student income with small drug sales to Western tourists in Istanbul, then becoming the protégé of the notorious heroin smuggler Abdullah Catli and, finally, rising to a prominent executive position at Ottoman Trading Company."

"Abdullah Catli has been long dead. I have risen to my current position of vice president of special operations by dint of hard work and my wits. I have not done badly for the son of a small shopkeeper!" he retorted.

"*Special operations* is only a euphemism for the illegal drug trade of the company."

The scorn in her voice finally put him over the edge. "I think you had better leave!" he ordered.

She rose from her chair, her head held high, and started walking toward the door. Suddenly, a crazy impulse overwhelmed his better judgment. He wanted to humiliate this proud woman.

"Wait!" he called out just as she reached the door. "I will reconsider helping your cousin on one condition. You must understand that I am reluctant to jeopardize my standing with Omer Tilki over some small matter. He prefers to use his political influence to sway decisions on lucrative business deals. However, I will intervene on your cousin's behalf if you are willing to pay me a price."

She paused at the door and turned toward him. "And what is that price?"

"That you agree to be my mistress. I would find an apartment where we could meet discreetly. Your parents and my wife would never need to know."

Fury contorted her face. "You disgust me! Have you no shame or honor? You are a disgrace to your family!" She seized an umbrella from the stand near the door and rushed toward him, thrashing him over the head and shoulders. He held up his arms to protect himself, finally wresting the umbrella from her hands. But she continued to attack, biting and scratching, causing him to fall back on his desk. His hand closed over a paperweight and he struck back, once and then twice, hitting her on her temple. She crumpled to the floor, silent, motionless, barely breathing, blood oozing from her head wound.

He stood there in disbelief, staring at her body. What madness had possessed him! It had all happened so quickly, and now his life was on the verge of ruin. Even though she was still breathing, he could not call an ambulance. But he could not dispose of her body on his own. He would need help.

Sitting down at his desk, he concocted a plausible story. She had tried to kill him with a gun that she had pulled from her purse, and he had been forced to defend himself by beating her over the head with his paperweight. He always kept a small firearm hidden in a secret compartment in the top drawer of his desk. After carefully wiping his fingerprints from the weapon, he placed it on the floor beside her outstretched hand. Then he called the night guards.

Chapter Thirty

In the tightly regulated world of Ottoman Trading Company, business meetings are normally held on Monday mornings in the conference room on the fourth floor of corporate headquarters at 80 Nuruosmaniye Caddesi. Smaller meetings sometimes occur in the fifth-floor office of Omer Tilki, the elder son to whom the patriarch, Emir Tilki, has yielded responsibility for daily operations of the firm.

By choice, the patriarch serves as chairman, limiting his role to attendance at monthly board meetings, making important strategic decisions for the firm, and supporting his favorite philanthropies. He still has an office next to his son's on the fifth floor, but it is rarely used.

Ozmen had a sense of foreboding as he rode the elevator up to the fifth floor. He had been summoned to the office of Omer Tilki on a Wednesday, which was most unusual. Although he prided himself on being methodical and reliable, recently, a number of his projects had gone awry.

He stepped out of the elevator into a large reception area bathed in afternoon light underneath a glass dome. Exquisite tiles with geometric designs covered the walls. Rare Turkish and Persian carpets converged on a central design in the parquet floor. In the center of the reception area was a large elegant desk—a gift from one of the last sultans of the Ottoman Empire—at which was seated a young man, who softly spoke into an intercom, announcing Ozmen's arrival. Two large men in business attire stood on either side of the lacquered, paneled double doors leading to Omer Tilki's office, their arms folded across their chests close to the guns concealed inside their suit jackets.

Ozmen heard the response on the intercom. "I will let you know when to send him in."

The failure of the receptionist to invite him to sit down while he waited confirmed his unease. Controlling his inclination to shift his tall frame from one foot to the other, he folded his hands in front of him and stared impassively at the carpeted floor, then at the tiled walls, and finally at the two guards. He brushed aside the idle thought that they would someday be his executioners. Had he not served the company faithfully for many years? Did it not have an obligation to him?

Twenty minutes passed before the double doors opened to admit him to a rare audience with Omer Tilki, who was seated behind a large antique walnut desk inlaid with silver and ivory.

"Please sit down!" A man of medium height, Tilki seemed taller than he actually was because he held himself stiffly erect. He had the bearing and clipped manner of speech acquired attending an academy for military cadets in his youth. His hair was now silvery gray, but the flesh on his face was firm. His mustache obscured the thin line of his lips, but his eyes were hard and angry. This was not a man to be trifled with.

"Well, Ozmen, what do you have to say for yourself?" Omer Tilki lacked the courtly mannerisms of his father, even though in ruthlessness, there was little to choose between them.

"In reference to what, sir?" Ozmen feigned deference to avoid further provoking the chief executive's wrath but resented it. He was, after all, a man of forty with the title of vice president for special operations and was accustomed to issuing orders to others.

"Shall we start with a little police matter? I was visited yesterday morning by Inspector Adem Polat of the Istanbul Police Department, inquiring whether a missing woman, Professor Hayat Yilmaz, had visited our offices last Thursday. I summoned the receptionist on the ground floor, who said that no one of that description or name had checked in at the reception desk during office hours. Anyone wanting admission after 5:00 p.m. has to ring the doorbell to be let in by one of the night guards. They were off duty on Tuesday morning so that I had to wait until the evening to interview them, which is just as well in view of what I discovered."

Ozmen swallowed hard, anticipating what came next.

"Apparently, a shopkeeper across the street, interviewed by Inspector Polat, thought he had seen a woman ringing the doorbell at our office entrance around 6:00 p.m. when he was locking up for the night, but he could not remember what she looked like. However, one of the night guards remembers admitting a woman who wanted to see you. She had introduced herself as Hayat Yilmaz. Why did she want to see you?"

"I can explain everything. She wanted my help in getting the release of her cousin Husayin Yilmaz, the captain of *Light of the East*. He was arrested by the Greek Coast Guard after they boarded the ship and discovered an illicit arms shipment."

"That was most unfortunate. Our Syrian customers are unhappy because they did not receive the weapons they ordered, and we are unhappy because we did not receive our normal payment in heroin. Moreover, one of our cargo ships has been impounded indefinitely. But tell me, why did she come to you? Did she know you?"

"Yes, since childhood. Her father and my father had shops next to each other at the Grand Bazaar. We were classmates at university and even became betrothed."

"But you never married. Why? You had known each other since childhood."

"She broke off the engagement because she disapproved of some of my activities. She discovered that I was peddling heroin, mostly to foreigners visiting Istanbul. She wanted me to stop, but I would not because I needed the money to finance my studies."

"Did you remain friends after the engagement was broken off?"

"No, she said that she never wanted to see me again, and we did not."

"Yet when she rang the doorbell to this building after all these years, you admitted her. You are a married man with three children, Ozmen. Are you tiring of your wife and looking for a diversion?" Tilki's thin lips twisted in a sneer.

Ozmen's face flushed at the half-truth in what Tilki said. But it was more complex. "It is not what you might think. I have always regretted the way our friendship ended."

Except it had been more than a friendship. He had once loved Hayat as a young man. Then a few days ago, that love had turned to hate.

"You are a sentimental man, Ozmen. It does not pay to be soft in our business. So what happened when she came to your office on the third floor? The night guard said he had heard loud voices. Did you argue?"

"When she explained the reason for her visit, I told her that there was little I could do for her cousin. She then threatened to expose Ottoman Trading Company to the Turkish authorities. She had heard enough from her cousin to convince her that our legitimate business is merely a front for our narcotics trade. I pleaded with her to be reasonable."

Ozmen might be a sentimental man, but he had always been a good liar. It was a trait that had facilitated his rise up the corporate ladder. To save his own skin, he twisted the facts about Hayat's visit without skipping a beat. The softening of the hostility on Tilki's face showed that he had scored an important point in his own favor.

"The registry of the Golden Horn Shipping Company is murky so that it cannot be easily linked to Ottoman Trading Company. However, if I intervened on behalf of her cousin with the Greek Coast Guard, their suspicions about our company would be aroused. She said that traces of heroin had been found on *Light of the East*."

"So how did she get that information? The seizure of the ship occurred only a week ago."

"She did not say."

"You must have been aware that this dangerous woman was one of the leaders of the demonstrations against our proposals to develop

Gezi Park! Yet you let her into your office. How do you explain your bad judgment?"

Ozmen remained silent. Any argument made in self-defense would be futile and might only stoke Tilki's rage.

"When the night guard came to your office door, he found this woman on the floor, bleeding profusely from a head wound. You told him that she had pulled a gun on you and you struck her with your paperweight to protect yourself. Is that correct?"

"Yes."

"The guard said he saw a gun lying on the floor when he first came, but it later disappeared."

"I put it in my desk."

"Or perhaps you planted the gun yourself."

Ozmen winced under Tilki's contemptuous gaze. "Here we have a well-educated woman teaching at a local university, formerly attached to the Turkish delegation to the United Nations in New York. Carrying a gun in her handbag? It does not seem plausible. So what really happened?"

Perspiring, Ozmen let the words spill out of his mouth. "She was screaming at me . . . telling me what scum I had become . . . betraying my family and my religion. She attacked me with an umbrella, which I tore from her grasp. But she kept coming at me, scratching and biting. I slapped her, but she kept shouting at me. Then I lost control . . . and picked up the paperweight and hit her on the head. I did not think I had hit her hard, but she was unconscious and bleeding."

"Then you asked for the assistance of the two night guards to take her down the elevator into the basement while you cleaned up the mess in your office? Fortunately, no one saw them."

"I also needed to decide what to do with her. I could not call for an ambulance. In the end, I decided I had to get rid of her as we have done before with others." Ozmen looked meaningfully at Tilki, who seemed unperturbed by the reference to prior executions.

"Through the secret tunnel leading from the basement to the Bosporus?"

"Yes. I swore the two night guards to secrecy. They threw her body into the Bosporus just before dawn." He said it calmly, without emotion; but inwardly, he felt numb. What kind of monster had he become? He barely recognized himself.

Tilki answered that question for him. "You are a cold-blooded bastard, but under the circumstances, you did the right thing. We do not want a vocal university professor getting on television to denounce Ottoman Trading Company or its affiliate, Galata Heights. We must protect our role in the consortium planning to redevelop Taksim Gezi Park."

Tilki drummed his fingers on his desk top while he thought out loud. "I think it is time to transfer ownership of Golden Horn Shipping to another shell company. It must disappear without a trace. As for Captain Yilmaz, I will speak to my father about using his political connections to get an exchange of Yilmaz for a Greek held in a Turkish prison. He has clearly been too talkative. Once he is back in Turkey, we can arrange an accident."

Ozmen began to breathe more easily. Tilki was regaining his composure. Fearing for his own life had been premature. He helpfully volunteered, "I will also speak to the personnel director about transferring the two night guards to another office to keep them away from that pesky police officer. I think there may be two openings in our office in Azerbaijan."

Tilki stared at the ceiling, ignoring Ozmen. "Thinking of Inspector Polat, we should also move swiftly to get him removed from this case. My father will have to use his political connections again to have this done. This will not please him. He prefers to use his political influence to catch bigger fish, such as a permit for a lucrative construction project, rather than to protect small fish like you."

Then Tilki focused his gaze once more on Ozmen, and when he finally spoke, his voice had a sharp edge. "We also do not want the police to question you about your former romantic involvement with Professor Yilmaz. If the police look for a motive for her murder—an old lovers' quarrel, for instance—and her parents tell them about her former engagement to you, you could become a suspect. I think you need to take a long trip. To Mexico City, where we are renewing our former ties with Diego Alvarez. He once did business with Abdullah Catli."

"Has Alvarez responded yet to the proposal that we left with Murat in New York? I think he planned to use that new employee, Bigelow, to carry the message to Alvarez."

"Yes, Alvarez will be meeting with Murat in New York in early September—next week in fact. You should be there. They have spoken by telephone. Alvarez accepts the broad outline of our proposal to ship heroin and cocaine from Mexico to the British market. The Serious Organised Crimes Agency has scored some regrettable successes recently in intercepting our vehicles carrying drugs from the European continent to Britain via the Chunnel. We need to establish an alternative route, shipping directly from Mexico to Britain via the Port of Liverpool."

"That was my idea," Ozmen said, hoping to ingratiate himself. "You may remember—"

Tilki cut him off. "We must make absolutely clear to Alvarez that we do not want to compete with Los Zetas in the American market. I may join your meeting via teleconference. We may want to arrange a few small shipments into the United States only to test whether we are using the right methods. But the big prize is the British market. Once we have refined our technique of concealing brown sugar within refined sugar, we can extend this strategy to the German market as well."

"Brown sugar?"

"Yes, that is American slang for heroin. Now, after the New York meeting, you should go to Veracruz to coordinate with Alvarez and his associates on the details. Nothing must be allowed to go wrong. We must repair our distribution system, which has encountered a number of setbacks recently—the boarding of the *Light of the East* in the Aegean Sea and the interception of one of our vehicles in London, to mention just two."

Ozmen rose from his chair, sensing the meeting was coming to an end.

"One more thing, Ozmen, before you leave. You should not become too relaxed on your trip. Your recent performance has been unsatisfactory." Tilki almost shouted, "The Ottoman Trading Company has not survived and prospered for nearly three centuries by making mistakes. If anything goes wrong with our new venture, I will have your head. *Quite literally!*"

Amateur Sleuth

Chapter Thirty-One

Ozmen pretended to doze on his cot, and Bob crouched against the wall, his head bent. Only Dave seemed awake with his thoughts. He got up to stretch his legs and silently paced up and down the length of the small room. He wondered what had ever possessed his brother to take a job with the Ottoman Trading Company—a very peculiar employer, as he had discovered when Bob had come to him six weeks ago to ask for a large loan. Bob had been with his employer for only eight months when the loan request was made, and Dave had done some due diligence.

A quick internet search had turned up some surprising information. An established trading company founded in the early eighteenth century, it had, over time, diversified into a broad range of products: foodstuffs, shoes, carpets, and in recent decades, electronics, chemicals, and pharmaceuticals. Headquartered on the Nuruosmaniye Caddesi in the Fatih district of Istanbul, its operations had spread globally to Beirut, Dubai, Karachi, Baku, Hong Kong, Marseille, Rotterdam, London, and New York.

Family-owned, the company was obviously well-connected politically. The website had carried a photo of the family patriarch, Emir Tilki, at a reception with Erdogan, the Turkish prime minister. Most senior executives in the company had the same surname, Tilki, suggesting a very tight-knit hierarchy dominated by the patriarch's sons, brothers, and nephews.

Most references to the company on the internet referred to business deals in the public domain. Its owners clearly preferred to keep a low profile, discreetly on the edge of the social whirl of Istanbul's business elite. But there were two references that had intrigued Dave. An article on the history of Turkish trading companies noted that OTC had been founded as a slave trader before slavery had been abolished in the Ottoman Empire in the nineteenth century.

The second article reported that the patriarch had been questioned during the investigation that followed the sensational car crash at Susurluk in 1996, which only his friend—a Turkish member of parliament, Sedat Bucak—had survived. Other occupants of the Mercedes-Benz who had died in the assassination attempt were Abdullah Catli, a notorious heroin trafficker and killer; his mistress, a former beauty queen; and the deputy police chief of Istanbul. The scandal had been Turkey's Watergate, revealing the deep linkage between the illicit drug trade and the Turkish state. But no charges had been laid against the owner of the Ottoman Trading Company, who, in the following eighteen years, had avoided even a whiff of scandal.

This background information had not influenced his decision on his brother's loan request. He agreed to the loan out of a sense of obligation to protect his brother. He felt that Bob was in trouble even though he did not know what. His private banker at Citibank insisted on an appraisal of the oil paintings before providing him with a loan, which would delay matters by weeks when his brother needed the money urgently. That was why he assumed some personal financial risk by using his own investments as collateral.

The Ottoman Trading Company would have faded from his memory except for what happened on the Aegean Sea cruise that he took shortly thereafter with his wife and daughter. Something unusual happened near the island of Rhodes. The passengers of the *Austral* leaned against the railing of the ship, cameras poised, eager to capture some unforgettable images of their cruise—a rising sun in a cloudless blue sky, casting rays of pink and gold onto a shimmering Aegean Sea. And in the distance were the imposing fortifications built by the crusading Knights of St. John on the site of the ancient acropolis of Lindos on the island of Rhodes, overlooking a medieval village and the white sandy beaches of St. Paul's Bay.

"Look, Dad, over there!" Helen called from the other side of the ship, facing the open sea. He turned to see what was arousing her excitement. Pulling abreast of the *Austral* on the starboard side was a Greek Coast Guard vessel escorting an old cargo ship flying a flag that he did not recognize with horizontal bands of green white and blue. Members of the Greek Coast Guard boarded the cargo ship and could be seen on deck. The ship had seen happier times. Emblazoned on its side was the name *Light of the East*.

Prompted by Helen, Dave asked the captain of the *Austral*, a genial Frenchman, who happened to be walking by, "Captain Rolland, do you know what is going on with that ship?"

"I am trying to find that out myself. I will investigate as soon as we dock in the city of Rhodes. That is the destination of the Greek Coast Guard and the cargo ship as well. Talk to me tonight. By then I should know."

That evening, the captain of the *Austral* hosted a cocktail reception for passengers on deck. Dave spied the captain standing near the swimming pool and made his way through the throng. The captain smiled at him as he approached.

"I have an answer—or perhaps I should say some hypothetical answers—to your question this morning. I spoke to the captain of the Greek Coast Guard. He told me—and this is off the record, you understand—that they had received a tip that the *Light of the East* was carrying weapons to the belligerents in Syria. When they boarded it, they discovered twenty thousand Kalashnikov assault rifles and explosives hidden in freight containers in the hold without proper documents. They also found traces of heroin in the hold, suggesting that the ship has been used in the illicit drug trade."

Melanie and Helen had, by this time, joined them and were listening wide-eyed.

"Where did the ship originate?"

"A Ukrainian port near Odessa. I am not familiar with the name."

"And the ship is Ukrainian? I did not recognize the flag on the ship."

"That is the flag of Sierra Leone, where the ship is registered. But the ownership appears to be Turkish. An obscure company I do not know—Golden Horn Shipping. The captain of the ship, Husayin Yilmaz, and his crew members are also Turkish."

"Has the captain explained what he was up to?"

"He apparently claims that his ultimate destination was the port of Iskenderun in Turkey, but the ship's papers listed intermediate stops in Tartus in Syria and Tripoli in Libya."

"So what do you make of this?"

Rolland shrugged his shoulders. "Who knows? But here are two hypotheses. If the weapons were to be delivered to the port of Tartus, they were probably intended for the Syrian government of Bashar al-Assad. Russia has a naval base at Tartus. A company acting on behalf of the Russian government—which supports the Syrian regime in the civil war—could have shipped the weapons out of a Ukrainian port to avoid implicating Russia."

The captain paused while a head waiter whispered in his ear that dinner would be served in fifteen minutes. He continued, "The second hypothesis is that the weapons were to be delivered in the Turkish port of Iskenderun, which is near the Syrian border, to Syrian rebels who control much of northern Syria."

"Which do you think is the more probable?" Dave asked.

"I am intrigued by the traces of heroin on the ship. The Syrian government would be able to pay for the weapons with cash. Those rebels supported by the United States and Saudi Arabia would also be able to pay with cash. On the other hand, if the weapons were intended for the Al-Nusra Front—rebels associated with Al-Qaeda—they would be most likely to pay with heroin. They control areas in northern Syria that are close to the supply lines of heroin flowing from Afghanistan through Iran and Syria into Turkey. In time, the Greek authorities will know which interpretation is correct. In either case, I fear for the future of the *Light of the East*. It will be destroyed."

"You mean blown up?"

"Oh no, that would be too obvious. The owners of the ship will not come forward to claim it. So the Greeks will permit it to founder and sink in a winter storm in the Mediterranean. But I am being too cynical."

"I have a final question," Dave said. "How could that ship have gotten by Turkish customs officials when it passed from the Black Sea through the Bosporus Straits into the Mediterranean Sea?"

The captain shrugged once more. "Perhaps the owner of the ship has friends among Turkish officials who do not object to having their palms greased with some extra cash."

Chapter Thirty-Two

The Golden Horn Shipping vessel *Light of the East* and its captain, Huseyin Yilmaz, were both linked to the Ottoman Trading Company, as Dave accidentally discovered in Istanbul. Before he left New York for the cruise, Jerry Braunstein—the consultant from SecurityNet who was in charge of the Europa Bank compliance project—offered to introduce him to a former neighbor and friend, Hayat Yilmaz, who had been attached to the Turkish delegation at the United Nations. She now taught urban and regional planning at Istanbul Technical University.

Dave emailed her immediately after his family and he disembarked from the *Austral* at the end of their cruise and offered to take her out for dinner at the Asitane, located in the old part of the city and featuring a menu worthy of a Turkish sultan. She was expecting them but prudently suggested eating at the restaurant in their hotel, the elegant Park Hyatt—a former palace overlooking Macka Park, which was popular with Turks as well as foreign visitors.

They were grateful for her suggestion. They had risen early that morning to witness the splendor of the former capital of Byzantine emperors and Ottoman sultans as their ship cruised up the Bosporus. After checking into their hotel, they had gone sightseeing: the Blue Mosque, the Hagia Sophia, the Hippodrome. Their hectic schedule had left them exhausted.

As Dave, Melanie, and Helen waited in the reception area on the second floor, a slender woman in a light linen suit, escorted by the concierge, approached them. She wore no jewelry or makeup, but she had a pleasant, smiling face. She held out her hand in greeting. "You must be the Bigelows. Welcome to Turkey's New York! I am Hayat Yilmaz."

After the introductions were completed, they sat in the reception area for a few minutes chatting about their impressions of Istanbul, which they unanimously agreed was an awesome city.

"I apologize for being late, but I was very busy with some administrative matters. This is the start of a new academic year at Istanbul Technical University, where I teach urban and regional planning."

When Melanie protested that they should not have taken her away from her work, she brushed away her concerns. "I am fine now. I finished my work. In fact, I have some free time tomorrow and would like to take you to see Topkapi, the palace of the Ottoman sultans, and then the Grand Bazaar for a little shopping for souvenirs. Would you like that?"

They were delighted.

"Good, then it is decided."

Melanie later confided to Dave that she guessed Hayat's age to be around forty. Hayat was still attractive but unmarried.

"Have you tried our Turkish wines?" Hayat asked, pointing to the nearby wine bar. "I am not a drinker, but they have an excellent reputation, especially those from Thrace on the European side of the Sea of Marmara and from our Aegean coast near Izmir."

Dave promptly ordered two glasses of white wine for Melanie and Helen, a red wine for himself, and a tonic water for Hayat. The wines were delicious.

After they were seated at their table in the restaurant, Hayat steered them through the menu. "You must try some of these dishes. They are from every part of the former Ottoman Empire. This is a puree of bread, nuts, and chickpeas. That is one of my favorites—apple stuffed with diced lamb, rice, currants, pistachio nuts, and rosemary."

As the evening progressed, the conversation turned to the recent riots at Taksim Square just south of their hotel. Hayat said, "The streets may be quiet now, but there is still a lot of resentment against the Erdogan government—which, from the start, had no sympathy for the young people demonstrating against a proposal by real estate interests to redevelop Taksim Gezi Park. For the last decade, there has been a huge building boom in Istanbul. Old neighborhoods that should be preserved and the few green spaces and parks that we have in the center of the city are disappearing."

"Did you participate in the demonstrations?" Helen asked.

"Not initially. But some of my students did, and I was very sympathetic to their cause. Eventually, I joined them. I even appeared on a number of television shows, arguing that any plans to redevelop Taksim Gezi Park should be halted to allow a study to determine what the impact would be on the neighborhood. But so far, to no avail."

"Why do you think the Turkish government is so opposed to the demonstrators' demands?" Helen was always interested in accounts of student rebellion.

"The current prime minister is a former mayor of Istanbul. His political machine and that of his party is oiled by money from powerful real estate interests. So the prime minister ordered the police to crush the demonstrations with clubs and teargas. The reaction surprised him, I think. What had been a fringe demonstration grew into something much bigger throughout the country. People who did not necessarily agree with the goals of the demonstrators were horrified by how the police treated them. Until now, opposition to the government has been weak, but things are beginning to change."

"Hayat, where is this money for real estate investment coming from?" Dave asked.

"Foreign investors from Europe--and, to a lesser extent, Asia and North America-- are putting money into Istanbul, which is the largest city in the region. But much of it is coming from Turkey too. The Turkish economy has been strong for some years now, and a rising business class is looking for new investment opportunities. Also, it is no secret that a lot of it is drug money."

"Drug money?" Dave became completely focused.

"As you may or may not know, much of the heroin from Afghanistan flows through Turkey before ending up in Europe. Turkish gangs control the trade and launder some of their profits by investing in real estate. Casinos used to be a favorite way of laundering money, but that avenue was closed when casinos were banned in Turkey in 1998. Of course, there are still illegal casinos and online gambling."

"Casinos and real estate investments abroad would be an alternative as well, wouldn't they? The illicit drug trade is so international now."

"Of course." Hayat nodded in agreement.

"I recently visited London and had one of the most interesting taxi rides I have ever had. We were halted on the way to my hotel by a police blockade because they had apprehended some drug smugglers in a truck with a Bulgarian license plate. The taxi driver began telling me how much of the drug trade in Britain is controlled by Turkish gangs who have invested their money in London real estate. He mentioned the name of the kingpin . . .?" Dave paused as he tried to recall it. "Baybasin . . . does that sound correct? Did I get that right?"

Hayat looked grave. "Yes, that name is well known in Turkey. It is a well-connected clan."

"What do you mean?"

"The illicit drug business in Turkey is often a family business. The Baybasin clan got their start in the drug business in the Kurdish part of Turkey, the southeastern corner, where there is a movement to secede from the country. The insurgents there have often financed their rebellion with drugs. But that is another story. The new wealth of the Baybasin clan has given them access to some very old, established families in Istanbul. For instance, the wife of the patriarch of the Tilki family is Kurdish and is related to the Baybasin clan."

"Tilki? Where have I come across that name before?"

"They started out as owners of the Ottoman Trading Company many years ago but since then have diversified into real estate, banking, and even shipping. They are like an octopus with tentacles everywhere. Their real estate company, Galata Heights Realty, is very active in Istanbul. Their shipping company is small, and you may not have heard of it: Golden Horn. My cousin works there."

"Would your cousin by any chance be Husayin Yilmaz? Same surname as yours?"

"Why, yes. Have you met him?"

"This is a remarkable coincidence. Earlier this week, we were in the Greek island of Rhodes. The Greek Coast Guard had boarded a cargo ship, *Light of the East*, which was suspected of carrying an illegal shipment of arms. A huge shipment of Kalashnikov rifles and explosives was found on board. There were also traces of heroin found on the ship. The captain of the ship was Husayin Yilmaz."

"Oh my god!" Hayat looked stunned.

"You did not know?"

"No, I have not heard from him for a long time."

"I am sorry to be the bearer of bad news," Dave apologized. He regretted ever bringing up the subject. An evening that had started out so well was ending on a somber note.

Chapter Thirty-Three

The following morning, Hayat showed no signs of being upset by the news about her cousin. She greeted the Bigelows cheerfully in the lobby of their hotel and thanked them profusely for dinner the previous night. Dave, Melanie, and Helen agreed beforehand that the plight of her unfortunate cousin would not be brought up again unless she first did. Hayat did not, so a conspiracy of silence on the subject prevailed all morning.

Of course, the splendor of Topkapi Palace—built by Mehmet the Conqueror on the ruins of the imperial palace of the last of the Byzantine emperors—was sufficient to push most unpleasant thoughts aside. Hayat was an excellent guide, explaining how this enormous complex of inner courtyards, ceremonial chambers, council rooms, and living quarters in the harem had served as the administrative center of the Ottoman Empire for four centuries. They could have spent more than the morning there, but eager to escape the busloads of tourists who descended on the palace, they decided to walk to the Grand Bazaar, stopping at a café along the way for coffee and pastries.

As they made their way through the crowded squares in front of the Hagia Sophia, Hayat maintained her bright chatter. But in front of the Blue Mosque, pathetic groups of beggars—often families with small children holding out their hands for alms from the faithful—caused her to falter. She dug in her purse for coins and placed them in the outstretched hands, tears in her eyes.

"It is so sad. These are Syrian war refugees. They have lost everything but cannot get work permits in Turkey, so they are forced to beg for a living."

When they approached the Grand Bazaar along the Nuruosmaniye Caddesi, her mood again darkened. They were standing by the display window of a design store, admiring some fine sculptures and furniture, when Hayat seemed startled by the reflection of a man getting out of a Mercedes-Benz across the street. She turned to look, her mouth compressed in anger, her face slightly flushed. The man briefly paused at the curb, and his eyes locked with Hayat's. They recognized each other. Dave was certain of that. Then the man entered the office building across the street, and his car pulled away.

Melanie also noticed the change. "Is anything the matter, Hayat?"

"No, I am fine." She forced a smile. "Shall we stop at a café for refreshments before we enter the Grand Bazaar? We will need all of our strength."

Over small black cups of steaming coffee and baklava, Hayat became talkative once more. "When I was a small girl, I came to the Grand Bazaar frequently. My father has a small shop there, selling carpets. I used to love it because I felt I was at the center of life—merchants shouting to lure potential customers into their shops and bargaining over the prices of goods, the milling crowds, the mingled aromas of food being cooked, the shops filled with beautiful silk scarves, gold jewelry, and ceramics. But as I grew older, my father thought that it was not appropriate for a young woman to be seen by many young men, so I stopped coming. My visits became very rare."

"Hayat, you make the Grand Bazaar sound so exotic!" Melanie exclaimed.

"Yes, it is exotic, but it can also be dangerous. How should I describe it—like the beautiful cove on an island? The waters can be very alluring, but they may also harbor sunken rocks where dangerous creatures like the shark and the giant octopus lurk."

"Oh, oh," Helen squealed. "I will be holding tight to my purse."

"Hayat, this is a personal question, but I hope you do not mind." Melanie blushed. "Those young men at the bazaar—did none of them interest you? They must have been interested in someone as attractive as you."

"Melanie, you flatter me. But it is true. There was a young man. His father's shop was next to ours in the bazaar. We entered university at the same time and even became betrothed. But we had a disagreement over the paths that our careers should take, his and mine. So I broke off the engagement. I have never married. I prefer my freedom."

"Well, that is a choice many professional women are making these days," Melanie agreed. "Pardon me for asking. I was just curious."

It was a conversation that Dave would try to recall in every detail in the days to come. But for now, they were content to wander the maze of streets in the Grand Bazaar for hours on end, looking for bargains and, for the most part, ignoring the pleas of merchants to spend their money. They limited their purchases to a beautifully embroidered shawl for Hayat, in appreciation for her hospitality, and several glazed porcelain pieces as souvenirs for themselves.

Then came the time to bid farewell. Hayat said that she would not accompany them to their hotel because she had an errand to run before going home. She advised that they take a taxi because the Metro did not extend to the Grand Bazaar, and the trams would be too slow. However, to ensure that the driver would not take them on a grand tour to pad his fare, she negotiated the fare with him before they got into the taxi. She stood on the curb, waving until they were out of sight.

Chapter Thirty-Four

The next morning, Melanie and Helen waited in the lobby with their luggage while Dave checked out. He had just finished paying the bill and was filing it away in his briefcase when a serious-looking receptionist informed him that the hotel manager would like to speak to him. Dave suddenly became aware of the hotel manager, who was standing quietly behind him.

"How was your stay, Mr. Bigelow?"

"Very pleasant, thank you."

"Excellent. Mr. Bigelow, I do not want to delay you unnecessarily because I know that you plan to fly back to New York today, but there is someone in my office who would like to speak to you."

"Yes, we need to leave in a few minutes. We have a 1:00 p.m. flight."

"I will mention that to the gentleman." The hotel manager opened the door to his office and invited Dave to step in. The sole occupant of the office was a police officer who introduced himself as Inspector Adem Polat. After the hotel manager explained the time constraints, he excused himself and left.

"Mr. Bigelow, I do not expect to detain you long. I just have a few questions concerning Professor Hayat Yilmaz."

"Yes, of course. My family and I had dinner with her two evenings ago, and then yesterday, she accompanied us on a tour of the Topkapi Palace and the Grand Bazaar."

The inspector nodded his head. "That confirms what her parents told us. Have you known her long?"

"No, we met her on this trip to Istanbul for the first time. We were introduced by a mutual friend, Jeff Braunstein, who resides in New York."

"Did she—during dinner or yesterday's excursion—express distress about anything or indicate fear for her personal safety?"

Dave looked curiously at the officer, a man of medium height, black hair, and a round and earnest face. He was close-shaven except for a neatly trimmed mustache. *Where were these questions leading?* he wondered. "She seemed to be in good spirits for the most part."

"Nothing at all? The reason I am asking, Mr. Bigelow, is that I am looking for clues to the brutal beating of Ms. Yilmaz last night. Her parents reported that she was missing when she did not return home by 10:00 p.m. A fisherman saw two men tossing her into the Bosporus at dawn this morning but rescued her before she drowned. She is in hospital now in intensive care, where she was identified as the missing person."

"Oh my god! How terrible! Which hospital is she at?"

"I am not at liberty to say. Only immediate members of her family know. Her life could be in danger."

"Is she able to speak?"

"No, she is unconscious. She was beaten savagely on the side of her head with some blunt instrument."

"But who would do such a thing?"

"That is why I am here to ask questions, Mr. Bigelow."

"You don't think that we . . .?"

"No, no, Mr. Bigelow. You are not a suspect," the officer said patiently. "I am just looking for clues . . . anything that she said or did."

"You don't think she was attacked for political reasons, do you? She participated in street demonstrations against development plans for Taksim Gezi Park."

Inspector Polat shook his head. "Most unlikely. Neither the government nor the developer would have anything to gain from hiring a thug to beat up a university professor, who was a leading figure in the protests, months after the demonstrations have ended. Of course, one cannot exclude the possibility of a crazy person acting on his own. But that is still a low probability."

"Okay, let me think. Yesterday afternoon, she was moved to tears by the sight of Syrian refugee families begging for their living in front of the Blue Mosque."

"You are suggesting that she befriended a Syrian refugee family, who then attacked her?"

"No, that seems as unlikely as a crazy person acting on his own." Dave paused then looked at his watch. The minutes were slipping by, and they needed to check in at the airport two hours before flight time. He thought hard.

"Okay, I have another idea. Yesterday, we were walking along the Nuruosmaniye Caddesi toward the Grand Bazaar, and we stopped to admire some furniture and decorative objects in the display window of one of the shops."

"Yes, there is a famous furniture shop on that street."

"Hayat saw the reflection of a man getting out of his car on the other side of the street. She turned to look at him, and they seemed to recognize each other."

"Anything unusual in her reaction?"

"What do you mean?"

"Did she smile and wave at him? Perhaps an old friend?"

"She seemed to get tense, even angry. Her face flushed, but she made no gesture toward him."

"What did the man look like?"

"I did not get a good look at his face, but he was tall and thin. Then he walked into an office building across the street. The entrance was to the left of a ground-level shop."

"His car? What kind of car was he driving?"

"A Mercedes-Benz. He had a driver who dropped him off."

"Nuruosmaniye Caddesi is primarily a shopping street. Corporate offices are usually located elsewhere in the city. Are you sure that it was an office building? Perhaps he was just stepping into one of the shops."

"No, I am sure that it was an office. It was a fairly modern building rising several stories above the shop. There was a brass plate to the left of the entrance, very discreet. No big sign that I could read, announcing the name of the company."

"That is helpful. I will check out the address. There is only one large company, to my knowledge, with corporate offices on Nuruosmaniye Caddesi. It is a very old company with roots going back to the eighteenth century—the Ottoman Trading Company."

"That could be relevant. Two nights ago, when we were having dinner with Hayat, she learned that her cousin was captain of a cargo ship arrested by the Greek Coast Guard for illicitly carrying an arms shipment, maybe destined for the Syrian rebels. That really upset her."

"How did she come by this information? Who told her?"

"Why, I did. You see, my family and I were on a cruise in the Aegean Sea last week, and we were in Rhodes when the arrest took place."

"The captain's name is . . .?"

"Husayin Yilmaz. The name of the ship is *Light of the East*."

"You think this is an Ottoman Trading Company ship?"

"Golden Horn Shipping, but Hayat said it is controlled by Ottoman Trading Company."

"Mr. Bigelow, this is very interesting. You have been very helpful. Here is my card if you remember something else and would like to contact me. You are free to go now."

Dave pulled a card from his briefcase. "Here is mine as well if you need to reach me." He walked out of the office to the lobby dreading what he would have to tell Melanie and Helen.

Chapter Thirty-Five

On Monday, Dave's first day back in the office after his return from Istanbul, he called Jeff Braunstein about the attack on Hayat Yilmaz. Horrified by the news, Jeff was determined to do something, even if he was thousands of miles from Istanbul.

"Look, some members of our team working on the Europa Bank money-laundering project have connections to the CIA. Why don't I ask one of them to contact Langley for a little background information on Golden Horn Shipping?"

At the initial organizational meeting for the Europa Bank project, at which Jeff presided, several representatives of obscure consulting firms located in the suburbs of Washington, DC, had sat through the meeting without uttering a word. Dave had wondered whether they were linked to the FBI or the CIA, and now his suspicions were confirmed. But Dave readily agreed with Jeff's proposal. It could provide a lead.

Jeff continued to prod. "Think, Dave. Did Hayat say anything that might give us a clue?"

"On the flight home from Istanbul, I racked my brain trying to remember everything she had said. When she told us that Golden Horn Shipping was owned by the Ottoman Trading Company, she referred to it as an octopus with tentacles stretching into trading, banking, shipping, and real estate. The next day, we were walking along Nuruosmaniye Caddesi toward the Grand Bazaar when we stopped at a shop window. She saw the reflection of a man across the street and turned to look at him. The sight of him bothered her. When I told the police officer about the incident, he thought the address across the street could be that of the Ottoman Trading Company. Right after it happened, we stopped at a café, and over coffee, she described her childhood memories of the Grand Bazaar, where her father owns a shop. She compared the Grand Bazaar to a beautiful cove where dangerous sharks and octopuses lurked."

"So your point is what?"

"Did you ever take a college course in psychology which explored the underlying meaning of word associations? Look, Wednesday evening, Hayat refers to the Ottoman Trading Company as an octopus. Thursday afternoon, she talks about the dangers posed by giant octopuses. You get it? Ottoman Trading Company equals octopus. Danger equals octopus. Therefore, Ottoman Trading Company equals Danger."

"Dave, I think you were reading too many novels on your vacation. This would never stand up in court. You ought to know that better than I do. You're the lawyer."

"I am not suggesting that this is evidence that could be presented in court. But it might give us some insight into what she was thinking a few hours before she was attacked."

"Okay, did the police officer provide you information where he can be contacted?"

"Yes, I have his card right here. Adem Polat, telephone number, email address."

"Good. Why don't you send him an email? See what he thinks. Did he tell you where Hayat is hospitalized? I'd like to send her flowers and a get-well message."

"No, he won't do that. Only immediate members of her family know because her life could be in danger."

"I see. Okay, why don't you call me when you hear back from the police officer?"

When Dave sent his email to Inspector Polat on Monday, he expected a quick response, certainly within twenty-four hours. The response did not arrive until Thursday, seventy-two hours later:

> *Mr. Bigelow, I appreciate your interest in helping the Istanbul Police Department in solving the case of Professor Hayat Yilmaz. Unfortunately, I no longer have operational responsibility for the investigation, and the case has not yet been reassigned to one of my colleagues. As of yesterday, I have been transferred to the division responsible for training new recruits. I can only report that Ms. Yilmaz is still unconscious so that she has been unable to provide us with details about her attackers. Doctors fear that she suffered brain damage and that she may never recover.*

Dave immediately forwarded the email to Jeff Braunstein. Within five minutes, Dave's telephone was ringing. It was Jeff.

"Dave, my sensitive nose smells a cover-up. Our friends in Langley have found very little on Golden Horn Shipping—how many ships they own, where they are registered. Even details about the Sierra Leone registry of *Light of the East* are murky. But this is interesting. Yesterday, in the legal notices section of one of the business newspapers in Turkey, there was a short item announcing the liquidation of Golden Horn Shipping. No information about where the assets are being transferred. Our friends also checked with the Greek Coast Guard. No one has come forward to claim *Light of the East*. It may now become the property of the Greek government."

"And now the police officer investigating the attack on Hayat has been reassigned," Dave added.

"Yes, that arouses my suspicions too. By the way, our friends in Langley found the trace of heroin on the *Light of the East* intriguing. This was probably not the first time the cargo ship had been used to ship arms to belligerents in Syria. They suspect the arms were destined for the Al Nusra Front, an al Qaeda affiliate in Syria. They pay for their weapons purchases with heroin. Whoever was selling the weapons is involved in the drug trade."

"That is what the captain of our cruise ship speculated as well."

"You know, Dave, I think it is time you and I made a site visit to Europa Bank's branch in Istanbul. While you were on vacation, I drew up a priority list of site visits that our anti–money laundering team should make. Istanbul and Mexico City are at the top of the list, followed by London, Hong Kong, Dubai, and Singapore. We can split up the team among the different sites. Any interest?"

"The second week in September would work for me. I am taking my daughter back to college right after Labor Day."

"The second week it is."

Chapter Thirty-Six

In the Sisli district of Istanbul, at the intersection of Buyukdere Caddesi and Levent Caddesi, are found many of the large plazas and high office towers housing major foreign and Turkish banks. The gleaming headquarters of Europa Bank's Turkish subsidiary are located at 159 Buyukdere Caddesi.

Dave and Jeff were invited to the top-floor office of the chairman of the Turkish subsidiary, Aydin Budak, toward the end of their week in Istanbul. For three days, they—with the assistance of a team of auditors—had interviewed staff at headquarters to determine whether appropriate procedures were being put into place to prevent money laundering and bribery by drug syndicates and terrorist organizations.

Aydin Budak gestured with his hands to emphasize the point he was making. "Let me assure you, gentlemen, that we are doing everything that is humanly possible. But, by now, you must recognize the magnitude of the problem. Turkey is not the United States. The underground economy accounts for half of all economic activity in our country, and most of it is unaudited. Knowing your customer is a goal that we are trying to impress on all of our staff, but old habits die hard. We have branches and millions of customers throughout the country. In small towns and villages, transactions are often based on trust, with no questions asked."

Jeff responded diplomatically, "We are impressed with your efforts in Istanbul. Nonetheless, I am puzzled why the Turkish government has not passed laws prohibiting the establishment of personal gold accounts by customers."

Budak grinned broadly. "For many of our women, especially in eastern Turkey, buying gold jewelry has always been like setting up a savings account. As they gain in financial sophistication, they may melt down the jewelry into ingots, which are then placed in a bank account for safekeeping."

Dave shook his head, "I don't think Jeff is talking about small savers. We noted several instances where foundations made large deposits of gold into accounts at your bank. For instance, in November of last year, gold ingots worth twenty million dollars were deposited into the bank account of the Emir Tilki Foundation."

"Ah yes, the Tilki Foundation is one of the largest philanthropies in our country. It has invested generously in medical research and hospitals in Istanbul, Ankara, and Izmir."

Dave persisted, "The point I wanted to make is that if large deposits of gold are accepted, without questions asked as to the origin of the gold, and the gold is converted into its equivalent in cash, then the money can be transferred anywhere in the world electronically. This concerns us because foundations, unlike businesses, are not audited."

"That's not true," Budak protested. "Some foundations are audited."

"But the vast majority of nonprofit entities are not because government auditors are too understaffed. Am I correct?"

"That is unfortunately correct," Budak conceded.

"Wouldn't you agree that this is a potential loophole in your anti–money laundering compliance system?" Dave asked.

"Well, be realistic!" Budak sounded annoyed. "If we do not accept gold deposits but other banks do, we will lose business!"

"You could lobby the government to change the law," Jeff suggested.

Budak rolled his eyes in dismay at the ceiling. "It could take years before agreement is reached in parliament. As Americans, you should appreciate that. You have political gridlock of your own."

"The name Tilki sounds familiar. Is there any connection to the Ottoman Trading Company?"

To Budak, the question seemed innocent, a curious offhand remark; but for Dave, it was loaded, enabling him to redirect the discussion.

"Oh yes. Emir Tilki is chairman of both the company and the foundation. He is one of the country's most prominent citizens."

"What other interests does he have?" Jeff joined in. He and Dave were two hunting dogs on the same scent.

"You mean business or personal?"

"Business."

"Well, there have been reports for some time that he has a controlling interest in Galata-Hatay Bankasi, a private bank that caters to wealthy clients. Tayfur Melek, its president, married Tilki's daughter. We have a correspondent banking relationship with that bank, as of course with many other Turkish banks."

"If Galata-Hatay Bankasi asked Europa Bank to make a money transfer on behalf of one of its wealthy clients, would you do the transaction without investigating their client?"

"Why yes. That would be normal practice. We are required by law to know our own clients, but correspondent banking relationships are unregulated."

Dave whistled under his breath. "What can you tell us about this bank? How long has it existed?"

Budak smiled. "Would you like a short lesson in Turkish history? Hatay is a small province in the southwestern corner of Turkey, bordered by the Mediterranean and Syria. Its largest city is the port of Iskenderun. After the dissolution of the Ottoman Empire, Hatay was briefly part of the French mandate in Syria. But in 1939, it was incorporated into the Turkish Republic after a popular referendum. The Hatay Bank was founded in the 1920s, and after the province became part of Turkey, it acquired the Galata Bank in Istanbul. The Meleks are a prominent political family in Hatay, which they represent in the Turkish parliament."

"What else can you tell us about the Tilki clan?"

"Emir Tilki's second son, Ahmet, is president of Mardin Sigorta, an insurance company serving the southeastern part of the country, where there is a large Kurdish population. Ahmet is a sober businessman who has stayed out of the limelight more than his older brother, Omer, spending much of his time in the provincial capitals of Mardin and Sanliurfa. Family connections probably helped his rise in the company. Ahmet's mother is Kurdish and the daughter of the founder of Mardin Sigorta."

"Aydin, you are an incredible source of information," Jeff exclaimed. "Now refresh my memory. Under Turkish law, isn't it true that electronic transfers of money by banks must be reported, but this requirement does not apply to non-bank financial institutions, such as insurance companies?"

"That is correct," Budak replied with a twinkle in his eye.

Chapter Thirty-Seven

On the day of his arrival in Istanbul, Dave sent an email to Inspector Polat, asking about Hayat Yilmaz and the police inquiry into the attack on her. Had any progress been made? The response came several days later, when Dave and Jeff were taking a taxi back to their hotel after the meeting with Aydin Budak of Europa Bank. It was from Inspector Korkut Tosun, to whom Polat had forwarded the email.

> *Regretfully, there has been no change in the condition of Ms. Yilmaz. She is still in a coma, so we have no new leads as to who attacked her. It is possible that she was robbed and was injured when she put up resistance. Thinking her dead, the robbers may then have panicked and thrown her body into the Bosporus. This, of course, begs the question what a respectable woman would have been doing in that part of Istanbul just before dawn. Moreover, forensic evidence indicates that she incurred the injury eight to ten hours before she was thrown into the Bosporus. We have considered the possibility that she was the victim of a lovers' quarrel, but her parents insist that she has not been seeing any man for years.*

Dave handed his phone to Jeff. "Look! Read this! What do you think we should do?"

Jeff wrinkled his face ruefully. "Is there anything we can do? Can two Americans who do not speak Turkish do better than the Istanbul police? We're amateurs."

Then Dave had an inspired moment. "See that?" He pointed out the window at a distinguished building. "Isn't that the College of Architecture of Istanbul Technical University? That's where Hayat taught!" He banged on the back of the driver's seat while pointing out the window. "Driver! Driver! Don't go to the Park Hyatt Hotel! Go there!"

The driver nodded to indicate that he understood. He maneuvered into a turning lane and, with squealing wheels, made a rapid U-turn before oncoming traffic. Depositing them at the entrance to the College of Architecture, he asked in English, "Would you like me to wait?"

Dave shook his head. "No, thank you. That will not be necessary. Our hotel is within walking distance from here."

"I was wondering what this building was," Jeff exclaimed. "I could see it from our hotel. Now I know." He read the sign at the entrance: Istanbul Technical University, Taskisla Campus.

The receptionist at the entrance asked them first in Turkish, then in English, "May I help you?"

Dave, who had decided to come to the building on impulse, now had to think up a plausible reason for their visit. His words came tumbling out. "We're visitors from the United States, friends of Professor Hayat Yilmaz."

The receptionist's welcoming smile froze. "Whom do you wish to see?"

"One of her colleagues, someone in the urban planning department with whom she taught."

"Of course." She spoke softly into the intercom, then she turned back to Dave and Jeff. "Professor Davut Oguz will see you. Take the elevator on the right to the second floor. His office is to the left of the elevator when you get off."

Professor Oguz was already waiting for Dave and Jeff in the hallway when they got off the elevator. A big bear of a man with a pleasant demeanor, he bounded forward to greet them, crushing their hands in his strong grip as they introduced themselves. After ushering them into his office and settling down behind his desk, he threw up his big hands and asked, "So what can I tell you about my dear colleague, Professor Yilmaz?"

Jeff and Dave began explaining the reasons for their interest in Hayat Yilmaz's welfare—Jeff's longstanding friendship dating back to her residence in New York and Dave's more recent acquaintanceship with her when he and his family were vacationing in Istanbul.

The professor nodded his head from time to time, and when they concluded, he remarked, "The particulars of Hayat's misfortune are very puzzling. When we began our classes for the fall term, there was no Hayat. She was always very conscientious, and if she needed to be absent, she would certainly have informed the department. Then the police came, and we learned, to our horror, that someone had tried to murder her."

"Who do you think might have done it?" Jeff asked.

Oguz shrugged. "They questioned many of us—faculty, students, and administrators—to find a lead but were unsuccessful. She was well-liked by both faculty and students, especially after she joined the demonstrations against the redevelopment of Taksim Gezi Park. The police did not seem interested in investigating whether the developers of Taksim Gezi Park might have tried to eliminate a critic. The developers are well-connected politically after all. They preferred to pursue a potential lead that she might have had a romantic liaison with a faculty member or student, which ended badly."

"Why do you think that was?" Jeff wondered. "There was clearly another potential angle."

"Pardon me for suggesting that they might be deferring to powerful interests. It may be a simple matter of probabilities. Murders or attempted murders are more likely to result from a lovers' quarrel than from a cold-blooded corporate calculation to dispose of an opponent. Moreover, no faculty member or student has an interest in the development of Taksim Gezi Park. A romantic entanglement with a faculty member or student is more likely."

"Was there any truth to their suspicions?" Dave asked uneasily.

"As far as the faculty is concerned, we are good friends and colleagues. Nothing more. My wife and Hayat are especially good friends. We were dinner guests a number of times at her parents' home, where she lives. As for students, I think it very unlikely. None of us has even heard the slightest rumor."

"Do you know where she is hospitalized? The police would not tell me because they said that her life could be in danger."

"They would not tell us either, but I know. Her parents told me. She is being kept at Istanbul University's Medical Faculty Hospital. It was the closest major hospital to the site of the attack."

"Have you seen her?"

"No, there are visitor restrictions."

Dave and Jeff looked at each other. They had learned a little more than they had known a few minutes before, but there had been no major breakthrough. Should they thank Professor Oguz for his time and depart? But something had been bothering Dave as they talked, a nagging thought at the back of his mind.

"Professor Oguz, thank you for generously spending some time with us. We do not want to impose. However, I just thought of something which might interest you. The afternoon before Hayat was attacked, my family and I were having coffee with her, and we got to talking about her youth. Her father has a shop in the Grand Bazaar. Eventually, she became engaged to the son of the merchant who had the shop next to her father's. They went to university together, but Hayat decided to break off the engagement because of some major disagreement. I forgot to mention this story to Inspector Polat when he interviewed me. Do you think this could be of interest to the police?"

Oguz stroked his beard as he thought. "Yes, it could be. In all the years that my wife and I have known her, she has never spoken to us about this engagement. She cannot tell us now, but her parents might." Checking the faculty directory, he dialed a telephone number. "Perhaps they are at home."

After speaking for a few moments in Turkish, he smiled at Dave and Jeff. "They will see us. I explained that two American friends of Hayat—who are visiting Istanbul from New York—want to extend their personal sympathy. Do you have the time, gentlemen? We will need to take the ferry across the Bosporus to Uskudar, the district of Istanbul where she lives with her parents."

Chapter Thirty-Eight

The ferry crossing from the dock at Beskitas to the dock at Salacak provided a spectacular view of Topkapi Palace, the Hagia Sophia, and the Blue Mosque across the water. How they shimmered in a golden haze as the setting sun swung lower in the western sky! If they had not had an appointment, it would have been tempting to linger at a café on the promenade along the water at Salacak. Instead, Oguz hailed a taxi, which took them up a steep hill to a pleasant neighborhood of wooden houses and streets lined by trees and parks dating from the Ottoman period.

When Oguz knocked on the door of one of the houses, they waited for a moment before footsteps could be heard. An old man opened the door. "I am Cengiz Yilmaz. Welcome to my home!"

They were ushered into a parlor where his wife, Oya, was waiting to serve them tea and sweet cakes. With Oguz acting as interpreter, they spoke in soft tones, as if they were in the presence of a hospital patient lying in bed. They talked a little about New York and the work Hayat had done there for the Turkish delegation to the United Nations. The parents expressed the hope that Hayat would soon be transferred to a hospital in Uskudar because it was difficult and time-consuming to cross the Bosporus to visit her at Istanbul University's Medical Faculty Hospital. Of course, they wanted only what was best for her. The old man, fatigue and anxiety lining his face, confessed that they were not sleeping well.

Finally, Oguz directed the conversation toward the police investigation after the tragedy and the questions that had been asked of faculty and students at the College of Architecture of Istanbul Technical University. The police had focused on a lovers' quarrel as a potential motive for the attack on Hayat. Had they been asked similar questions?

The parents nodded their heads in agreement. "We were asked the same questions," Cengiz Yilmaz said, "and we always gave the same answer. She was dedicated to her career. There was no man in her life."

Dave waited for Oguz to finish translating before he asked, "Ever? What about the young man to whom she was engaged when she was a university student?"

The parents looked startled when they understood the question. "How did you know that? But that was such a long time ago. She has not seen him for many years."

The old man shuffled over to a cabinet and, rummaging among papers, extracted an old photograph yellowed with age. He handed it to Dave, who passed it around for others to see. It was a photograph of a smiling young couple—Hayat and a tall, thin young man.

"It was their betrothal picture," the old man said.

"What was the young man's name?" Dave asked.

The parents looked at each other. The old man whispered, "Demir Ozmen."

Oguz, looking somewhat embarrassed, followed up with a question. "Do you know why Hayat broke off the engagement?"

The old man's lips twisted in disgust. "She discovered that he was a drug peddler."

Later that evening, Dave fired a response to Inspector Korkut Tosun's email:

> *I may have a lead for you in the Hayat Yilmaz case. You should investigate Demir Ozmen. He was formerly a lover of Hayat Yilmaz when they were university students.*

Breaking Point

Chapter Thirty-Nine

Maria Elena had not left her apartment since the beginning of the hostage crisis at the cathedral in Morelia. She had called in sick to the real estate office where she worked as a broker. Her illness had not been an exaggeration, even if it was only a symptom of her stress. She had lost her appetite, and the little food that she swallowed had nauseated her. She had sat on her living room couch for hours, newspapers strewn at her feet, a litter of cold coffee cups and stubbed-out cigarettes in front of her on the table, with her eyes fixed to her television set.

The continuous television coverage of the crisis included an address by the president of Mexico to the public, promising that everything would be done to gain the release of the hostages without bloodshed, but she had not felt reassured. She had not slept, afraid that she would miss a breaking development.

The tension was unbearable. Occasionally, she wept and then she prayed—mostly for her uncle, her father's brother, Father Cardozo, who had presided at the wedding at the cathedral. He had been appointed her guardian when she was still a young girl after her parents had been killed in a car accident. There was no doubt about the identity of the priest; several newspapers and television channels had confirmed it. He had been a loving guardian, invariably thoughtful and kind. In recent years, after she had moved to Mexico City, she had not been as attentive as she should have been; and now he was the hostage of a murderous drug gang that threatened to kill innocent people at random if their demands were not met.

The irony of this hostage crisis was that the murderous drug gang was Los Zetas—the group to which her lover, Diego Alvarez, was tied. She had never questioned him too deeply about what he did for the cartel on those occasions when he visited her in Mexico City. Because she knew him to be a decent man, she preferred to ignore media reports about the atrocities committed by Los Zetas against rival drug gangs. On a few occasions, she had even assisted Diego in avoiding a confrontation with members of other gangs, as had happened recently with that American, Bigelow, in the bar at the W Hotel. She had treated these occasions as amusing parlor games without serious consequences.

The hostage crisis in Morelia was different. She knew that even without talking to Diego, whom she had called to appeal for his help. He had seemed worried and had promised to do what he could. He had called back a few hours later reporting that he was still waiting to make contact with the man to whom the gang leader at the cathedral reported. He had not said who that man was. No names had been mentioned. His secretiveness had disturbed her.

Her mind was numbed by the frequent replays of video clips showing the initial seizure of the cathedral by the drug gang and by images of security officials arriving at the Palacio Nacional to consult with the president of Mexico. Would any progress ever be made? Her fear that something terrible was about to happen struggled with her hope that Diego would successfully intervene.

Several times, the television channels had shown the interview with the cameraman who had borne witness to the gang's seizure of the wedding party and who had been readmitted to the cathedral to make video clips of the hostages huddled in the nave near the altar. He had spoken briefly to the governor of the state of Michoacán, one of the hostages, who had reported no progress in contacting the kidnappers of Demir Ozmen. He had instructed state officials by telephone to use every unofficial link they had to the alleged kidnappers, the Knights Templar, to determine who was holding

Ozmen and where. The governor had said that this kind of delay was to be expected in a matter of this complexity and that he was still optimistic about a successful outcome.

The cameraman—who stood on the front steps of the cathedral, surrounded by a crowd of newspaper reporters from Mexico, the United States, and Europe—was enjoying his new celebrity. Yes, he answered, the hostages were being treated well. He had spoken to the priest, Father Cardozo, who had alerted the captors to water and food in the cathedral refectory that would be sufficient to satisfy the needs of the hostages. The prisoners were also permitted to take toilet breaks in groups of four, escorted by guards.

But what about the emotional stress? Were the hostages showing signs of their ordeal? That was to be expected, he replied. He had seen hostages hunched over in their chairs or stretched out on the floor, trying to get some badly needed sleep. And what about the bridal couple? How were they holding up? It had been a poignant scene, he admitted—the bridegroom sitting with his arms wrapped around his bride, who was resting against his shoulder, asleep from exhaustion.

Hours passed. Then a shot had been heard, and the body of a businessman had been thrown onto the front steps of the cathedral. The reassuring words of the cameraman now rang hollow. No one knew what would happen next.

Television anchors had given up on live reporting from the cathedral square and had resorted instead to documentaries on the virulent drug wars plaguing Mexico as gangs battled over lucrative trade routes to major markets in the United States and Europe. A learned professor from an American university and a fellow from a libertarian policy institute in Washington, DC, had debated the merits of legalizing drugs to break the hold of the gangs. Should governments tax and regulate drugs in the same way as alcohol?

Members of the Turkish media were also interviewed to elaborate on the impact of the hostage crisis on public opinion in Turkey, where it was receiving full coverage in all the major newspapers and television channels. They conceded that the Ottoman Trading

Company was not being forthcoming with information except to confirm that Demir Ozmen was a senior executive who had traveled to Mexico to negotiate some new business deals, pending official approval of a free trade agreement between Mexico and Turkey.

Maria Elena awoke with a start on her sofa. She was surprised that she had been able to doze off. Midday light was slanting through the blinds on her windows. The television set was still on. The hosts of the morning shows were almost apologetic in reporting that nothing had happened overnight or this morning, as if news should be entertainment. She stood up to walk toward the kitchenette. Her mouth was parched, and for the first time in more than a day, she felt a pang of hunger.

Then the news broke. She could tell from the excited pitch of the news anchor's voice that there was a major new development. She turned back to the television set. A reporter was standing in the square, pointing toward the pink cathedral bathed in golden light by the sun. The doors to the cathedral had opened. The masked leader of the gang, flanked by armed guards, emerged from the gloom inside, shoving the priest before him. The priest, whose vestments were torn and in disarray, was praying. The scream that Maria Elena felt rising in her throat died within her as the terrorist lifted his gun and fired into the back of the priest's head. The gunmen then withdrew into the cathedral, closing the doors.

"Oh my god!" She repeated it several times before collapsing on the sofa. She was in shock. It had happened so quickly that she wanted to believe that it was a bad dream. But bad dreams end, and the continuous television coverage made clear that this one would not. Within two hours, the cameraman who had been selected by Los Zetas to be their messenger to the world had heard their explanation of what had transpired.

The businessman had been shot because he had tried to escape during a toilet break. The priest had pleaded for the life of the businessman, offering himself as a sacrifice so that he would be spared. His request had been denied, but since he seemed to desire martyrdom, the leader of the gang had decided to oblige his death wish.

Maria Elena felt impotent rage rising within her. She knew her uncle. He would not have wanted heroic martyrdom. He was merely acting as a witness for his faith. His last prayers would not have been for himself but, rather, for the safety of the hostages and the souls of their captors. *Father, forgive them for they know not what they do!*

She wondered why Diego had not called her. Did he not know what had happened? She picked up the receiver to call him.

Chapter Forty

It was midafternoon when the solitude of the three prisoners, each withdrawn into his own thoughts, was broken by the sound of a key turning in the lock. They had become accustomed to the background noise penetrating the thin walls of their room—the voices of their captors, the ringing of phones, the occasional hum of a vehicle driving up to their motel unit and then departing, and in the distance, the relentless roar of traffic on the nearby highway. But the unlocking of the door riveted their attention. It was too early for their evening meal. What could it mean?

Two guards entered the room, their hands resting on the holsters of their guns. "Ozmen?" one called out to the Turk, motioning for him to come with them.

Slowly, as if fearing the worst, he got up from his cot and, without glancing at the Bigelow brothers, walked past the guards into the adjoining room. They quickly followed him and again locked the door.

Dave and Bob exchanged glances and strained to hear what was happening in the other room. The murmur of voices was audible, but they could not make out individual words. Neither liked the man, but to their relief, no shots rang out—nor did Ozmen cry out in pain.

Bob broke the silence first. "When you were questioning Ozmen about this woman you know in Istanbul—"

"Hayat Yilmaz?"

"Yeah, her. That jogged my memory. Just before I left New York, I was sitting in on a teleconference between Murat and Tilki to discuss what should be done about Ozmen's kidnapping. Ozmen is in deep shit with Tilki about some incident involving a woman. Tilki is so ticked off, he initially considered not ransoming Ozmen and leaving him to die."

"Was the woman's name mentioned?"

"No."

"Interesting."

The brothers relapsed into silence. Each man wondered who would be next.

When Ozmen, flanked by the two guards, entered the adjoining room, he saw a third man dressed in civilian clothes but whose erect, trim bearing and abrupt manner of speech identified him as a man who had once served in the military. Clearly in charge, he invited Ozmen to sit down and then introduced himself.

"My name is Pedro Guerra. I know who you are. The media has identified you as a Turkish businessman, Demir Ozmen, vice president for special operations of the Ottoman Trading Company. Your kidnapping has caused a lot of disruption in our country. The cathedral in Morelia was seized by a gang demanding your release. Two hostages have already been executed."

Ozmen eyed Guerra warily. Why tell him about the execution of hostages? Was this to intimidate him?

"Do the people who seized the cathedral belong to your gang?" he asked.

"No, they are much too stupid to belong to my gang. Vicious dogs sniffing at the wrong scent." He laughed contemptuously. "Tell me, what were you doing in Veracruz?"

"I was trying to arrange a trade deal with Veracruz Sugar."

"With Veracruz Sugar or with Los Zetas? The activities of you and your colleague—the one who was, unfortunately, killed—"

"Comooglou."

"Has aroused the curiosity of our informant in Veracruz. First, you were the guests of Diego Alvarez—an executive of Veracruz Sugar who is known to have ties to Los Zetas—at a heavily guarded luxurious villa. Each morning, you were picked up by a chauffeur-driven limousine with bodyguard and taken to the docklands, where you spent an unusual amount of time inspecting a cargo ship, the *Atlantica*, which had been selected for the transport of refined sugar. This is a relatively new ship, still in good condition and specially fitted, I believe, with secret compartments to conceal contraband. The ship was expected to leave port in ten days.

"You, of course, tried to disguise your real purpose. On the second and third mornings, you went to different parts of the docklands, where the papers you showed to the security guards indicated that you were two Turkish businessmen interested in either shipping Mexican automotive parts to Turkey or in exporting vegetables to the United States. These are standard procedures for someone trying to set up a highly sophisticated drug smuggling ring."

Ozmen sat impassively, not admitting to anything.

"You see, my organization knows everything about you. You may wonder who we are. We are Sinalo*a*, the main rivals of Los Zetas, and we will do anything to sabotage their plans to establish some sort of transatlantic partnership. Besides, you are dealing with the wrong people. We should be your partners."

Ozmen was impressed. "What are you suggesting?"

"In the exchange of messages over your release, Tilki, your boss, hinted that he might be interested in a long-term business relationship with Sinaloa. You may be unaware of this because you have not been able to talk to Istanbul this week. Our leadership agreed, provided that the ransom money for you was handed over without a hitch. I passed this message to Bigelow. Did he mention it to you?"

"No. We have talked only about how things went wrong."

"Yes, they did go wrong. There was a police trap. Someone tipped off the police. If Tilki changed his mind, he could have done it to make sure that he kept his money. But what is five million dollars compared to what he could earn over the long term dealing with us? No, it had to be someone else. What do you know about Bigelow?"

"He joined Ottoman Trading Company at the beginning of this year to handle our financial accounts in the New York office. The head of the office there has used him to carry some important messages, but I cannot vouch for his reliability."

"My hunch is that Bigelow is a police spy."

Ozmen nodded. "I share your suspicions. Either Bob Bigelow is incompetent or he is a police spy. I am also worried about his brother. He asked me some questions that could only be of interest to the Turkish police. I would not trust him. He could be dangerous."

"Both could be police spies. We will deal with them when the time comes."

"I could call Tilki to confirm his continued interest in working with Sinaloa," offered Ozmen, eager to align himself with his captors. "You still have my phone, don't you?"

"I have thought about that," replied Guerra, "but with both the Mexican and Turkish governments now on high alert, there is too much risk. Your call could be intercepted. Still, you could be helpful to us."

"How?"

"Talk to the Bigelow brothers. Get close to them. Maybe they will confide some secrets to you. If you succeed, then we can start thinking about how and where to release you. Understood? My boss and I have decided to spare you. We still have not made up our minds about the other two. I am inclined to shoot Bob Bigelow, but his brother—maybe I will let him live."

Ozmen was only too willing to comply. The solution to his dilemma had presented itself. After all, what were the Bigelow brothers to him—troublemakers at best and police spies at worst. He would happily betray both of them for his freedom.

"May I offer a suggestion?" he said. "If you shoot one of the brothers, it would be safer to shoot both of them."

Chapter Forty-One

When Ozmen was shoved back into the room, the curious Bigelow brothers waited only until the guards had left, locking the door behind them, before they fired questions at him.

"That took a long time. What did they want from you?" asked Bob.

"The same old things. Those guys are like an old record. They always ask the same questions." Looking disgusted, Ozmen sat down on his cot and sighed. "I am losing hope of ever getting out of here alive."

"Did they get rough with you?" Dave asked anxiously.

"Not this time. But who knows what will happen next time?" He crooked his index finger as if he was pulling a trigger. "Those guys are tough."

A key turned the lock to the door once more. This time, the guards pointed to Dave when they entered. He looked at Bob as he walked toward the door. "Keep the faith, brother!"

After Guerra introduced himself, he got quickly to the point, mixing his tactics to keep Dave mentally off balance.

"You are related to Bob Bigelow?"

"Yes, I am his brother."

"How long have the two of you worked together?"

"What do you mean?" The question puzzled Dave.

"For the police."

"You are mistaken. We have no connection to the police. I am a lawyer from New York in Mexico City on business, and my brother is chief financial officer for the New York office of the Ottoman Trading Company."

"What did you know about the police trap last night when the ransom money was transferred to us?"

"Nothing at all. I had nothing to do with it."

"Don't lie to us!" He walked over to Dave and hit him across the face. "You were seen at the restaurant last night sitting at the same table as your brother shortly before we picked him up, as agreed, for the transfer of the ransom money. What did he tell you?"

"He told me he was in Mexico City on a business trip and had a meeting after dinner last night. That was the last I saw of him until your men brought me here."

"Then why were you running after his car?"

"I wanted to return something to him that he had forgotten at the restaurant."

"It couldn't have waited until you were both back in New York?"

"It probably could have. I don't know why I did it. It was stupid of me."

"Do you know a Miguel Rodriguez?"

"No, I have never heard the name. Who is he?"

"He is an agent working for the Drug Enforcement Agency in the United States. My sources tell me that he tipped off the police about the ransom deal. What I am trying to find out is who told him about the ransom deal. Was it you or your brother?"

"I think you are mistaken about my brother and me."

"What kind of business did you say you are in? Why are you in Mexico City?"

"I am part of a team hired by the US Department of Justice to work on an anti–money laundering project at Europa Bank, which has a branch in Mexico City."

"Who is laundering money?"

"Drug gangs and terrorists."

Guerra laughed. "So you are one of the guys making life difficult for people like me." He walked up to Dave, who steeled himself for another blow.

"Do you have a family?"

"Yes, a wife and daughter."

"Look, if you want to see your family again, tell us what you know. Your brother is a police collaborator. Of that we are certain." Turning on his heel, Guerra tossed a final threat over this shoulder. "Think about my offer if you want to live. You still have a little time."

Chapter Forty-Two

Bob's interrogation came next, lasted longer, and was more brutal. It began with a blunt accusation: "Your brother told us you are a police spy!"

"That's not true! My brother would not tell a lie!" he replied with heat. It could not be true, even if he had reason to doubt his brother, because Dave could not have known about his FBI ties.

"Then what were you discussing at the restaurant last night? Instructions from the DEA?"

"Look, my brother and I met by accident at that restaurant. He did not even know that I was in Mexico City. We were just catching up on what was happening in our lives. Let him go!"

Guerra struck Bob across the mouth. "You expect me to believe that bullshit? Tell me the truth!"

"That is the truth!" Bob tried to avoid the second blow, but it glanced off his right eye.

"If your brother is what he says he is—a New York lawyer investigating Mexican banks and not a police liaison—then I will start believing in fairy tales. His life is hanging by a thread. If you want your brother to live, tell me who your police contact in Mexico City is and what you did to set up the trap."

"I don't know how the police found out."

"Ever hear of Miguel Rodriguez?"

Bob shook his head. "No, who is he?"

"Your phone records indicate that you received a call last night while you were eating dinner at Villa Maria. Who called you? We have not been able to trace it. It was from someone with an unlisted number."

"It was from my girlfriend. She wanted to check on me."

"You are lying. One thing I know for certain—you are a police informer. You are the only person who could have tipped off the police. None of my men would have done it. We have worked together for years. I completely trust them. You have one last chance. You may not give a damn about your own life, but do you want your brother's death on your conscience?"

Bob's voice shook as the threat to his brother hit home. "I was only following orders from my employer. I am not a police spy." Another blow fell on his head.

Then Guerra's mobile phone rang, giving Bob a temporary respite. He was certain that nothing was to be gained from a confession. The kidnappers did not live by a code of honor. If he admitted that he had had contact with Miguel Rodriguez, they might still kill his brother and him as well. Nonetheless, he knew that he would never be able to face Dave's wife and daughter again if his brother was killed by their captors and he somehow survived. He had made a mess of his life, and now he had dragged his brother into it.

When Bob was pushed back into the room after his ordeal, the other two prisoners could see evidence of his beating in the fading afternoon light—blood trickling from a bruised lip and a swollen eye showing the first signs of discoloration.

But Bob was still defiant, whispering to Dave, "I told that bastard Guerra the truth—that I was only delivering the money from Ottoman Trading Company for the release of Ozmen. I knew nothing about a police trap! But he did not believe me." His emphatic tone convinced Dave.

"What do you think they will do with us?" asked Ozmen, injecting himself into the exchange.

"Shoot us! When I was in there"—Bob motioned with his head toward the other room, where their captors kept guard—"Guerra received a telephone call. My knowledge of Spanish came in handy. I picked up enough from Guerra's responses to know that all the major highways leaving Mexico City have police or military blockades. Motorists are being stopped, and their vehicles are being inspected. Guerra's last question to his caller was what he should do with the excess baggage. He was looking at me when he asked that question."

Dave felt the muscles in his stomach tighten. He could not disagree with Bob's conclusion. Dead men did not talk and would not be able to identify the kidnappers to the police.

"We can either wait—hoping that we will be found and rescued in time—or we can plan our escape." It was Ozmen again. "Do either of you have friends in the US government or in the FBI who could pressure the Mexican government to act quickly? Your disappearance must have been reported by now."

It seemed to be an innocent question, and Dave responded without thinking. "I am sure my friend Jeff Braunstein, who is here in Mexico City with me, has contacted the US embassy by now. But the US government does not act quickly, so there is not much hope from that direction. Funny that you should ask about the FBI. My college roommate at Princeton joined the FBI after graduation. In fact, he had dinner at my house only a few weeks ago. But he is probably busy with matters other than freeing the hostages of Mexican drug gangs. Where are you, John Shafer, when I need you?"

Bob cringed inwardly at the mention of his FBI handler.

"Then we must plan our escape."

"But how can we, Demir?" asked Dave. "They always come in pairs and have guns. We have no weapons."

"Oh yes we do!" Ozmen turned his head, looking in the direction of the reeking chamber pot in the far corner, and guffawed. "This is not a time to be fastidious!"

Bob squinted at Ozmen with his one good eye. The dour Turk seemed unusually talkative and in good spirits tonight. He sensed that something was wrong. He put his hand on Dave's arm and whispered so that the Turk could not overhear, "Be careful what you say. I do not trust him."

Dave nodded to show that he understood. A silence fell over the room. The light dimmed as evening approached.

The sound of a key turning in the lock broke the stillness. It was around dinnertime, but the guards did not bring in their evening meal. Instead, they summoned Ozmen once more for further questioning by Guerra.

"What have you learned?" asked Guerra impatiently.

Ozmen smiled, relishing his role of *agent provocateur.* "I have some information which you may find useful. Dave Bigelow, as I suspected, has ties to senior police officials in the United States. He is a friend of John Shafer of the FBI."

"I do not know that name, but I will have my people check it. Go on!"

"The Bigelow brothers are planning to escape. They may do something desperate, even throwing the chamber pot at the guards to catch them by surprise and break out of here."

"Have some supper while I check on John Shafer." Guerra pointed to some food and beer on the table.

Ozmen ate rapidly while Guerra spoke to someone on his mobile phone. Before he finished, he heard Guerra swear in Spanish and then approach him with gleaming eyes.

"Ozmen, John Shafer is a senior narcotics official with the FBI in New York. You have done well, my friend. Tomorrow afternoon, we plan to leave this place, and we will take you with us. Then we can start work on planning the business relationship between Sinaloa and the Ottoman Trading Company. But tonight you must return to your cell so that the Bigelow brothers will suspect nothing. We will dispose of them in the morning."

When the guards returned Ozmen to their room, the Bigelow brothers did not ask how he had fared. Although he had been gone for about thirty minutes, he showed no signs of physical abuse or duress. Strangely, he belched as if he had bolted down food too rapidly. They waited in vain for their dinners to be delivered, their hungry stomachs growling. A wall of suspicion now separated the Bigelow brothers from Ozmen.

The thought occurred to Bob that their captors would not want to waste food on men who were about to die. Lowering his voice to a whisper too soft for the Turk to hear, Bob made a daring proposal. "We should jump the guards the next time they come in. Damned if I am going to sit here like a dumb duck waiting to be gunned down!"

"If I am going to die," Dave whispered back, "I want to go with dignity. No chamber pot." Then he had an idea. "What about the blanket on the Turk's bed? We could throw it over the head of the first guard to enter this room and tackle him before the second guard reacts. They probably are not expecting a fight from us, so we could catch them by surprise."

Bob shook his head doubtfully. "Less chance of success, I'd say. But if that's what you want, let's do it. But we do not bring the Turk into the plan!"

Hanging by a Thread

Chapter Forty-Three

Diego Alvarez was seething with anger. He felt like killing someone, especially Omar Morales, who had not returned any of his calls. This morning, he had had a long telephone call from a tearful and sobbing Maria Elena. Her favorite uncle—the priest presiding at the marriage ceremony at the cathedral in Morelia—had been executed by his captors. She had watched a television report in horrified disbelief as his body had fallen on the front steps of the cathedral.

"How could they do such a thing to this holy man? These Los Zetas people are animals! Diego, how can you work with such people? I have never questioned you before, but now I am. If you love me, you must break off with them at once!"

He had tried to explain to her that he was trapped—that once a drug gang owned you, you could never leave voluntarily. But his protestations had only made her more hysterical.

Then in the afternoon, he had received a summons from the military commander responsible for security in the state of Veracruz. The summons to the Municipal Palace had at first annoyed him. Had he not already shared everything he knew about the kidnapping of Demir Ozmen with the military police? What could he possibly tell them that they did not already know?

That was precisely what worried him as he parked his car near the Plaza de las Armas and walked quickly across the square to the Municipal Palace. The soldiers guarding the building looked straight ahead, observing whoever was entering or leaving. When he introduced himself at the reception desk, he was told, "Colonel Reyes is expecting you. Second floor to the right of the stairs." He knew Colonel Reyes well, but they had an understanding not to meet in public places, if at all possible.

His worries were confirmed when an aide ushered him into the office of Colonel Reyes. This was not going to be a private meeting. Two of those present he recognized: Captain Segundo of the Mexican Navy and Miguel Rodriguez, an agent of the DEA. The fourth person was not familiar to him, but he looked American.

Anticipating his question, Reyes said in English, "Allow me to introduce John Shafer of the FBI in New York."

"Mucho gusto, Senor Alvarez," said Shafer, shaking his hand. "Hablemos Espanol!"

Alvarez glanced nervously at Reyes. It was difficult enough leading a double life as a businessman and a member of Los Zetas. But there was a third dimension to his life—that of police informer—which, if it ever became known to Los Zetas, would mean instant death in the most grisly manner imaginable. Most probably hours of torture followed by beheading or being burned alive. Until now, he had sought to minimize the risk of leaks by always meeting privately with Reyes. Why was Reyes now putting him at personal risk by giving him no warning that other people would be present?

Again, Reyes seemed to read his mind. "You have no reason to worry about anyone here, Alvarez. We wanted this meeting because the circumstances are extraordinary. The president of Mexico has appealed to me to find a way to communicate with those members of Los Zetas who have seized hostages in the cathedral in Morelia. As you must know, two innocent hostages have already been shot and thrown out onto the front steps of the cathedral—one of them a banker who is a personal friend of the American ambassador to Mexico."

"The second victim, the priest, is the uncle of my girlfriend, Maria Elena," said Alvarez. "She called me this morning. It is very sad! She could not believe Los Zetas would do such a thing!"

"So we agree this carnage must stop. This catastrophe has been a horrible mistake. We have every reason to believe that the kidnappers of the Turk were not the Knights Templar but were rather Los Matas Zetas, working on behalf of the Sinaloa Cartel."

"So what do you want me to do?" asked Alvarez, pulling the cigarette from his mouth.

Reyes got straight to the point. "Do you know the leader of the group who seized the cathedral? Perhaps we can persuade him to abandon this mad venture. We would guarantee safe conduct for him and his men. Storming the cathedral could result in many casualties and do much damage to a historic building."

"Agreed," echoed Segundo, whose marines would probably have to carry out such an operation.

"I know him only by reputation. He is a hothead, a deserter from the military who is both bold and brutal. He goes by the nickname El Verdugo, the Executioner. I argued with our leadership against this mission, when I heard who was going to head it, but to no avail. Perhaps now they will be open to reason because this mission is directed at the wrong target and is also discrediting Los Zetas. I will do my best, but I can make no promises."

"Thank you, Diego. You have been very helpful to us in the past, for which I am grateful."

That was as effusive as Reyes would ever get, but his gratitude only made Alvarez wince. July 2013 was the month when the Mexican Navy had captured Miguel Trevino Morales, the leader of Los Zetas, on a rural road outside of Nuevo Laredo in the state of Tamaulipas bordering on Texas. Alvarez had provided the tip to the military. He was one of the few people within Los Zetas who had known the location of Morales at the time, but he had gained that information accidentally by talking to Morales's accountant, who was not even aware that he had betrayed his boss. Therefore, the finger of suspicion did not point directly at him.

Alvarez said nothing for a moment but kept his eyes focused on Reyes. "You and I have an understanding—that in return for helping you, you will help me to start a new life, maybe in another country.

When I got into this business as a young man, it was a gentler time. No longer. I think it may be time for me to leave."

"Help us one more time," countered Reyes, "and I will deliver on my side of the bargain. Perhaps with help from our friends." He glanced at Shafer.

"You must realize," pleaded Alvarez, "that every time I stick out my neck, I risk making a new enemy within Los Zetas. Since Trevino's arrest, the situation has become more unstable internally. My life could be in danger."

"Understood. But you agree to help us?"

"Yes. One more time." Alvarez got up to leave. "Will that be all? I need to get back to my office."

"Perhaps you can help with another matter," Shafer said. "An American, Bob Bigelow, was involved in a botched attempt to ransom Demir Ozmen. We believe he is being held by the Sinaloa Cartel at a location near Mexico City. The operation is being run by a man named Pedro Guerra, but he is not staying at the location which the Mexican Navy has under observation. What do you know about him?"

"Guerra is a former military officer whom we once tried to recruit into Los Zetas. He reports directly to Ismael Zambada, the right-hand man of Joaquin Guzman. If you capture Guerra, you may gain information that will lead to the arrest of Zambada and 'El Chapo' Guzman." Alvarez smiled. There was a hint of malice in his voice.

"Would you know where Guerra sleeps at night?" asked Miguel Rodriguez, who had listened silently up to this point.

"I can only guess. Guerra has a girlfriend, a bleached blonde named Marizol Flores. She is a cocktail waitress at a restaurant, the Villa Maria on the Avenida Homero. I do not know where she lives, but if you find out, you will know where Guerra is sleeping at night."

There was a ripple of laughter around the room.

"Did you know about the ransom plan by the Ottoman Trading Company?" asked Shafer.

"No, this is news to me. After the kidnapping, I called Omer Tilki, the president of the company in Istanbul, and gave him the best information that I had at the time. I said that Ozmen was being held by the Knights Templar—which, apparently, is wrong. He is a cool customer. He said nothing about his plans to attempt an initiative independently of Los Zetas."

"What is the relationship between Ottoman Trading Company and Los Zetas?" Shafer already knew, but he wanted confirmation.

"The exchange of goods between Ottoman Trading Company and Veracruz Sugar is to provide cover for the shipment of drugs by Los Zetas from Mexico to Europe. In fact, there is a ship leaving port tomorrow from Veracruz, destined for Liverpool, with a secret cargo on board."

"The name of the ship?" demanded Reyes sharply.

"*Atlantica*," responded Alvarez.

"We shall seize the ship immediately."

"Wait, Reyes. Don't be hasty," protested Shafer. "Let's think about this before acting. Wouldn't we gain more by letting the ship make its voyage? It might give our British friends an opportunity to do serious damage to Ottoman Trading Company's drug network in the United Kingdom."

Reyes nodded his agreement. "I see your point. It would also be better if we do not get distracted from our immediate priorities in Morelia and Mexico City. Thank you, gentlemen! Let's keep in touch."

Chapter Forty-Four

Now comes the hard part, thought Alvarez as he headed toward the door. He could feel Reyes's eyes following him. As soon as he had left the Municipal Palace, he walked across the Plaza de las Armas to his parked car. Before he could open the door, a man stepped out of the shadows, tossing his unfinished cigarette to the pavement.

"Hello, Diego. Visiting your friends at military security?"

Alvarez laughed nonchalantly, although inwardly he quaked. Within Los Zetas, this man had been nicknamed Lobo (the Wolf). He was used as an enforcer by Omar Morales, the brother of the captured leader and the head of the cartel's criminal operations. "I am seeing them more often than I would like, ever since the kidnapping of the Turk."

"Have you called your secretary for messages? Omar would like to talk to you."

"About what?"

"You will have to ask him. May I?" Before Alvarez had given permission, he had opened the passenger door and eased his slim frame into the car.

"Is Omar in Veracruz?"

"No, but he is not far away, on his yacht. Juan and Raul are with him."

The three main contenders for the succession to Miguel Trevino, thought Alvarez. "Having a strategy session?" he asked.

Lobo shrugged. "Perhaps." His face was inscrutable, his eyes hidden by his sunglasses.

"Where should we go?"

"There is a private airfield west of Veracruz. You have been there before. A helicopter will take us to the yacht."

An hour later, they were landing on the deck of an enormous yacht anchored in the cove of an island some fifty miles off the Mexican coast. Alvarez had no time to admire the lush vegetation of the island or the sparkling waters of the Gulf of Mexico. He was immediately ushered by Lobo below deck to the stateroom, where the leadership of Los Zetas was seated around a polished oak table. Their protectors sat against the wall by the windows, guns strapped across their chests, their hard eyes observing every movement inside the room and on deck.

After a brief exchange of greetings, Omar explained the reason for their summons. A brutal man who had stamped his character on the cartel, he did not mince words. "We have this little problem in Morelia. I personally approved this mission to seize the cathedral and selected El Verdugo to lead it. He is a good man who obeys orders without flinching. But Juan here has moral qualms about the shooting of innocent hostages until our demands are met. Raul is neutral, with no strong feelings one way or the other. What do you think, Alvarez?"

Juan interjected before Alvarez had a chance to speak. "I do not want you to misrepresent my position, Omar. All of us here are in agreement that we do not give a damn about the Turk. This is a turf battle, pure and simple, to show that Los Zetas cannot be trifled with by Sinaloa and its proxy, the Knights Templar. But turf battles need to be conducted with intelligence. Alienating Mexican public opinion on behalf of some Turk is stupid!"

Raul chuckled appreciatively over this comment while Omar glowered. It was a widely shared view within the cartel that Omar was less bright than his captured brother.

Alvarez could feel their eyes fixed on him. He had known Juan the longest, the man responsible for the financial operations of the cartel and generally more to his taste than Omar or Raul. He was a dropout from college rather than the Special Forces division of the Mexican military and had a touch of refinement. Although he was as cynical as the other two, he preferred to use bribery and blackmail rather than brute force to achieve his ends.

Alvarez looked at Raul as he spoke. If he could sway him with his arguments, then the hostage crisis in Morelia would end. "Do we even know for certain that the Knights Templar kidnapped the Turk and butchered some of our colleagues, leaving them to rot on some abandoned farm? I have information from an excellent source in Mexico City that the real criminals are Los Matas Zetas, acting as a proxy for Sinaloa."

Omar protested, "We had recently made incursions into the territory of the Knights Templar. Was it not logical to conclude that they were retaliating against us?"

"Logical, yes, but not necessarily correct," said Alvarez.

"How good is your source?" asked Raul.

"He has always been very reliable. He is a double agent working for both us and the DEA in the United States. I discovered his weakness, which made him sympathetic to our cause. He has an expensive taste for mistresses and fast cars."

Juan smiled approvingly.

Alvarez watched Raul for his reaction as his mind worked feverishly, in case more questions were asked about his source of information. To his relief, Raul's eyes moved from him to Omar. Raul was pursuing bigger game.

"Omar, the siege of the cathedral in Morelia would be a serious error of judgment, even a catastrophic mistake, if this information is correct." It was clear where Raul was heading—to undermine Omar's goal to succeed his brother as the leader of Los Zetas. "We should be attacking Guadalajara, the heartland of Los Matas Zetas, rather than Morelia."

Juan, recognizing that the alignment of forces was shifting in his favor, chimed in, "Better still. Since we know that Sinaloa is behind all this, we should strike at their leadership rather than at their proxies. We have a general idea where Guzman and Zambada like to hang out. If we tracked them down and passed the information on to the police, we could cut off the head of the Sinaloa Cartel. That is what they did to us. I am sure that they were responsible for betraying Miguel Trevino."

Thank you, Juan, for voicing that opinion, thought Alvarez. He offered a word of support to show his appreciation. "The advantage of Juan's proposal is that it could pay dividends with the Mexican police and the media, who generally have a more favorable opinion of Sinaloa than Los Zetas right now."

"Why?" growled Omar.

"They are considered to be less brutal." Those were dangerous words, Alvarez knew, but he did not waver. He had a personal score to settle. Omar's henchman had ordered the sickening and totally unnecessary killing of Maria Elena's uncle.

Omar glared at Alvarez. "I see no reason to end the hostage crisis in Morelia. What does it matter which proxy of Sinaloa we strike at or who kidnapped the Turk in Veracruz? The whole point is to make a statement that Los Zetas is not to be diddled with. If a few innocent people get shot along the way, so be it!"

Alvarez glanced at the faces of Juan and Raul and felt a grim satisfaction. Omar was fighting a losing battle and was about to be overruled.

On the flight back to the mainland, Lobo was silent until the helicopter had landed. "Omar did not appreciate what you just did. He will not forget." Lobo spoke in a low voice, but the warning was clear.

When Alvarez got back to his office at Veracruz Sugar, his secretary had already left for the evening. He shuffled through the messages on his desk and checked the emails on his laptop computer. At the back of his head was the gnawing fear that his life was in danger. It was not the first time. Years ago, when Los Zetas had broken with the Gulf Cartel, he had aligned with the more powerful faction to ensure his own survival, thereby incurring the enmity of a former associate who had then betrayed him to the Mexican military. To avoid arrest, he had agreed to cooperate with Reyes, but his usefulness was now over. He waited until he was back in his car, driving toward the center of Veracruz, before he called.

"Reyes? Good fortune was with us. I was able to act more swiftly than I expected. The siege in Morelia will be lifted on one condition: that the hostage takers be given safe conduct. The governor of Michoacán must accompany them until they have reached safety. Then he will be released."

Reyes's sigh of relief at the other end was audible. "Well done, Alvarez! I will inform my colleagues in Morelia and in Mexico City, who will be only too happy to grant the condition. The marines who have encircled the cathedral will be pulled back."

"Good! Now I have one more request. I have delivered my part of the bargain, and I want you to deliver on yours. I made an important enemy today in Los Zetas. I no longer have the luxury of time. My usefulness to you is finished."

Father Cardozo's prayer for a peaceful resolution of the crisis in the cathedral was answered. El Verdugo had already chosen his third victim for execution—the father of the bride, who was the brother of the governor—when he received a text message from Omar Morales to lift the siege of the cathedral. Fifty-four hours after their ordeal had begun, the wedding guests and the bride and bridegroom filed out of the cathedral, dazed and even hysterical with relief. No apologies were made by the terrorists, who were driven to an undisclosed location on the outskirts of Morelia, where their cartel had helicopters waiting to evacuate them. The governor was released unharmed.

Chapter Forty-Five

With the end of the hostage crisis in Morelia, top priority was now given to the rescue of the three kidnapped foreigners. The manager of the Villa Maria had been reluctant to divulge the home address of Marizol Flores. Her privacy needed to be protected. But then a small bribe had persuaded him to provide the information: a luxury apartment building in the Polanco district within walking distance of the hotel zone and the Paseo de la Reforma. It was only one block off the prestigious Avenida Presidente Masaryk, which was lined with multiple elegant boutiques. The building was clearly beyond the means of a cocktail waitress, but the manager had never been sufficiently curious to ask what her other means of support were.

The police in Mexico City had staked out their quarry carefully. Unmarked police cars were parked across the street and behind the building, guarding both the entrance and the exit. Plainclothesmen loitered inconspicuously on the street, watching her leave the building early that morning. She was a statuesque bleached blonde dressed in a chic Gucci jacket and short skirt and wearing very high heels. She did not go far—only to a small convenience store where she bought some breakfast items, presumably because she had a guest.

When she returned, nothing seemed amiss. The concierge, who had greeted her on the way out, now remained immersed in the morning newspaper, reading about the end of the hostage crisis in Morelia. The police had already won his cooperation with the flash of a badge, a wink, and a small financial inducement.

Only when she got off the elevator on the fifth floor did she begin to feel alarm. The man who had accompanied her on the elevator got off on the same floor and followed her down the hallway. She had never seen him before and knew that he was not one of her neighbors. It was not a large apartment building. When she placed her bag of groceries on the floor to fumble for the key in her handbag, the man paused behind her.

"May I assist you, senorita?" he asked.

She turned quickly, ready to swing her handbag at his head, when she noticed a number of men running down the hallway toward them. She opened her mouth to call for help, but then realized that this was more than an attempt to burglarize her apartment.

"Pedro! Pedro! Run! It's the police!" she screamed.

Her lover was shaving in the bathroom with the door open when he heard scuffling outside the apartment and Marizol's scream. Cursing, he grabbed his gun and phone and scrambled to reach the sliding french doors leading onto the balcony. The apartment faced the back of the building. Peering over the edge of the balcony, he dismissed the idea of jumping; the drop was too far. He also noticed the unmarked cars parked below and a sharpshooter huddled on the roof of a neighboring building. He was trapped.

However, he still had one option: to exchange the lives of the three hostages for his freedom. Quickly he dialed Ernesto's number. "Ernesto, are you there?" he shouted into his phone after several rings.

Ernesto finally picked up. "Pedro, what's going on?"

"Marizol's apartment is surrounded by police. My only chance to escape is to bargain the lives of the hostages for my release. You stay on this call until I give the order. If the police refuse to play along, shoot that bastard Bigelow."

"Anything you say, Pedro. But which Bigelow? We have two of them."

"If you don't know, shoot both of them!" bellowed Guerra.

"There is something you should know, Pedro. Something strange is going on. I was looking out the window when you called. There are helicopters hovering over our motel."

"Shit!" Guerra's cursing was interrupted by the booming voice of a police officer using a megaphone to speak through the open french doors.

"Pedro Guerra, you are under arrest. The building is surrounded. There are four police officers in this apartment. You cannot escape. Surrender peacefully if you want to live."

"Never! I will go peacefully on only one condition—that you give me my freedom in exchange for the lives of the hostages. Ernesto, are you still there?"

"I am still here," replied Ernesto calmly.

"Who is guarding the prisoners?"

"Diaz. They are in the other motel unit. I will walk over to carry out your orders, if necessary."

Guerra glanced at the open french doors through which he could hear voices speaking. "Hey, puerco, what do you say?" he shouted.

The police officer in charge ignored Guerra. He was on his phone talking to Captain Segundo, the navy officer in charge of the marines who had surrounded the Guadalajara Motel.

"Do not bargain with Guerra," said Segundo crisply. "We have used infrared sensors to determine where the hostages are being kept. They are confined to one room in unit 7. There are three of them—presumably the Turk and the two missing Americans. The guard is in the other room. In unit 6, there are three people who have free movement in the two rooms. They are probably the other kidnappers. Wait a minute! One of my helicopter pilots is reporting that one of the men has left unit 6 and is walking toward unit 7."

"So what do you intend to do, Captain Segundo?"

"Is it not obvious? Attack!"

At the Guadalajara Motel, Ernesto had just completed his call to Diaz when he became aware that the two helicopters, which had been hovering overhead at a distance, were suddenly diving toward him. He started running toward unit 7 just as rocket-propelled grenades slammed into unit 6. He heard an explosion and saw flames leaping into the sky behind him, then he collapsed to the ground in a hail of bullets. During the cover of night, the marines had taken up positions behind unit 5.

Guerra heard the explosion and the thud of the bullets on his phone. He swore a string of profanities as he leaped toward the open french doors, gun raised, hoping to catch the police inside by surprise. But he had forgotten about the sniper on the rooftop. He crashed into the french doors as a bullet slammed into his back.

Chapter Forty-Six

Dave and Bob had passed the second night of their captivity miserably, listening to Ozmen's snores on the sole bunk bed as they crouched uncomfortably against the wall. Groggy from lack of sleep, they still ached from the blows they had received while being questioned by Guerra the day before. This was not how they had expected to die—in some squalid, run-down motel in Mexico, the random victims of a murderous drug gang.

Until now, Dave had not thought much about death. His mind had been focused on ensuring the success of his career as a partner at a prominent New York law firm. To the extent that he had ever thought about death, he had expected to die in old age, like his father, in a hospital in an affluent Connecticut suburb of New York, surrounded by family and friends. Not in the prime of his life, in this stinking rathole. It was bizarre how an accidental encounter with his prodigal brother in a restaurant in Mexico City had sucked him into this death trap. What had he done to deserve this end? It was senseless. Perhaps if he had attended church more faithfully, this would not have happened.

Bob had retraced the missteps of his life several times before the heavy darkness in the room began to yield to the early morning light entering the dirty skylight in the ceiling. Then he realized that something unusual was happening as he noted the halt of traffic on the nearby highway and the clatter of helicopters hovering over the motel.

"Dave!" he whispered loudly, cupping his ear and pointing in the direction of the highway. His whisper was suddenly punctuated by gunfire, the breaking of window glass, and a terrific explosion, which blew a gaping hole in the wall separating the two rooms. Through the murk of swirling dust and teargas, he could see the guard who went by the name of Diaz approaching, his gun held ready. His mission was to kill the hostages. Of that Bob was certain. Diving over the debris that had fallen onto the floor, he snatched the blanket from the cot of an astonished Ozmen and hurled it in the direction of the guard.

Dave, who had been knocked to the ground by the force of the explosion, picked himself up and threw his body weight into the startled guard before he had a chance to shoot Bob. They wrestled for the gun, which skittered across the floor toward Ozmen. Diaz, a former wrestler, deftly pinned Dave to the floor. Bob lunged into the melee, grabbing the guard by the neck of his shirt as he tried to pull him off Dave.

Ozmen picked up the gun, his teeth clenched in anger, and aimed it at the writhing bodies. Bob was on top. *That bastard Bigelow*, he thought, his finger tightening on the trigger. Then he lowered the gun. Revenge would have to wait. The battle had shifted decisively.

Through the gaping hole, a number of anxious marines peered at them through the rubble and smoke, guns held ready. One of them advanced, asking in English, "Which one of you is Demir Ozmen?"

Ozmen—who only the day before had secretly cast his lot with his captors—handed them the gun. "This is the gun the terrorist wanted to use to execute us. But we managed to overpower him. I am Demir Ozmen, a Turkish national. I demand to be put in contact with the Turkish embassy immediately."

"That we will do as soon as we can," said the marine. Then he turned to the other two hostages, who by now had also risen from the floor, shaking the dust from their clothes and dabbing at their streaming eyes. "And you are?"

"We are the Bigelow brothers," Dave answered. "Bob and Dave. Arrest this man," he said, pointing to Diaz. "He is one of the kidnappers."

As Diaz was led away, the marine explained, "We tried to subdue your guard with teargas, but he threw a hand grenade at us as we battered down the door. Did you suffer any injuries?"

"No, we are fine," Dave assured him, "just a few cuts and bruises." He gingerly felt a lump on his head where Diaz had hit him.

For Dave, their rescue had been providential, coming only hours before their execution. But Bob had a more earthly explanation. "Saved by the Mexican marines and my Mama Bear app!" he chortled.

Dave looked at his brother quizzically. "Mama Bear app? What are you muttering about?"

Bob grinned. "My phone had tracking software on it. That is how the police were able to find out where we were being held by the kidnappers."

Dave's mouth sagged open in amazement. "You mean my chasing after you to return the phone was not a complete fiasco after all?"

For the moment, Bob was inclined to be charitable. "After your initial miscues, brother, you saved the day!"

But Ozmen was less forgiving. He glared balefully at the Bigelow brothers. They should not celebrate too soon. He still had some scores to settle with them.

A Second Chance

Chapter Forty-Seven

For Diego Alvarez, the Turkish affair—as he hereafter referred to it—ended successfully. Although he had played an important role in defusing the hostage crisis in Morelia and in the rescue of Demir Ozmen and the Bigelow brothers in Mexico City, he was never lionized by the press, nor did he want to be. Anonymity was the key to his plan to begin a new life, far away from Veracruz Sugar, Los Zetas, and the Mexican military. Celebrity would make his escape impossible and his execution by Los Zetas a certainty.

The important thing was that Reyes, the commander of the Mexican military in Veracruz; Shafer of the FBI; and Rodriguez of the DEA knew what he had done. Moreover, Captain Segundo of the Mexican marines had been very pleased with the telephone numbers and records of calls discovered on the mobile phones of Pedro Guerra and his men. They provided a trail that could lead them to the leaders of the Sinaloa Cartel: Zambada and Guzman.

Alvarez did not hear from Reyes after his appeal, but this did not surprise him. Frequent communications between them would only arouse suspicion. Then a plain vanilla envelope from a travel agency arrived at his office. It contained an open round-trip air ticket to Mexico City on a commercial flight. He had not ordered or purchased the ticket, so he knew it was the signal from Reyes.

His secretary, who had opened the envelope, seemed surprised. "You did not tell me that you were going to Mexico City on business."

"It is a personal matter." When she arched her eyebrows to show that she did not find his explanation sufficient, he added mysteriously, "An affair of the heart."

She had never pried into his personal life. Being discreet was a prerequisite for her job and the reason why Alvarez had kept her on his payroll for years. Nonetheless, she was dumbfounded because she had assumed that he was a confirmed bachelor who preferred living alone.

"You are engaged?" she asked curiously.

"Let us say that I am considering it," Alvarez said smilingly. "If I do not return next week, you can assume that I am on my honeymoon. Thank you, Margherita."

The message was clear. Ask no further questions.

A day later, he received a hotel brochure for the St. Regis Hotel on the Paseo de la Reforma in Mexico City from the same travel agency that had sent him the air ticket. It was the hotel where Reyes expected him to stay. He called the hotel directly, using his mobile phone, to reserve the bridal suite. He could never be certain that someone—his secretary, a business colleague, someone working for Los Zetas—was not eavesdropping on his calls whenever he used the office telephone. His personal phone was safer.

Reserving the bridal suite was consistent with what he had told his secretary, and it was also part of his escape plan. He had given some thought to what it would be like to live as a Mexican exile in some foreign country. He needed a companion, and no one was better suited to fit this role than Maria Elena, with whom he stayed whenever he came to Mexico City. She knew about his double life as a businessman and a facilitator for Los Zetas. What he had never told her was that he also had a third life—as a police informer. Could he count on her loyalty?

When he checked into the St. Regis Hotel that Friday evening, there was an innocent-looking package waiting for him containing a passport and resident visa for Argentina, which would enable him to start a new life in Buenos Aires as Juan Mendoza. He frowned when he looked at the passport; the photograph made him look twenty years older than he was—gray hair, a wrinkled forehead, shadows under his eyes. Also in the package were a debit card and checkbook drawing on a Citibank account that had been opened up for him in Buenos Aires. Taped to the passport was a typed note with a telephone number to call on Saturday afternoon at 3:00 p.m.

Then he called Maria Elena. She still seemed distraught over the death of her uncle, whose funeral she had attended only days before. She apologized for having become hysterical when they last spoke on the telephone. She seemed surprised to hear that he was in Mexico City. Normally, he gave her advance warning, but he explained that for business reasons, he was staying at the St. Regis Hotel. She was relieved. Her apartment was in a mess because she had been too despondent to clean it up, and she would not let him see it.

Undeterred, he responded smoothly, "I have a proposition that you may find irresistible. Have dinner with me in my hotel suite. We will have room service, including the best champagne and wine. We need to talk about our future."

"Our future?" She wondered where this was leading. "But this is so sudden! I need time to get ready. Give me two hours."

"Good. I will meet you in the lobby when you arrive. Chilled champagne will be waiting."

It was a whirlwind romance. Within hours, he had proposed marriage, and she had accepted. He cautioned her that there was one condition, and she could still change her mind: she would have to leave Mexico.

"But why? Are the police about to arrest you?"

"No, my love, quite the opposite. I have had a falling out with one of the leaders of Los Zetas over the seizure of the cathedral in Morelia and the murder of your uncle. My life is in danger. I will have to leave Mexico incognito under a false identity. Will you come with me?"

"How could you not have a falling out with beasts like them? But where will we go?"

"I have some friends who will help me. They do not know yet about our plans to marry. I will surprise them tomorrow. You too will need to assume a false identity so that no one in Los Zetas will be able to find us. Promise me you will tell no one."

"I promise."

They were married on Saturday at twelve noon at a civil registry office in Mexico City, followed by a lunch for two served in their bridal suite at the St. Regis. Shortly before 3:00 p.m., Maria Elena excused herself. She had to return to her apartment to collect things that she would need for the trip.

"Be careful," he whispered as they embraced. "You never know who might be watching."

Chapter Forty-Eight

When Alvarez called the number that had been inserted into his new passport, a familiar voice answered, "Shafer here. Who is this?"

Alvarez answered without hesitation, "Juan Mendoza."

"Ah, Juan. Colonel Reyes told me to expect your call. Can we meet?"

"I am at my hotel now. Where should I go?"

"We have an office on the twenty-first floor of the Torre Mayor building, not far from the St. Regis. When you get off the elevator, you will see a plaque by the door for the architectural firm of Albertson & Associates. Ring the doorbell. Someone will admit you."

Alvarez left the St. Regis by an indirect route through the adjacent Torre Libertad before exiting onto the Paseo de la Reforma and making his way to the Torre Mayor. Several times he stopped to make sure he was not being followed. He knew that Los Zetas often used young children to spy on their targets. Then he walked past the Torre Mayor and doubled back, entering through a side door. The elevator banks were cordoned off, as was to be expected on a weekend, but it made him nervous because he would have to introduce himself to a security guard.

"Your name, please?" asked the guard at the reception desk. "I will also need some identification."

Alvarez took a deep breath. "Juan Mendoza." He pulled out his new passport, which, fortunately, he had remembered to take with him.

The security guard smiled as he looked at the passport photograph. "You apparently have discovered the fountain of youth since this photograph was taken. You look much younger."

Alvarez grinned. "It is amazing what a vacation and rest can do for one's appearance."

"Whom are you seeing this afternoon?"

"Albertson & Associates, an architectural firm."

"I will call them to let them know you are here."

The security guard dialed a number and waited for a response. When someone finally answered, he said, "There is someone here to see you—a Mr. Mendoza." There was a pause. Then he handed the passport back to Alvarez. "You are expected. Take the elevator to the twenty-first floor."

It was Alvarez's first experience with using an assumed name, and it was one to which he would adapt quickly. For much of his life, he had practiced deception successfully, serving several masters simultaneously. Escaping to Argentina under a false identity would not be a radically new step for him.

When he rang the doorbell on the twenty-first floor, Shafer opened the door almost immediately and ushered him into the office suite. Several smaller offices were darkened and unoccupied. Only the large corner office, which had breathtaking views of the Paseo de la Reforma and the Angel of Independence monument, was being used. The two men who were already seated in the office rose to greet him.

Shafer spoke in English. "Miguel Rodriguez you have already met. Allow me to introduce my colleague from the DEA in New York, Jim Connors." Then he sat down behind the desk and motioned Alvarez to take a seat.

Shafer did not waste time. "Colonel Reyes requested that we help you to start up a new life in another country because your life is in danger. We owe him a number of favors, and you as well. I hope you like our selection of Argentina as your new home."

Alvarez nodded appreciatively. "I have visited Argentina on business. Buenos Aires is a very elegant city. I am delighted."

"Good. I apologize for the photograph in your new passport. It does make you look older, but in time, your appearance may begin to resemble the photograph. In the short term, you may need to use a little makeup and a wig to disguise your appearance. We have a number of experts who can help you in that regard. To complete the disguise, we would like you to travel as an invalid confined to a wheelchair. How does that sound?"

"I am open to your suggestions," replied Alvarez.

"Good. Now for the logistics. Jim and I thought initially that the easiest way to get you into the United States would be to fly you in a private jet to Ciudad Juárez on the Texas-Mexican border and then drive you across, but Miguel Rodriguez does not think that is a good idea."

"It is too risky," said Rodriguez emphatically. "Ciudad Juárez has become the murder capital of Mexico during a turf battle between drug cartels. It is probably a city which Diego Alvarez has visited. He might be recognized by someone, even if he is disguised."

"The better plan," continued Shafer, "is to fly you in one of Captain Segundo's military transport aircraft to a base in Baja California. From there, you will be flown across the border in a US Navy helicopter to a base near San Diego. At that point, my colleague, Jim Connors, will take charge."

Connors picked up where Shafer had left off. "Once you are in the United States, you will be taken to a safe house, where we will provide you with details on the life of the man whose identity you are about to assume. It will help you in answering questions at customs and passport control and, once you are settled in Argentina, from local officials as well. Our makeup specialists are pretty good, but a beard would be helpful. Don't shave for the next week or two."

"Any questions, suggestions?" asked Shafer. "We would like to move you out of here tomorrow if possible. For your safety, we need to act quickly. Once you are reported missing, your friends at Los Zetas will be scouring Mexico looking for you."

"I have only one problem. You have made no plans for my wife."

"Your wife? I thought you were single."

"I got married this morning to Maria Elena Cardozo. She will be accompanying me."

"That will complicate matters," Connors rebuked him, "and it increases your risk."

"I apologize, but I will not leave without her. She must have special papers too."

Connors grimaced and looked at Rodriguez. "Can we do it?"

Rodriguez nodded.

"How long would it take?"

"Two days. It would delay their departure until Tuesday."

Shafer shrugged. "It's your decision, Diego. My only suggestion is lay low for the next few days. Extend your reservation at the hotel through Tuesday night, although you will be departing in the afternoon. We will figure out a way to smuggle you and your wife out of the hotel without anyone noticing."

When Alvarez returned to the hotel by the same indirect route that he had taken to get to the Torre Mayor, he found that Maria Elena had not yet returned. He waited nervously as time passed. When he called her apartment, no one answered. Three hours later, he heard a sound at the door. When he opened the door, she flung herself into his arms.

"You are safe! I was so worried! When I left my apartment and hailed a taxi to take me to the hotel, you will not believe whom I met! It was Lobo. He had been waiting outside the building. The most evil-looking man I have ever seen!"

"What did he say?"

"He asked where you were. He said that he had heard you were in Mexico City this weekend and wondered if you were staying with me. I said that was news to me. When he noticed my suitcase, I said that I planned to spend the weekend with a girlfriend in one of the northern suburbs of Mexico City. I don't think he believed me. He stood there and waited so that he could overhear the instructions to the taxi driver. Don't worry! I did not say the St. Regis Hotel. I instructed the driver to take me to the Buenavista train station."

"Good. Did he follow you?"

"I do not know. But to make sure, I took the Metro north, switched a couple of times, and doubled back to Buenavista Station. From there, I took a taxi here. That is why it took me so long to get back!"

"Good girl! I am so sorry to put you through all of this!"

"It was nothing, Diego. I love you!" She paused to catch her breath. "What did you learn from your friends?"

"We will be leaving Tuesday for the United States aboard a military aircraft, compliments of the Mexican Navy. You will be given a new passport and papers—"

"The Mexican Navy? Diego, who are you?"

"Now is not the time for explanations!"

She threw up her hands in exasperation. "Okay. And where to after that?"

"Argentina."

She screamed with delight. "I have always wanted to see Buenos Aires."

Two weeks later, at Los Angeles International Airport, passengers were milling in front of a gate waiting to board an American Airlines flight to Buenos Aires. "First-class passengers, parents with small children, and those needing assistance will be given priority in boarding," boomed the public address system.

"Make way! Make way!" shouted an airline attendant, pushing a passenger in a wheelchair toward the gate. The passenger was an old man, his gray head bent low so that his beard touched his chest. Walking slowly behind the attendant, supporting herself with a cane, was an elderly woman. A filmy scarf partly covered her gray hair and face, and sunglasses shielded her eyes against the bright light. They both disappeared down the gangway leading to the aircraft.

Although Diego Alvarez was forced to flee Mexico, he exacted his final revenge on the murderers of Maria Elena's uncle. Using information he provided, the Mexican Navy tracked down and killed Heriberto Lazcano in a shootout. Bringing Omar Morales to justice took longer, but he was eventually captured and imprisoned.

As for "El Chapo" Guzman, the head of the Sinaloa Cartel, he too was arrested. He managed to escape his luxury accommodations via a tunnel, which his accomplices had dug underneath the prison walls—only to be recaptured again after a brief period of freedom. His lieutenant, Zambada, remains at large.

Chapter Forty-Nine

On the flight home from Mexico City, Bob Bigelow came to the unshakable conclusion that now was the time to make a complete break with his past life. He would never return to Ottoman Trading Company. Any firm that would blithely send him off on a mission to negotiate with murderous Mexican drug cartels to obtain the release of a hostage could not be trusted. Murat had assured him that all he needed to do was drop off a briefcase filled with cash to rescue Ozmen. There would be no personal risk to him. The Mexicans were a charming, delightful people, Murat had said.

Like hell they were!

The fury welled up inside him. His jaws clenched, and his face reddened; a vein prominently distended on his forehead, giving the impression of a man about to suffer a stroke.

"Are you feeling well, sir?" asked a stewardess who was looking anxiously at him. His discolored eye and the cut in his lower lip had already attracted her attention when he first boarded the flight.

"Not at all," he said sarcastically. "I am having murderous thoughts!" He visualized Murat hanging from a lamppost.

"Oh dear!" She seemed alarmed. "You are not intending to do anything violent, I hope?"

"You have nothing to fear. I will control my anger and channel it constructively before I gird myself for my next battle. My last dragon put up a hell of a fight!" he said, pointing to his cuts and bruises and giving her a crooked grin.

"That's a relief." She smiled at him.

The other passengers, who were looking nervously at him, began to relax.

"And how do you propose to do that this time?" she asked pertly.

"If you had an air ticket and could fly anywhere in the world, where would you go?"

"I vacationed in Tahiti last year. It was wonderful! The beaches, spectacular sunsets, the feeling of being far away from everything!"

"Could you imagine living there for the rest of your life?"

"It could get boring after a while. You could try Italy—glorious cathedrals, art museums, delicious food and wine!"

"I would like that, but Italy has one problem. It is much too close to Turkey!" Bob was beginning to calm down.

"You must know Mexico. Any interest in returning?"

"Not in a long time."

"You have me stumped. But I have an idea. There is a travel magazine in the pouch on the seat in front of you. At the back of the magazine is a world map showing all the routes that Delta flies. That could be a start." She smiled and turned to walk down the aisle.

He did not want the conversation to end. "Where are you from?" he asked.

"Vancouver."

"Vancouver must be a nice place. Washington state or British Columbia?"

"North of the border, if you please. You know—beautiful coastal views, fishing, hockey, Mounties in red tunics."

"I get the picture. So why are you a stewardess if Vancouver is so great?"

"Just trying to see a little of the world before I settle down. Delta has a direct flight every morning from Kennedy to Vancouver, by the way."

"I will check it out, I promise. If you give me your telephone number, you can be my guide," he said hopefully.

"I will think about it." She was laughing and shaking her head as she walked away.

When he exited the airplane at Kennedy, she slipped a piece of paper into his hand and winked at him. It had her telephone number and name written on it. *Becky Moran.* He liked the sound of her name and her appearance too—red hair, green eyes, freckles sprinkled over the bridge of her nose, and an infectious smile.

True to his decision, Bob never worked again at Ottoman Trading Company. He sent an email to Murat that he would be collecting disability pay for a few weeks because he was suffering psychological trauma after his ordeal in Mexico City. When Murat tried to call him, he refused to pick up the receiver because he did not want to engage in conversation with a man he loathed.

It occurred to him that his absence from work could make Connor and Shafer's job of tracking Murat's activities more difficult, but he did not give a damn.

Early October can be very pleasant in New York—warm Indian summer days followed by cool, crisp nights, the leaves on the trees starting to turn color. For a few days, he took long walks in Central Park with Jack, who was in dog heaven chasing every squirrel he saw. Bob even attended a few Broadway shows, but he soon tired of his relaxed regimen.

On impulse, he called Andrea Williams and invited her to have lunch with him. To his surprise, she agreed. He had expected her to be aloof, but she was curious about his experience as the hostage of a Mexican drug cartel and his rescue by the Mexican marines, which had been reported in the *New York Times.* She even gave him a hug before they sat down at a table at an outdoor café near Lincoln Center.

"My god, Bob! What have you been getting into? I really felt for you when I read the *Times* article about your experiences. Perhaps we should make it an episode in my program, *West Side Follies.*"

"It might not be funny enough for your program, believe me. Thanks to your friend Murat, I played with fire and nearly got myself killed." He sketched a few details of his captivity with as much humor as he could muster.

"How is Murat? Have you seen him since you got back?"

"No. Officially, I am on disability leave, but I will not go back to Ottoman Trading Company."

"I don't blame you," she said sympathetically. "I haven't talked to him in weeks. The last time was just before you got that loan from your brother. What do you think you will do next?"

"I am still sorting things out." A few ideas were bouncing around in his head, but he did not want to share them with her. Nor did he mention the upcoming Sotheby art auction.

"Do you want to talk about us?" she asked. "I thought that might be why you called. I'm sorry about the way I behaved, slamming down the phone on you. I just went ballistic when I saw that video clip."

"I can understand your shock. I didn't tell you about the nightclub in Mexico City because I didn't think it was that important. That's the style of business in Mexico. Rest assured, I do not intend to return to Mexico anytime soon." He gave her what he hoped was his most appealing smile.

Andrea returned his smile tentatively, then she became serious again. "After you called this week, I thought about us starting over. The more I thought about it, the more I wondered whether Humpty Dumpty can be put together again. We were sort of rushing into marriage without having talked about the trade-off between children and careers."

"I thought we would get around to it when the time is right. I don't have children from my first marriage to complicate matters."

"I appreciate that, Bob. But my career is very important to me, and it has taken off in the last two years. I don't want to go on maternity leave in the foreseeable future to have a child. Your career is—how would you describe it—unsettled. You're smart and ambitious, and I'm sure you will be back on your feet again soon. It's only a matter of time. But let's face it. We really don't know each other that well."

Bob swallowed hard. Was this why he had called Andrea? To flush out the issues and deal with them? He sensed that he was at a tipping point. Did he want to start over with Andrea, or did he want a clean break with the past?

As he pondered how best to respond, Andrea pulled her phone from her purse to check her emails. She squealed with delight. "Great news! Dwayne Nelson has agreed to replace Fred Sanford on my television program. What a relief. I have been interviewing dozens of job applicants, and he seems perfect for the role."

"That's great," said Bob. "How did you manage to find him in such short order?"

"Derek Taylor introduced him. He's known him for a few years. Derek has been just wonderful, giving me moral support and helping me to think through the kind of person I would need to replace Fred," she gushed.

"Have you started seeing Derek socially?" Bob asked since Andrea's eyes lit up when she talked about him.

"Yes," she admitted with a hint of embarrassment. "We have so much in common. We dated a lot years ago, and when you and I broke up . . ." She hesitated, not wanting to venture any further into tricky waters.

The expression on her face resolved any lingering doubts that Bob had about the end of their engagement. He acknowledged that she was physically attractive, even glamorous, but he wondered how he could ever have thought that he loved her or that she loved him. She could sense his waning interest. He asked a few polite questions about her old flame but could only think about Becky Moran. The conversation faltered. She cut the lunch short, claiming that she had to attend to urgent business.

The past could not be kept at bay forever. He received a telephone call from Connors and an email from Shafer asking why he had not contacted them after his return from Mexico City. They suggested a debriefing session at the Hilton Garden Inn near his office. He wanted to rebel, but he feared their power to destroy his life by pressing criminal charges against him. He decided to stall for time until he figured out what to do next.

He rented a Ford Mustang at a Hertz agency, packed his bag, and headed north on the New England Thruway with Jack beside him. He stopped at a gas station to send an email to Shafer and Connors that he was traveling. He did not say for how long, but he promised to get back to them after his trip. He toyed with the idea of crossing the Canadian border from Vermont but decided to check into a hotel in Boston instead.

For two days, he explored the possibility of establishing a false identity in Canada. His internet research—using a computer at a branch of the Boston Public Library—revealed that there were seven men with the name Robert Bigelow in Vancouver. One of them, a man in his early thirties, had recently died unexpectedly from a stroke. He had lived at 95 Cedar Crescent. But to pose as this man, he needed to get his date of birth and his Canadian social security number. How could he do that? There were a number of websites offering assistance in creating a false identity, but he concluded that they were mostly scams.

Still, he did not despair. The Sotheby auction of his father's paintings would be in a matter of days. Once he had his share of the money, he would have international mobility. He could travel anywhere in the world and go into hiding before the FBI and the DEA could find him. However, he needed a bank account that they did not know about.

Walking back to his hotel, he noticed branches of both TD and Europa Bank on opposite corners of the street. TD, a Canadian bank, would have branches in Vancouver; but Europa Bank, a British institution, had operations in many countries, including both Canada and Switzerland. A Swiss bank account appealed to him because Switzerland's bank secrecy laws would protect his identity. He might need that as a last line of defense.

By the weekend, an escape plan was beginning to take shape in his mind. To avoid arousing their suspicion, he sent an email to Shafer and Connors agreeing to meet Friday afternoon at the Hilton Garden Inn. That would give him a few days of leeway to establish an account at Europa Bank and to purchase a one-way Delta ticket to Vancouver departing Thursday morning. On Tuesday, he would attend the Sotheby auction with his brother, Dave, who had suggested in an email that they meet for dinner immediately after.

Chapter Fifty

Both Bob and Dave greeted each other somberly before the Sotheby auction began. Apart from an exchange of emails, they had not spoken to each other since their return from Mexico City. Bob was preoccupied with his secret plans and said little. Dave was moody, finding it difficult to adjust to the stark contrast between the elegant salon, filled with art connoisseurs and enthusiasts, and the squalid motel room in which they had so recently been imprisoned.

Memories of his near brush with death still depressed him. At times, he felt remorseful. He thought about the two hostages who had been executed at the cathedral in Morelia: Fernando Velasquez and Father Antonio Cardozo. If only he had not encountered his brother at the restaurant in Mexico City. If only the concierge at the Four Seasons Hotel had recommended a different restaurant to him. Then Bob's ransom of Demir Ozmen would have gone smoothly, and no innocent lives would have been lost. Bob's gratitude for saving his life was misplaced. Their unexpected meeting at the Villa Maria had caused Bob to forget his mobile phone, and his chasing after his brother's car to return the phone had aborted the ransom attempt.

"Are you all right, Dave?" Bob asked.

When Dave revealed his thoughts, Bob gave him some good advice. "You're going to drive yourself crazy if you keep thinking that way. Accidents happen. You are not responsible. We survived, thanks to a lot of people. Some of their names we will never know. Now we need to get on with the rest of our lives."

As the auction proceeded, with the final bids exceeding their expectations by nearly 10 percent, their spirits rose. Bob and Dave were euphoric, shaking hands and slapping each other on the back. For a moment, their differences melted away. Then the old differences started resurfacing.

"Bob, would you mind if we skipped dinner tonight? Next week would work better for me."

Bob's voice revealed a hint of irritation. "I won't be here next week, Dave."

Dave seemed surprised. "Going on a business trip? We can always have dinner when you get back."

"I may be gone for some time."

"An around-the-world cruise perhaps?"

"Something like that. That's why we need to talk now. It will only take a minute." Bob pulled a piece of paper from his wallet. "I would like to have my share of the money—less the one million dollars that I owe you—deposited in my Europa Bank account. This is the account number."

"Europa Bank? Didn't you use to have a Citibank account?"

"I switched."

"I hope that you are not thinking of hiding your money overseas. The IRS is cracking down on Americans who fail to reveal foreign bank accounts."

"The IRS is not my main worry."

Dave looked warily at his brother. "You're not in trouble again, are you, Bob?"

"No more than usual. I've got to go, Dave."

Dave grabbed his brother's arm. "I need an explanation. What's going on?"

Bob's gaze faltered, and he looked away. "I'll give you a hint. Your friend, John Shafer!"

"What has Shafer got to do with you?" exclaimed Dave.

"Shafer has got me by the balls! He is blackmailing me to force me to inform on Ottoman Trading Company!"

"What does he have on you?" The words exploded from Dave's mouth. He felt as if someone had slugged him in the stomach. The pieces of the puzzle were falling into place—the call from Shafer in August asking if he and his wife could stop over at Dave's house on the way back from New Haven, the familiarity Shafer had revealed with the details of Bob's life and movements, even though they had never met. Shafer had been stalking his brother!

"I would rather not say. Look, Dave, I've got to go. Thanks for giving me that loan when I needed it. I haven't apologized before, but I am really sorry about dragging you into that trouble in Mexico City! Melanie and Helen will probably never forgive me."

"They were pretty shaken up, but they are getting over it. They are happy that we are both safe."

Bob swallowed hard. "They are more forgiving than I would be. Give them my best!"

"You are not saying goodbye, are you?" asked Dave. Then sighing in resignation, he gave Bob a hug. "Look, you do what you've got to do, but remember—I'm your brother. If you ever need help, you call me, understand?"

"Thanks, Dave."

As Bob turned and walked away, there were tears in his eyes.

Chapter Fifty-One

Dave watched Bob head to the exit. Then his mind switched back to Shafer. He would call him and demand an explanation. What in the hell had been going on behind his back?

Shafer and he went back a long way. They were not only roommates at Princeton but fellow members of the University Cottage Club, one of the oldest eating clubs on campus for third- and fourth-year undergraduates. They had also played together on the varsity football team, which won a coveted Ivy League championship after decades of drought. Dave still remembered the days of celebration that followed. They had been heroes on campus. At one of the parties, Shafer had introduced Dave to an acquaintance of his girlfriend, who later became his wife, Melanie. Shafer had been the best man at his wedding.

For a while, their careers had followed similar paths. Both had gone to law school—Dave at Harvard and Shafer at the University of Chicago. Thereafter, their lives had diverged. Dave had found the lure of a corporate law practice at a major firm in New York City irresistible and had urged Shafer to make a similar choice. But Shafer had decided otherwise. He came from a family that had a strong tradition of public service in the military, so his decision to join the FBI after graduating from law school had not come as a complete surprise.

Dave thought he knew Shafer as well as anyone and had never had a reason to distrust him. But there was one trait he had noticed about Shafer from their football days. Shafer played to win. He was an offensive tackle who did not necessarily play by the rule book. On the field, he did whatever he thought he could get away with, just short of incurring a penalty. His competitive spirit won him the complicit winks and laughing admiration of his teammates and the coaching staff, but his furious opponents dubbed him “Cheating Charlie.” Charles was his middle name.

Dave tried Shafer at his office first. Shafer picked up on the first ring. Dave heard voices in the background. “Am I calling at a bad time?” he asked. “This is Dave Bigelow.”

“No, my meeting is just finishing.” Then, almost apologetically, Shafer added, “Dave, let me congratulate you on your narrow escape. Just like the good old days, miraculously escaping tackles when it looked like you would be thrown for a loss.”

Dave had played halfback on the football team. “The Phantom” had been his nickname.

“You’re working late tonight.”

“Yeah, things have been crazy at the office lately. Otherwise, I would have called you right after you got back from Mexico City.”

“I thought about you in captivity. I needed a helpful tackle to spring me loose.”

“We did our bit,” replied Shafer without elaborating. “What’s up?”

“Look, John, I just had a chat with my brother, Bob. Do you mind telling me what’s been going on? He said you were blackmailing him into spying on his employer.”

“Well, *blackmail* is a strong word. Let’s just say we persuaded your brother to cooperate with us. He should part company with his employer anyway. A shady bunch of people we are going to put out of business.”

“What are you holding over his head?”

“I am not at liberty to say. FBI policy, you know.”

“Not even off the record?”

“Minor drug offenses. That’s as much as I will say.”

"Minor drug offense, like hell. A minor drug offense would not get him to willingly put his life at risk dealing with Mexican drug cartels."

"Dave, the FBI did not send your brother to Mexico. His employer did that."

"Okay. Still, why are you hiding behind FBI policy now? I've never known you to strictly abide by the rules."

"I also never knew you to complain when one of my questionable tackles sprung you for a big gain."

"So you're not going to tell me."

"I've said all I am going to say."

Dave felt his anger building. He needed to know badly. How could he help Bob if he was kept in ignorance? But first, he needed to remove the last vestige of doubt about the time John Shafer had invited himself and his wife over for dinner in August. The dinner talk had dwelt for some time on his brother—his latest activities, the turmoil in his personal life. It was Shafer who had injected Bob into the conversation. Dave had attributed his interest to friendly curiosity, nothing more.

"Were you trailing my brother already when you came over for dinner a couple of months ago?" he blurted out.

"He was on our radar screen," admitted Shafer.

"You shit! How could you abuse my friendship and hospitality that way?" shouted Dave.

"Keep calm, Bigelow. My job requires that I sometimes do things which are not quite kosher."

"Well, you can consider our friendship over."

Shafer's voice remained steady even though he was annoyed. "I hope that will not be the case. Besides, I need your help. What's Bob up to? He has been avoiding me ever since his return from Mexico City."

"I wouldn't know. I don't keep my brother's schedule."

"Would you know if I told you your brother's life is at risk?"

Dave gulped. "At risk? What do you mean?"

"One of the Mexican cartels is ticked off over the role that Bob played in the tracking down and killing of the kidnappers. They have a price on his head."

Oh god, thought Dave. *Was this nightmare ever going to end?* "He had nothing to do with that," he said defiantly.

"Oh yes he did," countered Shafer. "Why do you think he had a tracking app on his phone?"

"Because you put it there?"

"Not me personally, but one of my Mexican associates suggested it to him."

Dave could no longer deny to himself what should have been obvious: his brother had been a police informer, just like Demir Ozmen and Pedro Guerra had suspected. That would explain why the two police cars had trailed him when he left the restaurant in Mexico City. He took a deep breath, and in a shaky voice, he divulged what he knew. The Sotheby auction had given Bob financial freedom, and he was about to leave New York on a long trip. Maybe he would never return.

When Dave got off the phone, the euphoria of the Sotheby auction had vanished. He had betrayed his brother. Whatever his brother had done, he wanted him away from New York, the FBI, and the drug cartels. Should he have kept silent, gambling that Shafer was lying about the death threat? But if he had refused to cooperate and the worst had happened, could he have forgiven himself? He had caved in because he had no choice.

Of one thing he was certain: he would never speak to Shafer again.

Chapter Fifty-Two

Bob kept his contacts with people on Wednesday to a minimum. There were no farewells to neighbors. He did not bother to stop his mail. He did not pay the rent on his apartment early. He intended to simply disappear. His only unusual activity was to stop at a pet shop to purchase a portable kennel for Jack. He would not leave his dog behind.

The line at Kennedy Airport on Thursday morning was short when Bob checked into the Delta flight to Vancouver. He had arrived early at the airport because he had to allow extra time for checking in Jack. Everything was going as planned, or so it seemed, until he heard a familiar voice as he turned to head in the direction of airport security.

"Bob, good morning! Fancy meeting you here!" It was the unmistakable voice of John Shafer.

Bob turned warily, his heart pounding. Standing ten feet away were Shafer and Connors, looking very serious. He wanted to run but decided that would be futile and unnecessary. Flying to Vancouver was not illegal after all.

"What a coincidence!" he said, trying to sound as casual as possible. Then he struck himself on the side of the head. "I completely forgot! We have a meeting tomorrow, right?"

"We do," responded Shafer. "But when we discovered you were leaving town, we decided to change the venue and time of our debriefing session."

"But how did you . . .?"

"Your brother called me last night. He was very testy, calling me a shit for abusing his friendship. I tried to calm him down, explaining in very general terms the basis for the cooperation between you and me. No details, you understand? Nothing that will embarrass you. I then asked him whether he had seen you since your adventure together in Mexico City. He was evasive at first, even suspicious, trying to protect you."

"Then he squealed on me?"

"Go easy on your brother. I played rough. I told him that I had heard Sinaloa had put a price on your head and that I wanted to warn you. He became more talkative after that. He said that he had gotten the impression that you were leaving on a long trip."

"So my life is in danger?"

"Not as far as we know. However, we wanted to see you because we felt hurt by your deliberate avoidance of us over the last two weeks. After the tip from Dave, we took the precaution of checking the passenger lists of outgoing flights from New York. There you were, Robert Bigelow, heading for Vancouver! You weren't planning to do some business for Ottoman Trading Company, were you?"

"Hell, no! I never want to see them again."

"You won't have to. Have you heard? Your brother said you haven't been back to the office since your return from Mexico City. We issued an arrest warrant for Recep Murat for running a drug-smuggling operation, using Ottoman Trading Company as a front, and ordering the murder of Tony Santelli. He, unfortunately, sensed what was about to happen and caught the first flight to Istanbul before we could get to him. It's too bad you didn't go back to work. You might have been able to tip us off about his plans to flee."

Bob would have liked to see Murat behind bars, but he expressed no regrets. Let Shafer and Connors deal with him. Someday they would get Murat. He would have a target on his back for the rest of his life. "What happens to the New York office?" he asked.

"It has been shut down. You are now officially unemployed, although that should not inconvenience you too much. Your brother told me about the Sotheby art auction."

"The timing could not have been better," agreed Bob. He looked warily at Shafer and Connors. "So that's it? You came to the airport just to tell me this?"

"Keep in touch," said Connors. "We will try to get Murat extradited to stand trial in the United States. We would like you to be a witness for the prosecution if we ever get that far. Cooperation from the Turkish government is not certain even though they will receive a complaint about Ottoman Trading Company."

"There is one more thing," added Shafer. "I owe your brother a favor. When you and I first met in the bar at the Edison Hotel, I told you that the bartender at the Bar Boulud had identified you as the man who had a drink with Fred Sanford shortly before his death. It was a little white lie designed to make you cooperate with us in shutting down the Ottoman Trading Company operation here. None of the bartenders in the Lincoln Center area could recall who had met with Sanford before his death. Whatever happened is between you and your conscience, but there is insufficient evidence to bring charges against you. You are free to go!"

"You did what?" sputtered Bigelow indignantly over Shafer's admission. "You cynically used me for your own ends, putting my life at risk?"

"I was just doing my job," responded Shafer without any sign of remorse. "Besides, what happened to you was deserved punishment. You engaged in illegal drug peddling. I don't feel guilty."

"By the way," added Connors, "Vancouver has an active drug scene. If you want a job with my Mountie friends, just let me know. I will make the introductions."

With that final jibe, Connors and Shafer walked away.

Unfinished Business

Chapter Fifty-Three

For a few days, Ozmen was feted as a celebrity. He was received as a guest at the home of the Turkish ambassador to Mexico and lionized by a Turkish media that had flocked to Mexico City. It was a drama made for television—his escape from the hands of a thuggish drug cartel and the lifting of the hostage crisis at the cathedral in Morelia. Knowledge of his treachery had died with Pedro Guerra. He had even been given a police escort by an apologetic Mexican government to Benito Juárez International Airport for his flight back to Istanbul.

It was on the long flight home that sober reality began to return. Several weeks had elapsed since he had left Istanbul for New York, eager to avoid being incriminated in the attack on Hayat Yilmaz. He had hoped to fade into obscurity but instead had become a darling of the media, which was eager to interview him, even offering contracts for the publication of a book on his experiences as a captive of a Mexican drug cartel.

What worried him were the stone throwers—journalists who asked awkward questions about why he would have been kidnapped by a drug cartel in the first place and why a second cartel would have seized a cathedral filled with wedding guests to bargain for his release. One of those stone throwers had even interviewed Omer Tilki, who was quoted in an article saying that Ottoman Trading Company would dismiss any employee suspected of having connections with the illicit drug trade. Of course, there would be a thorough investigation. Ozmen would be considered innocent until proven guilty.

Tilki's blatant hypocrisy almost made him smile. On the other hand, he knew how publicity-shy Tilki was. Would he have given an interview to a journalist unless he was embarking on a scheme to throw Ozmen overboard to the sharks in order to save the Ottoman Trading Company from a ruinous scandal? It was not a comforting thought.

Ironically, he would have been in a stronger position with Omer Tilki if he had never been rescued and if Pedro Guerra and he had been able to escape the clutches of the Mexican military, permitting them to work together to build ties between the Ottoman Trading Company and the Sinaloa cartel. His employer would then have embraced him as a hero.

He had talked briefly by telephone to Tilki a day after his rescue. He had expected at least a few words of sympathy for the ordeal that he had undergone, even if they did not reflect genuine feeling; but Tilki's remarks had been perfunctory, almost cool. No promise had been made that anyone from Ottoman Trading Company would be welcoming him at the airport. A number of matters would be waiting for his attention when he returned to the office. It was as if nothing extraordinary had happened to him. His first day back would just be another day at the office. Ozmen had been tempted to ask if there was any new information about Hayat Yilmaz since they had learned that she was still alive, but he decided against raising this awkward subject with Tilki.

Ozmen was able to push these questions to the back of his mind during his first week back in the office. He had his hands full dealing with the shock of British authorities seizing the *Atlantica* when it arrived in Liverpool. How could this have happened? He told a furious Tilki that he had personally inspected the cleverly disguised secret compartments where the heroin and cocaine would be stored, but the police had had no difficulty in finding them. There must be an informer, he had asserted to Tilki. Perhaps the assistant to Alvarez who had shown them around the docks.

"Possibly, but it is more likely that Los Zetas is incompetent. Our alliance with them is worthless, even dangerous!" Tilki barked. "Who knows, this shipment on the *Atlantica* may have been a sting operation, designed to entrap us. Because of this botched operation, Mehmet, my personal friend and second-in-command in our British organization, has been jailed. Other arrests have been made as well because the police followed up with some of the suppliers who were supposed to receive this shipment."

"I am very sorry to hear about Mehmet," said Ozmen with genuine regret. "I last talked to him during my trip to London in August, when the police seized one of our vans."

"We have some smart lawyers working on his release, but it will take time and cost money. He is not easily replaceable." Tilki looked at Ozmen with narrowed eyes. "Isn't it a remarkable coincidence that trouble strikes wherever you are? What a pity that I have lost Mehmet."

Ozmen sensed the uncharitable drift of Tilki's thoughts—that Mehmet would have been a good replacement for him. His resentment was building, but he controlled the tone of his voice when he said, "I called Diego Alvarez, the manager at Veracruz Sugar who is part of the *Los Zetas* cartel, to ask him how the British police had found out about the *Atlantica*."

"So what did he say?"

"I could not reach him. His secretary said that he had suddenly announced that he was getting married this week and would be leaving on his honeymoon. The announcement caught her by surprise because she had not known that he even had a fiancée. She had not seen him in two days and did not know how to reach him or when he would be returning."

Tilki was disgusted. "Bah! That is no way to run a business. We should be dealing with the other Mexican cartel, Sinaloa. If only we had succeeded in ransoming you, we would have opened up lines of communication that could eventually have resulted in a business deal. But that was botched too by the American, Bigelow. Whom can I trust in this organization?"

It suddenly occurred to Ozmen that he had forgotten to voice his suspicions about Bigelow to Tilki after his return to Istanbul. He still had scores to settle with that impudent American.

"I think Bigelow deliberately betrayed our ransom attempt. He is a police informer, in my opinion."

"Why do you say that?" snapped Tilki.

"The plans to ransom me were known only to you, Murat, and Bigelow. Only Bigelow could have tipped off the police."

"You do not suspect Murat?" asked Tilki mockingly, knowing only too well the rivalry between Ozmen and the head of the New York office.

"Whatever my differences with Murat, I would trust him before Bigelow."

"Fair enough," replied Tilki. "So would I. When I talked to Murat earlier this week, he mentioned that Bigelow is absent on sick leave. He has not returned to the office. I will call Murat again and relay your suspicions. But he is fully occupied now dealing with subpoenas from the FBI. Shooting Bigelow may have to wait."

"Whatever you think best," said Ozmen, deferring to Tilki's judgment. "But I would not give up on the idea of an alliance with Sinaloa. When I was in captivity, Pedro Guerra, the man in charge, told me that Sinaloa would still like to do business with us, despite the botched ransom attempt."

"But Guerra and his men were killed when you were rescued. There is now bad blood between Sinaloa and us. An alliance with them is not worth pursuing."

Tilki drummed his fingers nervously on his desk top. "Enough of that for now. We have some unfinished business to attend to—namely, Hayat Yilmaz and her cousin, Husayin."

"How is she?" asked Ozmen anxiously.

"When I called you in Veracruz shortly before your kidnapping, we knew that she is still alive, but we did not know where she is being kept. Then a simple solution occurred to me. The Tilki Foundation is a major benefactor of hospitals in Istanbul. I did not want to involve my father directly. But I know the director of programs, Agah Taner, who is familiar with all of the major hospitals in the city.

"A few discreet telephone calls by Taner as a friend of the family, interested in determining the health of Hayat Yilmaz, sufficed. Within hours, he discovered that she is being kept at Istanbul University's Medical Faculty Hospital.

"Until recently, she was in a coma and kept under tight security, so there was no reason to act hastily. Why run the risk of stirring up a hornet's nest when she might die of her injuries naturally? However, this last week, she has shown signs of coming out of her coma. That could be bad news for us. Fortunately, security around her room has become more relaxed. If she starts talking to the police, we will need to act.

"There is also the matter of her cousin, Husayin Yilmaz, the captain of *Light of the East*, who will be released from a Greek prison in Rhodes tomorrow. My father used his political connections, and the Turkish government has arranged a prisoner exchange. Yavuz, my personal bodyguard, will lead a welcoming committee in Iskenderun to drive home the point to Yilmaz that in matters relating to the Ottoman Trading Company, silence is golden."

Ozmen shuddered inwardly. He had seen that mirthless smile on Tilki's lips before. *But better Yilmaz than me*, he thought.

Chapter Fifty-Four

Husayin Yilmaz savored the smell of freedom as the Greek Coast Guard vessel approached the Turkish Port Authority terminal in Iskenderun. For weeks, he had been interrogated by Greek officials about his ship's mission, but he had not cooperated, withholding any details that would incriminate the Ottoman Trading Company. Kept in solitary confinement, he had not been permitted to fraternize with his crew at mealtimes or during exercise periods in the prison yard, but he had not been mistreated. Still, he had had little reason to expect an early release. There had been no indication that his routine was about to change until this morning, when he had been taken to the prison director's office and told that he would be released to Turkish officials in Iskenderun.

He and two other Turkish prisoners were taken on deck shortly before the Greek vessel docked. They were marched into the terminal building by two armed guards, who were greeted by the sole Turkish official in the empty waiting room. Shortly thereafter, they were joined by Turkish policemen guarding three Greek prisoners. The exchange of prisoners and documents was completed in a matter of minutes. The Greek guards and their charges then departed for their ship for the return trip to Rhodes.

Yilmaz was relieved to be back on Turkish soil, but he did not know what would happen next. The Turkish policemen consulted in hushed tones with the Turkish official. He could feel their eyes on him. The Turkish official shook his head and then shrugged his shoulders. The policemen approached and gave curt orders to the other two prisoners to move to a waiting police van. They said nothing to Yilmaz, who started to follow them. He paused when the official shook his head and winked at him.

"You are free to go. Your uncle is waiting outside."

Yilmaz picked up his bag and started moving toward the open door. He could see a stranger standing outside, away from the police van, smiling broadly and beckoning to him.

"Welcome home, nephew!" he boomed.

Yilmaz did not show the surprise that he felt. He did not have an uncle in Iskenderun. Moreover, he had never seen this man before—of medium height, powerfully built, a long scar running from his right eye down his cheek. Not a pleasant-looking man. He was probably someone acting on behalf of the Ottoman Trading Company.

Yilmaz moved toward the man and embraced him. "Uncle, it is good to see you again!"

Yilmaz looked back at the official, who had already turned away from the open door, his job done and rapidly losing interest in the matter. The official had only followed orders, and it was not the first time that a prisoner release had occurred without explanation. The police van pulled away from the curb as Yilmaz was escorted to a waiting Mercedes-Benz.

Yilmaz dropped his bag into the open trunk, pressed the lid shut, and got into the back seat next to the man who had greeted him. The driver stared straight ahead, not acknowledging his presence with a greeting.

"You are from Ottoman Trading Company?" Yilmaz asked the scarred man, who had not yet bothered to introduce himself.

"Yes," he replied. "As you may or may not know, Golden Horn Shipping no longer exists. I do not know the details. But you still have an employer who will take care of you."

The car had by now exited the yard of the Turkish Port Authority terminal and had merged into traffic on a main road.

"Where are we going?" asked Yilmaz.

"We have organized a welcoming party for you, outside the city." As the man smiled, his scarred cheek pulled down the lid of his eye. It was a sinister face, but Yilmaz was not alarmed. In his career as a sea captain, he had met many sailors whose scars bore witness to their brawls. It was only after the car had traveled about twenty minutes and was approaching a dilapidated warehouse district on the outskirts of Iskenderun that Yilmaz began to sense danger.

Chapter Fifty-Five

"This is a strange place to welcome a returning sea captain—no nightclubs, no dancing girls!" Yilmaz chuckled as he turned to his companion but then froze. He was staring into the barrel of a small handgun.

The car halted in front of a gate guarded by two armed men. When the driver lowered his window to identify himself, the gates opened, and the car proceeded to a building that looked in poor repair—broken windows, peeling paint, and rusting, exposed beams supporting the roof.

The driver, pulling a handgun from inside his coat, came around to Yilmaz's door and opened it. "Get out!" ordered the scarred man. He motioned with his head toward the door of the warehouse. "In there!"

Climbing out of the car, Yilmaz glanced in the direction of the gate, calculating his chances of escape. They were not good. He felt a blow to the back of his head.

"Move!" shouted the driver.

As they entered the dimly lit interior of the warehouse, the scarred man called out, "We have your friend, Yavuz!"

As Yilmaz blinked to adjust his vision from the bright sunlight outside, he could make out four dark figures. Two of them advanced toward him and, grabbing his arms, pushed him toward a tall, burly man whom he had seen before on the few occasions he had visited corporate headquarters on the Nuruosmaniye Caddesi in Istanbul.

“What do you want from me? Why are you treating someone who has loyally served his company like this?” he protested.

“Because you talk too much, scum, that’s why!” sneered Yavuz.

“I told the Greek authorities nothing about our operations. Believe me,” pleaded Yilmaz.

“Liar! We know that you told that woman professor, your cousin, far too much. If you want to live, you had better tell us the truth! What did you tell the Greeks? Encourage him, boys!”

Blows rained down on his head before he could ask how they knew about his cousin Hayat. His assailants threw him to the floor, kicking him in the chest and then in the groin. Screaming with pain, he shouted his innocence but to no avail. He tried to rise from the floor but was hurled back against sacks of merchandise stacked against the wall. He recognized the smell of the merchandise. Heroin! It was his last thought before he blacked out.

He slowly regained consciousness, rising through layers of pain. How much time had passed he did not know. Cautiously he opened his swollen left eye a slit, not wishing to alert his assailants, who were standing a short distance away. Yavuz was talking.

“Attila! Sirhan! Naim! You come with me! Omer would like us to make a courtesy visit to a customer who has been slow to pay for shipments received. Korkut, Veli—you stay here and guard our guest! We will be back in a couple of hours.”

Yilmaz closed his eyes, listening to the footsteps recede and a door slam shut. So there were only two left. That improved his odds of escaping. Then he remembered there had been two men at the gate to the warehouse, which was surrounded by a high wire fence. Four in total. The odds were stacked against him unless he created a diversion that would distract his guards. But how? He waited, not stirring. Minutes slipped by.

Then his opportunity came. One of the guards began pacing back and forth. The other guard stirred restlessly in his chair.

“Hey, Korkut, I am going outside to have a smoke.”

Yilmaz did not need to open his eyes to identify the man who had spoken. It was the man who had driven the car to the warehouse.

The second man responded gruffly, "Don't take long. I need to make a pit stop. Do you know where the toilet is?"

It was the voice of the man with the scarred face, who had unwisely eaten a whole package of dates while waiting for Yilmaz to arrive at the Turkish Port Authority. His stomach was now in a state of rebellion.

"It's over there, in the corner near the exit."

Yilmaz again peered through his eye slits and made out the dark silhouette of Veli retreating in the direction of the exit.

Korkut got up from his chair. Turning his back to Yilmaz, he shouted to Veli before he opened the door, "Five minutes! No longer!"

Yilmaz moved his head slightly to survey the interior of the warehouse, which was dimly lit by a few overhead light bulbs and whatever daylight could pass through the dirty windows. On the small table next to his chair, Korkut had placed a kerosene lamp to provide additional light so that he could read a tabloid newspaper that now lay on the floor.

Fortunately for Yilmaz, the weather outside was beautiful, a sparkling sunny afternoon, although that was not obvious inside the gloomy warehouse. Veli enjoyed his first cigarette so much that he decided to have a second. One of the gatekeepers, bored with his undemanding duties, wandered over and struck up a conversation with Veli about the prospects for the local football team in the Turkish Second League. Meanwhile, Korkut was impatiently waiting inside, cursing Veli under his breath.

Korkut walked over to peer at Yilmaz, who was lying very still, barely breathing. He muttered out loud, "We beat up that bastard pretty good! Still out cold!" He shook his head, spun on his heel, and walked rapidly toward the toilet.

Yilmaz did not stir until Korkut's back disappeared through the toilet door. He suppressed a groan as he pushed himself up from the floor. His head was throbbing. He gripped the chair for support as he lurched to his feet. He had only minutes to act. If Veli returned, his opportunity would be lost.

He painfully bent over to pick up the newspaper from the floor. He then grasped the handle of the kerosene lamp on the table and moved toward the bags of heroin stacked against the wall. He lifted the lamp chimney and applied the exposed flame to the newspaper, which he tossed next to the pile of bags. The flames flickered brightly as they consumed the paper. Then he hurled the lamp into the flames, smashing its glass body and spilling its combustible contents.

Shielding his face with his arms as the flames shot into the air, Yilmaz backed away and ran toward the toilet door. The sound of smashing glass would surely have been heard by Korkut. If he jumped on Korkut as he emerged from the toilet, he might be able to wrestle his gun from him. It was a desperate plan, but it might work. Then a better plan came to him in an instant. Good fortune was with him. As he crouched by the toilet door, his foot came to rest on a piece of iron pipe that had been left in the corner. This was a much better weapon than his bare hands.

"Veli, is that you? What's happening?" shouted Korkut as he opened the toilet door while pulling up his pants. His scarred face contorted in pain as the metal pipe smashed into his temple. This was one brawl that he would not survive. He collapsed into a crumpled heap at the feet of Yilmaz, who bent down to extract the gun from the shoulder holster of the dead man.

The door to the warehouse opened. An astonished Veli wheeled and shouted over his shoulder to the gatekeeper with whom he had been engaged in conversation, "There's a fire! The warehouse is burning down! Korkut, where in the hell are you?"

Yilmaz had to act quickly. The interior of the warehouse was now brightly lit by the flames engulfing the stacks of heroin bags. Oblivious to his pain, he moved rapidly toward Veli, hurling the iron pipe at him to catch him off guard. Veli stumbled as he reached for his gun, but he was too late. Yilmaz was on top of him, firing his gun at point-blank range into his chest. He caught the slumping Veli and, holding him in front as a shield, turned to face the gatekeeper, who had come charging through the door. Two shots rang out. One bullet pierced the body of Veli, and the other ripped through the throat of the gatekeeper, who crashed to the floor in a pool of blood.

Three down and one to go.

Yilmaz dragged Veli away from the door and waited for the second gatekeeper to come. After several minutes, it was apparent that the gatekeeper was biding his time, expecting Yilmaz to flee the burning building. When Yilmaz peered around the edge of the open door, he was greeted by a hail of bullets, and he pulled back quickly. The man was shooting an automatic rifle, probably a Kalashnikov, so he had a distinct advantage in firepower. Somehow, Yilmaz would have to dash through that door to Veli's car without getting shot.

The smoke inside the warehouse was now becoming unbearable, making breathing difficult. Yet it could also provide a screen. It had begun billowing in thick plumes through the open door.

Yilmaz extracted the car keys from Veli's pocket and also picked up his gun where it had fallen on the floor. A second handgun could be useful if Korkut's gun ran out of ammunition.

Placing a handkerchief over his mouth and nose, Yilmaz began to prepare his escape. Several times, he extended his arm around the side of the door, firing in the general direction of the gatehouse before ducking back to avoid the retaliatory salvo. Then at a moment when the smoke was especially thick, he darted through the door and fell to the ground, crawling toward Veli's parked car. By the time the gatekeeper realized what had happened, Yilmaz had reached the car and opened the driver's door.

Bending low over the steering wheel, Yilmaz started the engine and accelerated the Mercedes-Benz in the direction of the gate. A burst of gunfire shattered the windshield and riddled the passenger side of the car, but through the thick smoke, Yilmaz was able to make out the shadowy figure of the gatekeeper standing in the middle of the road near the gatehouse. The car hit him with a sickening thud then crashed through the gate to freedom.

But his problems were not yet over. In the distance, he could hear the sirens of approaching fire engines and police vehicles. Yavuz and his men would be returning soon, and the police would inevitably defer to them. Yilmaz would be the fugitive trying to elude the reach of both the Ottoman Trading Company and the police.

Chapter Fifty-Six

Hayat Yilmaz stirred and groaned in her sleep on the narrow hospital bed. Her brow was damp with perspiration, a sign of her distress, and with a cry, she raised her right arm as if to ward off a blow. Memories of her past, including a traumatic event whose details were still dim, were beginning to seep back into her consciousness.

Bilge, the nurse on duty, paused by the open door to her room and entered to check on her. She had taken a special interest in Hayat ever since she had been moved from the emergency ward to this wing of Istanbul University's Medical Faculty Hospital weeks before. Now, she noted with satisfaction, Hayat was showing signs of improvement. Three days before, she had emerged from her coma, opening her eyes and following the movement of the doctor's hand over her face. Then yesterday, as her visiting mother had hovered over her, she had smiled in recognition. The old woman had been ecstatic, tears of joy welling from her eyes.

Bilge glanced at her watch. She had been on duty since early morning, and her shift was almost over. In a few minutes, she would be free to leave on a week's vacation, although first, she would need to instruct the substitute nurse, Melek, on the specific needs of each patient. She smoothed the sheets on Hayat's bed and checked the tubes taped to her left arm, to ensure that they had not been disturbed by the woman's tossing. Everything seemed in order. She walked briskly from the room, smiling in anticipation at the progress she expected to see when she returned from vacation.

Melek rose from the desk at the nurse's station as Bilge approached and greeted her. She was a trim woman, middle-aged and experienced, who had formerly worked in a military hospital. Bilge did not know her personally since she was not one of the regular substitute nurses, but she had come highly recommended. Bilge had been surprised that someone with Melek's credentials would be available to work as a substitute but had not pursued the question. Melek was a reserved woman who tended to deflect questions about her past or her personal life.

"I am about to leave, Melek. Would now be a good time to do a final tour of the ward, in case you have some questions that I have failed to answer?"

"Why, of course, Bilge." Melek's lips twitched in a brief smile.

The two nurses walked down the corridor, stopping by each patient's room to go over the routine for the evening shift. When they halted by Hayat Yilmaz's door, Bilge murmured softly, "I have prayed for this woman every day since she arrived. She teaches at the Istanbul Technical University, a brilliant woman who has been through so much! But at last she is showing signs of recovery!"

"Does she have any special meal requirements?" asked Melek, her pen poised over her notepad to write down instructions.

"For the time being, she is being fed intravenously, and the daytime nurse, Esin, will be taking care of that. But your responsibility will be to administer the medications—again intravenously—because she has been unconscious until a few days ago and still cannot take them orally."

Melek nodded. "I understand. And the prescriptions?"

"They are listed in her file at the nurse's station. Would you like me to go over them with you?"

"That should not be necessary. It should be self-explanatory. The medications should be in a plastic bag supplied by hospital administration and kept at constant temperature. All I need to do is to substitute a new bag for the old bag, attaching it to the infusion pump beside the patient's bed."

Melek's calm voice impressed Bilge with its quiet confidence and professionalism.

The two nurses moved on down the corridor. Their final stop was by the door of Temel Kaplan.

Bilge spoke in a hushed voice. "He is suffering from terminal cancer and is in great pain. There is nothing that we can do for him except to give him powerful medications administered intravenously to dull the pain while we wait for the end. That will be your responsibility as well. Any questions?"

Melek shook her head. "It sounds routine. His prescription will be on file at the nurse's station."

After Bilge departed, Melek went about her chores methodically, stopping occasionally to chat with a patient or with a doctor completing his rounds. By nine o'clock, the ward settled into silence. Visitors and doctors were gone. The telephone had stopped ringing. Melek sat at the nurse's station, poring over patients' files and her daily checklist. It would be three hours before the night nurse arrived.

At ten o'clock, Melek took a key from the desk drawer and unlocked the door to the room where medications were kept under refrigeration in separate trays labeled with each patient's name. She looked for the tray marked with Temel Kaplan's name. Putting on surgical gloves, she removed a plastic pouch from his tray and left the room, locking the door behind her.

Deliberately she walked down the corridor and stopped by the door of Hayat Yilmaz. She looked over her shoulder to make sure that there was no one in the corridor who might see her. Then she entered the room and walked softly to the side of the bed. In a matter of minutes, she had exchanged plastic bags attached to the infusion pump. Then she waited for the patient's reaction.

Hayat Yilmaz woke with a start, her body rigid with panic. She felt a crushing pain in her chest. She saw someone standing by her bed and wanted to cry out for help, but the sound died in her throat as darkness enveloped her. The angel of death tiptoed as quietly out of the room as she had entered.

Once again, Melek went to the room where the refrigerated medications were stored and removed a pouch from the tray carrying Hayat Yilmaz's name. Then, locking the door, she proceeded to the room of Temel Kaplan. Would the change of medications kill him? Would she have two deaths on her hands? No, she would not feel remorse. He was going to die in any case. Mercy killing—isn't that what they called it in the Netherlands?

When Melek returned to the nurse's station, she sat down to collect her thoughts. Her hands were trembling. She thought about going to the nurses' washroom to splash cold water on her face but could not bear the thought of looking at herself in the mirror. In the morning, Hayat Yilmaz's death would be discovered.

What would her alibi be? That she had mistakenly substituted Kaplan's medicine for the woman's? Since both patients were only a few rooms apart, she would say that she had intended to refresh their medications on the same trip and had carried both pouches with her. It was against regulations, she knew, but she had been rushed for time since this was a new job, and she was still struggling to learn what was expected of her. Out of consideration for Ms. Yilmaz, she had not turned on the lamp on her nightstand, and in the darkness, she had confused Temel Kaplan's medicine for hers. It was a dreadful mistake that would haunt her to the end of her days!

Yes, she thought, that would be a plausible alibi which should help her to avoid prosecution, although it would certainly ruin her nursing career. What hospital would want to hire her? Her reputation for competence would be irredeemably destroyed.

Needing reassurance, she picked up the receiver to the telephone and began dialing. Suddenly, she stopped and hung up. Using the hospital line would not be wise because there might be a record of her call to someone outside the hospital at the time of Hayat Yilmaz's death. Fishing her phone from her purse, she called the man with whom she had been living for several years.

"The deed is done. Tell me, Yavuz, that I did the right thing. Was this necessary? I need your support." Her voice shook as she spoke.

He told her what she wanted to hear. “You have done well, Melek. Our master will be pleased. We had no choice but to obey. He demands complete loyalty from those who serve him.” Then he hung up.

Chapter Fifty-Seven

Dave was astonished to read the obituary for Hayat Yilmaz, which appeared in the *New York Times* two days after her death. She had made many friends at the United Nations, where diplomats who had worked with her in the past said uniformly that she was a brilliant woman who had served Turkey well. There was only one sentence in the obituary about what had caused her death—an accidental substitution of medications at one of Istanbul's leading hospitals at a time when she had begun showing signs of recovery from a near-fatal beating in August. That had left him incredulous. But what could he do about it?

An angry Jeff Braunstein had an idea when Dave called him. "Let's go public! There is no point in talking to the Istanbul police because any investigation is going to be obstructed by officials higher up. So let's get our story into the media—the Turkish media—to light a fire under the Istanbul police."

"How do we do that?"

"Years ago, Hayat introduced me to a journalist who works for one of the Turkish news agencies here in New York. He still works here because I bump into him from time to time. His name is Ahmet Ozak. Why don't I call him and suggest that he interview you about your experience as the prisoner of a Mexican drug gang? I think you will get a good reception because his agency is associated with the secularist, moderate opposition to the current government. They publish one of the largest daily newspapers in Turkey. They are still smarting over some trumped-up charge of tax evasion, which they suspect the government is using to intimidate them."

A week later, Ahmet Ozak was sitting in Dave's office. He was exploring the human-interest angle of the friendship between Hayat Yilmaz, a leader in the Taksim Gezi Park demonstrations, and Dave Bigelow, a fellow prisoner of the celebrated Demir Ozmen. But he suspected that this was not why he had been invited to make this interview.

"Is there another side to this story that we have not yet covered, Mr. Bigelow?"

"I believe there is. We have talked about my friendship with Hayat Yilmaz and my shared experience with Demir Ozmen as prisoners of a Mexican drug gang. There is a third side to this triangle that is less well known—the relationship between Hayat Yilmaz and Ozmen."

"Did they know each other?"

"Yes, they were childhood friends who were once betrothed. But their engagement was broken off when she discovered some activities of an unflattering nature about him."

"Such as?"

"Drug peddling."

"Aha! So what is the connection to the present?"

"Hayat's parents swore that she was not seeing any man and that she had had nothing more to do with Ozmen after the engagement was broken off. Yet the officers of the Istanbul police force who questioned me and others felt that a lovers' quarrel was the most likely explanation of Hayat's savage beating in August. I cannot be certain, but I suspect that she reached out to him again recently."

"Why would she have done that?"

"To ask for help for her cousin, Husayin Yilmaz." Dave related how he had told her about the seizure of the *Light of the East* and how her cousin's plight had upset her.

"When Ozmen and you were prisoners of this drug cartel in Mexico City, did you ask him about Hayat Yilmaz?"

"Yes, and he denied ever knowing her."

Ozak arched his eyebrows in surprise. "The fish smells. But why has this information not come out in the media? Did you tell the Istanbul police what you know?"

"I did, and I believe both the officers with whom I spoke were conscientious policemen. But their investigations were thwarted by political interference."

"You mean a cover-up? But Demir Ozmen, despite his recent celebrity, is not powerful. Who could be pulling the political strings?"

"His employer, perhaps."

"Yes, that would make sense. But tell me, what did you think of Ozmen as a man?"

"He was rather disgruntled, which is to be expected, given his experiences after his kidnapping in Veracruz. But when he lied to me about Hayat, I no longer trusted the man. What was he trying to hide? My brother, who worked for Ottoman Trading Company at the time, also did not trust him. We sensed a change in his behavior toward the end of our captivity, almost as if he had come to an agreement with our captors. He wasn't on our side anymore. He was on their side. But that just may have been our paranoia. We all thought we were going to be killed."

"Very interesting. Mr. Bigelow, I will have to do some additional research before my article is published, to satisfy my editors. But I can assure you, this information will be made public. Perhaps we can lead off with the headline 'Official Obstruction of Criminal Investigation!'"

Ozak laughed, knowing that the odds were heavily stacked against that happening in a country where press freedom was under attack by the government.

"How soon do you think your article will appear?" Dave was anxious to avoid further delays. He breathed a sigh of relief when Ozak answered.

"Within a week would be my guess."

Chapter Fifty-Eight

Cengiz Yilmaz was sitting on the front step of his house in the Uskadur neighborhood of Istanbul. It was a pleasant evening in early fall, mild temperatures and a soft breeze blowing off the Bosporus, but the old man's heart was heavy. He could no longer bear to stay inside the house filled with mementos of happy moments past, which mocked the weeping of his wife. Their world had been shattered by the events of the last week. Lost in his thoughts, he did not immediately raise his head when he heard footsteps approaching.

"Uncle Cengiz?"

The sun had now set behind the hills to the west, and in the dusk, he did not immediately recognize the battered face of the man who spoke. But the voice he knew.

"Husayin, is that you? How did you make it to Istanbul? There have been police reports on television and in the newspapers that you are wanted for murder in Iskenderun."

"It was self-defense. Thugs tried to kill me and brought blood down on their own heads. It is a long story. Can we go inside so that we do not arouse the curiosity of your neighbors?"

The old man hesitated. "Our house is in mourning, but please enter. You are welcome." As he opened the door, he called out, "Oya, it is Husayin, my brother's son."

"Are you mourning Hayat?" asked Husayin as Cengiz closed the door.

"Yes, Hayat has died. How did you find out?"

"Only a few days ago, after my release from a Greek prison. The Greek Coast Guard impounded my ship last month because they objected to some merchandise that we were carrying. I was held in Greek custody, with no access to Turkish media, until last week, when I was released in Iskenderun. Since then, I have been on the run from the police, hiding during the day and moving around only at night. But I got a prepaid disposable phone and was able to catch up on news on the internet."

Husayin did not reveal that he had robbed a shopkeeper of both cash and the prepaid phone at gunpoint. That would have shocked his uncle.

Oya, her eyes red-rimmed from crying, joined them. "Welcome, Husayin," she said. "Hayat was attacked in August by an unknown assailant who inflicted serious head injuries. She was taken to Istanbul University's Medical Faculty Hospital, but for weeks, she remained unconscious. Then last week, she regained consciousness. I think she recognized me for the first time. I was overjoyed. But my hope that she would recover was destroyed days later when the hospital called us to report that Hayat had died. It was so strange, so unexpected, that she should suddenly die after clinging to life for weeks."

"Why do you say that it was strange?" asked Husayin after her sobs had subsided.

Cengiz answered for his wife, "Her body was strong, despite her head injuries, but she died of a heart attack. Professor Oguz, her friend at Istanbul Technical University, made some inquiries. On the night she died, she was given her medications by a substitute nurse who may have been inexperienced. The medications were intended for another patient. That is what is strange. You would think an inexperienced nurse would be given closer supervision to avoid tragic mistakes like this one. There will be an official investigation, but whatever they decide, it will not bring back our daughter."

Husayin sank down on the sofa, covering his face with his hands. When he finally spoke, his voice trembled. "Did Hayat know anyone at the Ottoman Trading Company?"

"No one that she ever mentioned to us. Why do you ask?"

"When I was released last week in Iskenderun by the Greek Coast Guard, I was met at the Turkish Port Authority by employees of the Ottoman Trading Company, which controls my firm, Golden Horn Shipping. I was taken to a run-down warehouse, where the chief bodyguard of the president of the Ottoman Trading Company and his henchmen beat me mercilessly. They wanted to extract a confession of what I had told the Greek authorities while I was in their custody. I told nothing, but they did not believe me. The chief bodyguard, named Yavuz, claimed that I had once revealed company secrets to my cousin, the woman professor, who could only have been Hayat."

"Did you ever talk to Hayat about your company's business? What does it do?" asked Cengiz.

"Yes, I did. It trades in many different products around the world, but its most profitable line of business is the illegal drug trade—heroin, cocaine, amphetamines."

"But how could you work for such a company?" demanded Cengiz. "My brother was an honorable man, and I know that he raised you to live by his example."

"Hayat asked me the same question. She said that she had broken off an engagement many years ago with a man who was selling illegal drugs. I have forgotten his name."

"Would it be Demir Ozmen?" whispered Oya.

"Why, that's the name! He is head of a division at Ottoman Trading Company—vice president for special operations or something. I never had direct contact with him."

"He was recently released by a Mexican drug gang who kidnapped him while on a business trip to Mexico. Have you not heard?" Cengiz was amazed because the story had been front-page news in the major Turkish newspapers.

Husayin shook his head in embarrassment. "My Greek hosts never provided me with Turkish newspapers. I saw some headlines on the internet after my release, but I did not understand the connection to Hayat until now."

He remained silent for a moment then continued, "Do you not think it odd that Yavuz should have known that I had talked to Hayat about company operations? He is a rough, coarse man—not the sort Hayat would have associated with. He could have picked up that information only from Demir Ozmen. When did the attack on Hayat occur? Was it before or after Ozmen was kidnapped in Mexico?"

"The story about the kidnapping broke one or two weeks after she was attacked," said Cengiz emphatically.

"Do you think Hayat was attacked by Ozmen?"

Cengiz shrugged his shoulders. "Who knows? That possibility was raised by two American visitors from New York who came to our house a few weeks ago."

"Americans? Were they the police?"

Cengiz shook his head. "No, lawyers, I think. Professor Oguz brought them here because they were friends of Hayat."

"Of one thing I am certain," exclaimed Husayin. "Yavuz would not have beaten me unless he was given orders by Tilki, the president of Ottoman Trading Company. Tilki might have been upset about the loss of a ship, but he could simply have dismissed me. He had Yavuz beat me because he was afraid of what I might have told the Greek authorities. Who put that suspicion in his mind? Who made the connection between me and Hayat? It had to be Ozmen!"

"But Ozmen could not have been responsible for the medicine overdose that killed Hayat," said Cengiz.

"I agree. That was Tilki. When I escaped from his thugs in Iskenderun, he turned on Hayat."

"Nephew, I fear for you." Cengiz shook his head sadly. "You have very powerful enemies. The Tilki family is wealthy and well-connected. But are they guilty of Hayat's death? It is possible. They are benefactors of Istanbul University's Medical Faculty Hospital."

"I know what I face. I am a fugitive from the law. I cannot expect justice from this government or the legal system. Of necessity, I will join the opposition—you know, Hayat's people, who demonstrated in Taksim Square against the government and powerful real estate interests."

"You are in danger," said Oya. "Please spend the night with us."

"No, I must go. I have brought enough dishonor and grief to our family and this home. But I swear to you, the death of Hayat will be avenged! May Allah bring you peace in your time of mourning and give me the strength to fulfill my duty!"

Husayin rose from the sofa, bowed to his aunt and uncle, and disappeared into the night as swiftly and unexpectedly as he had come.

Chapter Fifty-Nine

Ozmen's head was spinning as he took the elevator to the fifth floor, where he had been summoned by Omer Tilki. He had just learned that the New York office of the Ottoman Trading Company had been shut down by court order and that Murat had fled to Istanbul to avoid arrest by the FBI. But that was of less concern to him than a front-page story in one of Istanbul's leading newspapers based on an interview with Dave Bigelow in New York and tying Ozmen to the death of Hayat Yilmaz.

When the elevator doors opened into the reception area, he was immediately escorted into Tilki's office by two bodyguards. Already seated inside were Omer and Emir Tilki, Murat, and Yavuz. He overheard Emir Tilki admonishing his son: "Success does not go to the fainthearted. Sometimes one must be resourceful and ruthless! You have disappointed me."

Omer Tilki did not appreciate being humiliated in front of his employees. His voice was tinged with rage as he confronted Ozmen with the newspaper article. "Have you read this article? Too bad that your confinement together did not make comrades of you and Dave Bigelow."

"Yes, I have read it. Bigelow only said that I am a suspect in the initial beating of Hayat Yilmaz, that I was once betrothed to her, and that he could not understand why the Istanbul police had not made progress in their investigation. He did not say that I am guilty of her death from an accidental overdose of medications at Istanbul University's Medical Faculty Hospital."

"The police have not succeeded only because we have done our best to obstruct their investigation. But the cost of protecting you has become too high. Hayat Yilmaz's obituary was in all of the newspapers last week. Even the *New York Times* carried her obituary. Now this article has unleashed a media frenzy. When I arrived at the office this morning, my limousine was besieged by reporters. My father even received a call from the prime minister's office."

Emir Tilki interrupted, "The call did not come directly from the prime minister but, rather, from one of his personal aides. The message was very clear. The prime minister will not tolerate a hint of scandal involving any of his major donors. We have contributed generously to the election coffers of the ruling party."

Tilki provided the background for the prime minister's concern. Since the demonstrations at Taksim Square, the prime minister had been subjected to increasing criticism for his authoritarian style of rule and for the corruption seeping into his administration. The opposition had accused him of deliberately thwarting investigations into corruption by reassigning thousands of police officers and members of the judiciary. The prime minister had lashed out furiously at his critics, accusing them of being part of a foreign conspiracy to undermine the Turkish Republic. So far, his political support had held, but he recognized that he was vulnerable.

"You know what that means, don't you? I do not care about not being invited to receptions at fund-raising events and being photographed with the prime minister. But I do care about a drying up of zoning decisions favorable to our real estate investments. Major construction projects await official approval in Istanbul, Ankara, and Izmir."

"Thank you, Father," Omer said deferentially. "But did you not protest that we are the innocent victims of an incompetent and corrupt employee at Ottoman Trading Company?"

"Yes, I did, and the prime minister's aide even seemed to believe me. But this controversy must be stopped now to avoid damage to our interests."

Ozmen felt like a condemned man as Omer Tilki's eyes bored into him. "Adding to our grievance is that we have reason to believe that Husayin Yilmaz, after escaping Yavuz's men in Iskenderun, has made his way to Istanbul."

"How do you know that he is in Istanbul?"

"He had the audacity to call my office, introducing himself as a friend of the martyred Hayat Yilmaz. I had Yavuz take the call. He recognized the man's voice. It was Husayin Yilmaz."

"That explains the call my wife received from a stranger last night. He introduced himself only as a friend of Hayat Yilmaz and wanted to know when I would be returning home from the office."

"Husayin Yilmaz is clearly bent on mischief. He does not know for certain what happened, but he suspects. However, you will not need to worry about taking evening strolls on dark streets until he is apprehended. I have decided to relieve you of your duties as vice president of special operations. Yavuz, take him away."

Yavuz was already on his feet, jerking his head in the direction of the door, where two bodyguards were waiting. Ozmen appeared ready to comply, turning toward the door. His worst fears were being realized. He felt overwhelmed, but he was not resigned to his fate. He would not go down without a fight.

Ozmen had no illusions about what would happen to him. He knew too much about the illicit activities of Ottoman Trading Company to be simply dismissed. Omer Tilki feared that he would seek vengeance by talking to the police. Since the Mexican terrorists had not obliged by relieving him of his troublesome employee, Tilki would initiate action himself, using the call from Husayin Yilmaz as an opportunity.

As he was pushed out of Tilki's office, Ozmen caught a glimpse of the normally inscrutable face of Recep Murat, now altered by a small triumphant smile. He felt the anger surge within him. They had been rivals within the company for years.

He halted and turned back toward Tilki, pointing an accusing finger at Murat and shouting, "Don't forget, Tilki, this man showed the bad judgment to choose Bob Bigelow to deliver the ransom money. Because of his mistake, your Mexican venture went up in smoke. He is the one you should be punishing!"

Murat stood up as if to challenge him, and Ozmen did not hesitate. He unleashed a powerful blow that smashed the cartilage in Murat's nose. Out of the corner of his eye, he saw one of the bodyguards lunging toward him. He sidestepped and tripped him just in time, grabbing him around the neck and pulling the gun from the holster inside his jacket. Ozmen only had time to point the gun in the general direction of Omer Tilki before Yavuz clubbed him from behind. The gun fired harmlessly into the ceiling. Then everything went dark.

The police, the media, and Ozmen's family were soon informed that he had left the company under a black cloud, terribly despondent about his personal situation. An internal investigation had turned up disturbing evidence of Ozmen's involvement in the illicit drug trade. He had also confessed under questioning that he had broken off an affair with his former college sweetheart, Hayat Yilmaz, when she threatened to talk to his wife. This might explain why her body had been found, badly beaten and on the verge of death, in the Bosporus in August. He had denied his guilt but had revealed that he was receiving abusive calls from her cousin, Husayin Yilmaz, a man wanted for the murder of four Ottoman Trading Company employees in Iskenderun.

Two weeks after Demir Ozmen returned to Istanbul, his body was found floating in the Bosporus, a gunshot wound to the head. Yavuz had seen to that. In its press release, the Ottoman Trading Company called his death a revenge killing and urged the police to redouble their efforts to capture the most likely suspect, Husayin Yilmaz. It was a sensational theme quickly picked up by the press, as Tilki had anticipated.

A Fishing Expedition

Chapter Sixty

Bob was sitting at a table in Tommy's Pub—a restaurant and bar catering primarily to locals in the small town of Agassiz, about an hour's drive east of Vancouver—when the past intruded. It was not the most remote town in the world that he could have chosen, but it was three thousand miles from either New York or Mexico City and probably twice that distance from Istanbul. Located in the majestic Fraser River Valley, the town was a magnet for fishing enthusiasts from around the world, attracted by the abundant salmon, sturgeon, and trout in nearby lakes, streams, and rivers.

He had not expected to meet Buzz Malone here. After working up an appetite fly-fishing that morning, he was ravenous and tucking into his fish and chips when four men walked into the pub and pushed up to the bar. The four men were laughing back and forth about their encounter with a monstrous sturgeon that had managed to get away. Bob would not have heeded them except for the loud voice of a big, burly man who had an unmistakable Boston Irish accent. The shock of seeing Murat's former bodyguard brought back a painful memory—the death of his friend, Tony Santelli, who, according to John Shafer, had last been seen in the company of Buzz Malone. Shortly thereafter, Malone had left for a fishing vacation in Canada, or so Murat had said, never to return.

Surveying the four men from a distance, Bob guessed who they were. The man with the weather-beaten face and faded jacket and pants was a local fishing guide. The two men standing between him and Buzz Malone were probably corporate executives on a fishing trip. Their faces were too pale and their gear too new for them to be regulars. Bob overheard references to Las Vegas several times. Possibly magnates escaping the air-conditioned chill of their gambling casinos in the Nevada desert for the boreal green and mountainous splendor of British Columbia?

By habit, Buzz Malone pulled away from his clients and surveyed the other customers in the pub. It was what any bodyguard would have done. His gaze swept over the customers in the pub twice before settling on Bob, who did not duck to avoid being seen. He had never had an open feud with Malone at Ottoman Trading Company. For the most part, they had ignored each other. Muttering a few words to the other men, Malone swaggered over to Bob's table. He moved with surprising lightness for a man of his bulk. This was a man who prided himself on his physical fitness.

"You're a long way from New York, aren't you?" His pale blue eyes peered at Bob from a bright red face—a pugilist's face with a short, flattened nose.

"I'm as surprised to see you as you are to see me!" replied Bob calmly. "You suddenly disappeared last summer, and a Russian took over your job. What happened?"

He was not about to provoke a confrontation. He had only John Shafer's word about the most likely suspect in the murder of Tony Santelli. That was not proof, and he knew from past experience that Shafer did not always tell the truth.

"Mind if I sit down?" asked Malone. He did not wait for Bob's answer and eased himself into a chair. "I got tired of New York and went on a fishing vacation in Quebec, just north of Montreal. I liked the fishing life so much that I called Murat and told him I wasn't coming back." His words came with practiced smoothness. "After that, I bummed around and moved west, doing a few odd jobs and finally ending up here."

"You haven't been in touch with Murat after you left?"

"A few times. Murat owed me some back wages. Not recently."

"Well, the New York office of Ottoman Trading Company shut down last October." Bob did not say it had been shut down by federal order. He did not want to get into a discussion of the illegal drug business of Ottoman Trading Company, about which Malone would have known, or that Murat had fled the United States to avoid arrest as a suspect in the murder of Tony Santelli.

"Why did that happen? Not enough business?" asked Malone innocently.

"Something like that."

"So you're working up here now?"

"No, I came up here on an extended vacation so that I could be close to my girlfriend, who lives in Vancouver. I don't have a work visa yet. What about you?"

"I've never bothered. No one has asked. I get paid in cash."

Malone looked at Bob skeptically and then grinned. "So that's your story, huh? You're up here on vacation and have a girlfriend. You sure you're not here on the lam?"

Bob was taken aback. "Why do you say that?"

"Wasn't your buddy trying to get away from the New York police after they seized drugs in his apartment?"

"You mean Tony Santelli?"

"That's right. I had trouble remembering his name."

"So the police were his problem. What has that got to do with me?"

Malone smiled knowingly. "C'mon. Don't try to play cute with me. The two of you were going fifty-fifty on the stash of drugs in his apartment."

Bob snorted. "Wherever did you hear a cock-and-bull story like that?"

"I got it straight from him."

"No kidding. You mean you guys knew each other?"

"Not really. I took a call from him for Murat. He was hard up for money and offered to sell me his Rolex watch. I said sure and agreed to meet him at a Starbucks in Chelsea. We got to talking. To make a long story short, I got his watch and he got my cash. I paid him a good price. I never heard from him again. He disappeared. Who knows, he might be up here in Canada and will come walking through the door at any moment." Malone chortled to himself.

Bob's heart was pounding, but he kept his voice calm. "Do you still have the watch?" He remembered Tony's watch, a very expensive and unique Rolex, which he had given to himself as a birthday present.

"Nope. I didn't need another watch, so I traded it in for cash at a pawnshop in Montreal when I came up here."

"So how was he when you talked to him? I haven't heard from him either since he took off."

Malone did not blink, looking steadily at Bob. "Very nervous. Scared as hell." Then he smiled. "But he pulled himself together again after he got my cash."

"That may explain why he told you those wild stories. Nervous, huh? Poor guy. But thanks for helping him out."

Bob felt that he had gone as far as he could go without asking Malone bluntly whether he had killed Tony. That question could trigger an attack, which he would not win. He decided to change tack.

"So who are those guys at the bar?" Bob looked in their direction and saw that they were staring back.

"Some dudes from Las Vegas who are up here for a little R & R while they investigate some opportunities in the hotel and casino business. I joined up with them a month ago as their bodyguard."

One of the men at the bar called out across the room, "Hey, Buzz, time to go!"

Malone pulled up the sleeve of his jacket to look at his watch. "One twenty p.m. Duty calls!" He shoved back his chair and swiftly moved back to the bar. In a minute, the four men had disappeared through the door.

Bob was stunned. Malone's story did not jibe with Murat's. Murat had said that Tony had never showed up at the Starbucks in Chelsea. But apparently he had met with Malone. The proof that they had met was that Malone knew about Bob's agreement with Santelli to split the stash of drugs in his apartment fifty-fifty. Bob had never told that to anyone except Andrea Williams, and then only on the evening of the day that Tony was murdered. She would not have had a chance to pass that information to either Murat or Malone, even if she had been so inclined, which he doubted.

It was also doubtful that Tony had volunteered that information during his meeting with Malone. It was more likely that it had been extracted from him through torture before he was killed. But what was the motive for the killing? To prevent Tony from surrendering to the police and telling them that the source of the stash of drugs was Murat and the Ottoman Trading Company? There was no longer any doubt in Bob's mind about who had committed the murder. But what should he do?

A curious young waiter came over to his table to give Bob his bill. "You know those people, eh?" he asked.

Bob shook his head. "Only the guy who sat down at my table. Why?"

"Oh, nothing really. They've been coming in here almost every day for the last week. They're from out of town—the States, I think."

"Any idea where they might be staying?"

"Yeah, they're over at the Paradise Valley Lodge a few miles from here. My girlfriend works in the restaurant there. She says they've just about taken over the top floor. Big spenders, eh? I saw them over there earlier this week."

That did not surprise Bob. The Paradise Valley Lodge was the only luxury resort in the area; it was several cuts above the motel that he had checked out of this morning.

He had expected to drive back to Vancouver for the weekend because Becky Moran would have the next few days at home before flying off again on Tuesday. Now he was beginning to have second thoughts as he walked out of the pub to the parking lot. He needed to stay in Agassiz until Buzz Malone was arrested and in police custody.

After all, Tony had been his friend. If he had succeeded in turning himself in to the police, who knows what would have happened? He might have squealed on Bob and implicated him as a joint owner of the drugs that the police had seized in his apartment. But that was not certain. In any case, Tony deserved justice.

Walking out to the parking lot, Bob was greeted by the reproachful barking of Jack, who had tired of being confined to the car while his master had lunch. However, his protests quickly changed to barks of delight when Bob produced the takeout cheeseburger he had brought with him and placed it on the pavement next to the car. Jack was a great fan of burgers.

While Jack devoured his lunch, Bob sat in his car, his forehead furrowed as the memories he had tried to forget flooded back. *Healing can take a long time*, he thought. *Maybe it never happens. The scar tissue that forms over old wounds may make us believe, falsely, that it has occurred. Memories fade. Our former life begins to feel like the life of another person experienced vicariously. Then the past comes back to haunt us. Old wounds are reopened. Our wounds bleed again.*

He shook off the feeling of depression that descended like a mist from the mountains. He had to do something, quickly. Buzz Malone was a dangerous man, powerfully built, and probably armed with a gun. If Bob tried to tackle him physically and beat a confession out of him, he would be the one bludgeoned to death or shot. He did not want to be a dead hero, especially since Becky had given him a reason to live. If he went to the local police and asked that they arrest Malone, they would want to check his story, which could take days. By the time they were prepared to act, Malone might have slipped through their fingers, departing with his new employers to an unknown destination.

Bob knew what he had to do even if the thought sickened him. There was a man in New York to whom he had resolved never to speak again. But that man had the authority to make events move quickly. With shaky fingers, he dialed a number which he had memorized and which was still embedded in the recesses of his brain. It was 2:00 p.m. in Agassiz and 5:00 p.m. in New York. Maybe he could still catch him, although it was a Friday afternoon in May, and he might have left the office early.

The telephone at the other end rang four, five, six times. He had probably missed him, Bob thought, and was about to leave a voice-mail message when someone picked up the receiver.

"John Shafer."

Bob took a deep breath. "This is Bob Bigelow."

"Who?" When Bob repeated himself, Shafer exclaimed, "I'll be damned. I hadn't expected to hear from you after all this time. How long has it been? Nearly seven months?"

"Are you still working on the Tony Santelli case?"

"Yeah, although for the time being, we are not making any progress. No new leads."

"I have a tip for you. Remember Buzz Malone, Murat's bodyguard, who you said was the last man seen with Tony Santelli before he was killed? I met him today, quite by accident, in a pub in Agassiz, British Columbia—a small town about sixty miles east of Vancouver."

"How do you spell the town's name?"

Bob spelled it for him.

"Do you know where we can reach him?"

"He is staying at the Paradise Valley Lodge just outside Agassiz. He is currently employed as a bodyguard by some gambling casino executives who are up here on vacation."

"We will start working on this immediately. I remember you telling us that Murat had told you Malone had gone to Canada on a fishing trip. We notified the Mounties, who had an eye out for him, but no luck. Canada is a big country. One small minnow is easy to miss in an ocean."

Bob was about to end the call when Shafer came back with one more question. "Is there a telephone number or email address where we can reach you if necessary?"

Uneasily, Bob provided the information. He had wanted to escape Shafer and did not want to be trapped by him again.

Sensing his hesitation, Shafer assured him, "Don't worry. The Mounties may need to contact you to confirm the identity of Buzz Malone. Otherwise, we will not call on you again unless we can extradite Recep Murat from Turkey and bring him to trial."

Chapter Sixty-One

Bob Bigelow waited a few minutes after the call with Shafer ended before ringing the Paradise Valley Lodge. "Do you have a double room available for tonight and tomorrow night?" he asked the receptionist.

"I am sorry, sir. We are almost sold out for tonight. But the honeymoon suite is still available. It is lovely and very private. Would you be interested?"

"I'll take it." What the hell, it would cost only a few hundred dollars more, and his future was on the line.

Then he called Becky. He had guessed correctly that she would already be home. "I have had a change in plans. I will not be driving back to the city tonight. How would you like to spend a weekend in Agassiz at the Paradise Valley Resort? We can go fishing, or we can just take it easy, admiring the scenery. What do you say?"

"I think that's a wonderful idea!" Her enthusiasm lifted his spirits. "So how have you spent the last couple of days? Productively, I hope."

He laughed. "I caught a few salmon, which I have packed away in ice, and I am laying to rest a few ghosts from the past."

"Ghosts from the past? That sounds mysterious. You will have to tell me about them."

"I will tonight. When do you think you can get here?"

"Around eight o'clock. I need to clean up and wash some laundry before I can drive out."

Bob had not told Becky much about his past life, except for a brief recounting of his ordeal as the prisoner of kidnappers in Mexico City. The Mexican capital was where they had first met when he boarded the flight back to New York City, and he had needed to explain his reason for being there. On one occasion, she had asked why he had decided to leave home for his extended stay in Vancouver. Was he running away from something? He had given a brief explanation—a divorce, his employer going out of business. His parents had died. Home no longer held any attraction for him. There was nothing to go back to. Thereafter, she had not probed.

They had dinner that night in the honeymoon suite. Bob did not want to risk an encounter with Buzz Malone in the lobby or the bar. But he also wanted to talk privately with Becky, to make a clean slate. Marriage could not be based on evasions. Jack did not try to impose himself on them and kept a discreet distance. She listened quietly to Bob and then assured him that she still loved him, despite what had happened in the past. He proposed and she accepted.

The next morning, while Becky still slept, he put on his gym clothes and went down to the fitness center one level below the lobby. As he had expected, Buzz Malone was already there, lifting weights and running on the treadmill, sweat glistening on his brow and soaking the shirt that clung to his lean, muscular torso. He was surprised to see Bob.

"I didn't know you were staying here."

"I had a change of plans. I was going to go back to Vancouver, but my fiancée and I decided to spend the weekend here instead."

"Your fiancée? You mean she's for real?" Malone's voice was envious.

"Yeah, I am happy to say she is for real," replied Bob. He was about to start the treadmill when Malone made a statement which froze him in mid-motion.

"I called Murat last night after I met you."

Bob turned toward him, trying to sound casually interested. "I thought you said yesterday that you weren't keeping in touch."

"Not recently. But after I met you yesterday, I was curious. His New York number is no longer working, but I had his mobile number in Istanbul. We did a lot of catching up. He told me interesting stories about the closing of the New York office and about you."

"About me? Such as?" Bob hoped that the nervous tension he felt did not show.

"I guess Demir Ozmen and you did not become pals during your captivity in Mexico. Demir told Murat that he thought you are a police spy and recommended that you be shot." Malone had a lopsided grin on his face, but the smile did not extend to his eyes. "You really have a knack for getting into trouble, don't you?"

"Don't believe every bullshit story you hear," Bob retorted. "He blames me for the failure of the ransom attempt and wants to get even."

Malone silently spun on his heel and walked toward the locker room, leaving Bob in confusion as to whether he believed Ozmen's accusation. Had Murat offered Malone a reward for killing him? If so, he did not have much time. Becky and he had better check out of the hotel immediately.

But maybe not. Help should be arriving soon.

At that moment, Bob's phone rang. He jumped even though he had been alerted by email the night before to expect a call. He heard a clear, crisp voice: "Mr. Bigelow, this is Sergeant Baker of the Royal Canadian Mounted Police. We went to the suite where Buzz Malone is staying, but his employers said that he is in the gym."

"Yes, I can confirm that. I am in the gym now. He just went to the locker room and is probably taking a shower."

"Please do not leave the gym before we arrive. We need you for positive identification."

Moments later, two Mounties arrived. Bob pointed in the direction of the locker room. "He is still in there."

When Malone emerged from the locker room fully clothed, handcuffed, and flanked on either side by a Mountie, he seemed startled when Bob said, "This is your man."

Malone could not contain his fury. "You Judas! You piece of shit! I will get you for this!"

The two police officers advised him to keep quiet or he would be gagged. Bob resisted the impulse to lift his middle finger to Malone in contempt. He waited for the police officers and Malone to get into the elevator before he took the stairs to the lobby.

Two police cars with flashing lights were parked in front of the lodge. Curious guests gathered at the entrance to see what was happening. One policeman stood by the cars, and a second took up position in the lobby to provide cover if necessary. The doors of the elevator opened, and Malone was marched across the lobby to one of the waiting cars. He would be extradited under police escort on the next flight to New York.

When Bob got back to the honeymoon suite, room service had already delivered breakfast. Becky flashed a grin when he reported on the morning's events. "The Mounties always get their man!"

Some of the burden of guilt resting on Bob's shoulders began to lift. A smile of relief spread across his face. The capture of Malone had happened so fortuitously that he wondered whether life was a series of random events after all. It was the sort of philosophical question that his brother, Dave, would appreciate.

Rough Justice

Chapter Sixty-Two

Dave Bigelow had not seen Ahmet Ozak for months, ever since his interview with the Turkish journalist in New York, when he had revealed his suspicions about Demir Ozmen. Now the occasion of Dave's second site visit to the headquarters of the Europa Bank subsidiary in Istanbul had given them an opportunity to meet again. They were sitting in a coffee shop as the journalist related the tumultuous events in his life that had followed the publication of the article connecting Ozmen to the brutal beating of Hayat Yilmaz. He had tried to interview Ozmen before the release of the article, but his requests for a meeting had been met with silence. Days later, Ozmen's dead body had been retrieved from the Bosporus.

The manner of his execution was typical of the slayings that occurred during turf battles between Turkish drug gangs. That had intrigued the editors at Ozak's news agency, who had transferred him back to Istanbul to begin a series of investigative articles about the Ottoman Trading Company. The question they had posed was whether Ozmen had been a rogue employee, as the company claimed, or was there a deeper, more sinister link between the company and the international drug trade?

"Would I have undertaken this assignment if I had known how it would end?" Ozak shook his head ruefully. "At first, I had the support of my editors. But months later, they fired me under political pressure. I am now a freelance journalist making out as best I can. My former newspaper will accept occasional articles from me on cultural or sports events, but not on politics or the international drug trade."

"What do you mean by political pressure? What happened?"

"I started my investigation by contacting the father of Hayat Yilmaz. He confirmed what you told me about the reason for the breaking off of the betrothal between his daughter and Demir Ozmen. I gained his trust. He introduced me to his nephew, Husayin Yilmaz, who is in hiding because he is accused of killing a number of the company's employees, including Ozmen. I asked him whether he had shot Ozmen in revenge for the death of Hayat Yilmaz, as the company claims. He denied it. He suspects that the company killed Ozmen. I believe him."

"Was there ever a thorough investigation into how Hayat died?"

"There was an investigation, but not a thorough one. The conclusion was that Hayat Yilmaz died from an accidental substitution of medications, not from her injuries. The medications were administered by a temporary nurse, who was subsequently dismissed for incompetence, although no charges were pressed against her by the police or public prosecutor. She has disappeared, according to my acquaintances at the hospital. The official explanation was not satisfactory. Apparently, this nurse was not some inexperienced young girl but, rather, a matron with twenty years of nursing behind her."

"But shouldn't that raise all kinds of questions?" Dave was shocked.

"Officially, no—but privately, yes. I checked into the personal life of this matron and discovered an interesting link to the Ottoman Trading Company. She is the mistress of a man who is the personal bodyguard of Omer Tilki, president of the company."

"Omer Tilki? But what would be his motive for wanting Hayat killed?"

"She knew something that he did not want to become public."

"Such as what?" The answer came to Dave as soon as he finished the question. "Drugs?"

Ozak nodded. "There is a family connection between the Tilki clan and the Baybasin clan, which runs the British drug trade. Birds of a feather flock together."

"It makes sense that Ozmen could not have planned the overdose of medications administered to Hayat. He was a hostage in Mexico. Planning something like that would have taken more time than the one or two weeks he had after his return to Turkey."

"Agreed. When I raised some of these questions in the articles that I wrote, my editors started receiving death threats in the mail. They feared that a lawsuit by the Ottoman Trading Company against the newspaper was imminent. But the Tilkis abhor bad publicity and retaliated by getting their friends in government to revive the bogus tax evasion case against the newspaper. It was much more effective. The message was clear. Drop this line of inquiry or you will get hurt. My editors caved in and fired me."

"So what hold do the Tilkis have on the government?"

Ozak smiled cynically. "Money. They are major contributors to the prime minister's campaign to change the constitution so that he, as president, can become the elected sultan of a revived Ottoman Empire." His face tensed. "But perhaps I have said too much. I must watch what I say if I want to avoid arrest for treason."

The two men finished their remaining coffee in silence. Dave glanced at his watch, thinking about an early morning meeting he had scheduled.

Ozak gestured to him. "I promised Cengiz Yilmaz that I would take you to see him. Do you have the time? He wants to thank you for your friendship and support for Hayat. He would also like you to meet someone."

"At his home?"

"No, at his shop. He is a carpet dealer in the Grand Bazaar, not far from here."

Chapter Sixty-Three

Many of the shops in the Grand Bazaar were already shuttered for the evening when they arrived. They were greeted warmly by Cengiz, who conversed with Dave in the front room of the shop using Ozak as an interpreter. The mysterious person whom he had wanted Dave to meet was not present. Cengiz assured Dave that he would arrive soon.

A loud creaking noise from the back room—as if from the unoiled hinges of a door—heralded the arrival of the stranger. Cengiz pushed aside the hanging carpet that separated the front of the shop from the back and motioned to Dave to follow him. The dimly lit storage room was filled with carpets rolled up on the floor and stacked against the wall. No one was evident until a large carpet in one corner of the room began to move. A tall, bearded man suddenly emerged from the dark shadows into the light.

He greeted Cengiz and then strode toward Dave with an outstretched hand. In halting English, he introduced himself. "I am Husayin Yilmaz."

Dave had guessed the stranger's identity the moment he saw him. He hesitated, then reached out to grasp the hand of a wanted murderer.

Cengiz directed a request at Dave, which Ozak translated. "My nephew is in a very difficult situation, wrongfully accused of murder when he was only acting in self-defense. He cannot expect true justice in our country. For Hayat's sake, can you not help him as well?"

"How can I help?" asked Dave when he understood the question.

"You must have powerful friends in the US government. Could you use your influence to help him gain asylum in the United States?"

Dave had not expected this appeal and was unprepared to respond immediately. A minute elapsed before he responded, "It would be difficult. There is a 1979 extradition treaty between the United States and Turkey in murder cases. However, there are political exceptions. A request for extradition can be refused if it is politically motivated, and that assumes that you had already gained entry into the United States, Husayin. That is a separate issue, which I will discuss with the information officer at the US consulate in Istanbul. She was a classmate of mine at Princeton. We are having lunch later this week."

After Cengiz and Husayin had expressed their gratitude for whatever he could do, Dave excused himself. As he walked with Ahmet out of the Grand Bazaar to a nearby taxi stand, Dave could no longer contain himself. "Ahmet, where in the hell did he come from? He appeared out of nowhere."

Ozak laughed. "It is a well-kept secret. At the back of Cengiz's shop is a door with steps leading down to the Yerebatan Sarayi, which means 'sunken palace.' It is better known in English as the Basilica Cistern. It was built by the Emperor Justinian I to provide water to his great palace. It survived the Ottoman conquest and, for many years, also served the needs of the sultans' Topkapi Palace."

"Now why has no one ever mentioned it to me before?"

"Most tourists miss it. They walk above it not even knowing that it exists, even though it has many wooden bridges over the water that permit exploration."

"And hiding too?"

"Yes, and that too."

"But I think Husayin must be spending much of his time above ground. He looks too sunburned to be hiding during the day in the Basilica Cistern."

"That he does," agreed Ahmet. "I feel sorry for Husayin. The last few months have been very frustrating for him. If he is thinking about gaining asylum in the United States, he must be giving up on ever bringing the Tilkis to justice. Omer Tilki is a very elusive man. He rarely appears in public, and when he does, he is surrounded by bodyguards."

"And apparently, he does not respond to telephone calls. Elizabeth Waters, the information officer at the US consulate, mentioned to me when I called her that she has been trying for months to set up a meeting with Omer Tilki to explain US reasons for requesting the extradition of Murat, the former head of the company's New York office. His secretary's standard response is that he will get back to her, but he never does.

"Finally, this week, her anger boiled over. She offered Tilki's secretary time on three different days when she could meet with him. His schedule was completely booked, she was told. 'Even on Friday?' she asked. Especially on Friday, because Tilki, apparently, is going to announce in front of the Blue Mosque, with the media present, the funding by his company of the Turkish-Syrian Friendship Foundation to assist Syrian refugees who have fled the civil war in their country."

"This Friday?" asked Ahmet curiously. "Do you know what time?"

"Around midday, I assume. Elizabeth said she would be able to have lunch with me because Tilki cannot meet with her at that time."

Ahmet was silent as he opened the taxi door for Dave. He knew someone who would be very interested in that information.

"Can I offer you a ride somewhere?" asked Dave.

"No, thanks. I just remembered I forgot my cigarette lighter at Cengiz's shop. I will need to go back before he closes for the night."

It was minutes later when Dave recalled that he had never seen Ahmet smoke a cigarette.

Chapter Sixty-Four

Two days later, Dave was sitting on the terrace of the Sultanahmet Palace Hotel restaurant, which had views of the Blue Mosque and the sparkling Sea of Marmara in the distance. He was chatting with Elizabeth Waters about Husayin Yilmaz's chances of being given asylum in the United States.

"I am not hopeful. Relations between Ankara and Washington are already strained. Whatever the merits of Husayin Yilmaz's case, Washington will hesitate to make things worse. But I promise you that I will test the political waters and make some inquiries on his behalf."

Waters was a personal friend of Professor Oguz of Istanbul Technical University, who had suggested the restaurant to them. Professor Oguz had not yet joined them because he had been delayed in traffic. It was a pleasant day in May with bright sunshine and a soft warm breeze blowing from the south. The murmur of street noise drifted up to them, punctuated by the persistent calls of muezzin to Friday prayers.

"What a perfect choice," said Elizabeth in her cheerful Midwestern voice. "So atmospheric—and the menu looks interesting too. It's too bad about the traffic, but Professor Oguz should be here shortly. Have you known him long?"

"A business associate, Jeff Braunstein, and I were here on a business trip last September for some meetings at the Turkish head office of Europa Bank. On impulse, we stopped at the College of

Architecture of Istanbul Technical University to ask about Hayat Yilmaz, a friend of ours who had taught there. That's how we met him."

"Wasn't that extraordinary? Hayat brutally beaten and tossed into the Bosporus, rescued by a fisherman, only to die at one of the best hospitals in Istanbul from an accidental dose!"

"At least that is the official explanation," responded Dave just as Oguz joined them at the table. "I am skeptical."

"My apologies for being late," said Oguz, "but the traffic today in Istanbul is horrendous. I overheard your comment. I do not have much confidence in the official findings either."

"Do you think there was a cover-up?" asked Jeff.

Oguz grimaced as he spoke. "There was speculation in the press, encouraged by a report from the Ottoman Trading Company, that Demir Ozmen was responsible for Hayat's death and that her cousin then killed him in revenge."

"There is one problem with that speculation, Professor Oguz," retorted Dave. "As someone who shared his captivity in Mexico, I am confident he had no opportunity to plan Hayat's death from an overdose of medications. After his return to Istanbul, he would not have had enough time to come up with some elaborate scheme."

"I could not agree more, Dave." Oguz chuckled. "I do not endorse the company's explanation. It is another of those Turkish mysteries."

"I wonder if it really is a mystery," Dave countered. "Ozmen's employer has to be the primary suspect both for her death and for the cover-up."

Elizabeth Waters glanced at Dave and nodded in support. "In the United States, the Department of Justice has shut down the New York office of Ottoman Trading Company as a front for an illicit drug operation. The head of that office, Murat, escaped arrest and fled back to Turkey, where he succeeded Ozmen as vice president for special operations at corporate headquarters. The Turkish government has not yet acted on a US request for the extradition of Murat. In fact, our ambassador to Turkey has urged an investigation into the operations of Ottoman Trading Company several times, but he is being stonewalled."

"Relations between Turkey and the United States are somewhat troubled right now over Egypt and the Syrian civil war—"

"Don't make excuses for the Turkish government, Professor Oguz," interrupted Waters. "This goes much deeper than differences over foreign policy."

Oguz sighed. "Unfortunately, yes. Emir Tilki and his son, Omer, are important supporters of the governing party, holding fund-raisers which helped it to win our recent local elections. The anti-government demonstrations in Taksim Square have been crushed through the arrest of many of its organizers and supporters, who now await trial for sedition and even treason. The prime minister has his eye set on becoming our next president in August, and he will not act against any of his important business supporters in the forthcoming election campaign."

"In other words, the Ottoman Trading Company is protected against an official investigation unless there is a change of government in Turkey?" asked Dave.

"Precisely, Dave," agreed Waters. "And from what Professor Oguz has said—and I concur completely—that is unlikely to happen."

"I have faith in my country, and justice will happen, sooner or later," opined Professor Oguz. "But why don't we place our orders for lunch? Our waiter has been waiting patiently for us. Would you like me to recommend some of our Turkish specialties?"

Chapter Sixty-Five

A few hundred yards away from the restaurant, throngs of the faithful were exiting onto the public plaza in front of the Blue Mosque after listening to Friday prayers. Some of them stopped to press coins into the outstretched palms of beggars, whose numbers had swelled since the start of the Syrian civil war.

Most of the beggars were regulars, but within the last month, they had been joined by a man named Hussein, who claimed that he was a refugee from Aleppo, the commercial center of Syria. He had lost everything, he said—his home, his family, his business—in a bombing attack by the Syrian air force directed against the insurgents who had gained control of the city. He had fled to Turkey with only the clothes on his back. None of the beggars doubted his story; it was only too familiar. However, some of the regulars who hailed from Aleppo wondered about his accent. He spoke Arabic fluently, but with inflections that were Turkish, not genuinely Aleppine. He explained that he had grown up in a small village near the Turkish border but had moved to Aleppo as a young man.

Hussein sat slightly apart from the other beggars, as was his custom, carefully studying the faces of pedestrians who walked by. His hair was tousled, his heavy beard flecked with gray, his face sunburned and creased, but his eyes were ever watchful, not dulled by misfortune. Whenever a policeman approached to urge the beggars to make way for pedestrians, he complied quickly, never engaging in verbal confrontation with him, as some of the other beggars did.

Among the faithful attending prayers this Friday was Omer Tilki, accompanied by Yavuz and a second bodyguard. In recent months, he had become a regular attendee at prayers on Friday because he recognized the benefits of burnishing his image as a pious man with the media and the government. Frequently he would stop to press a coin into the outstretched hands of the beggars assembled outside the Blue Mosque, although he was not a particularly generous donor.

Tilki had good reason to feel pleased with himself. Business was going well. The company's real estate investments were booming, and the profit margins on merchandise trading were strong. Moreover, illicit operations—what the company referred to as "special operations"—had recovered nicely from the depredations of the police in Greece, the United Kingdom, and the United States. The New York office was not essential to the company's worldwide operations, and Recep Murat, freed from his duties there, had proved to be a fine replacement for Demir Ozmen. As long as his father remained in the good graces of the prime minister, they had nothing to fear from any official investigation.

Within minutes, he expected to announce, in front of the Blue Mosque, the creation of a fund by the Ottoman Trading Company to help Syrian refugees. It was a brilliant publicity coup that would erase any memory of the unfortunate events of the last year. He noticed that members of the media were already gathering outside the entrance to the Blue Mosque.

Omer Tilki heard the shrill cry of an old woman begging for alms. He paused and walked over to her, fumbling for a coin in his pocket. His bodyguards remained behind, amused smiles on their cynical, hardened faces. As he pressed a coin into her frail, wizened hand, she whispered blessings on him. A toothless smile lit up her sad wrinkled face. Looking into that face, Tilki felt a chill. Her eyes were opaque—the eyes of a blind woman. He turned to get away. She reminded him of death.

He was unaware of a bearded beggar who approached swiftly from behind, his hand outstretched. His palm was not open to receive alms but held a gun that he had pulled from within his tattered jacket. Three shots rang out, and the heir to the Ottoman Trading Company lay dead in the plaza, his sightless eyes staring up at the startled pigeons circling overhead. It happened so quickly that his bodyguards, looking in the opposite direction, had no time to react.

Pedestrians screamed as the bearded man lunged through the crowd and disappeared down a side street, with Yavuz in pursuit. Policemen came running. Distant shots could be heard, then silence.

Chapter Sixty-Six

Dave and Elizabeth—sitting on the terrace of the Sultanahmet Palace Hotel restaurant—heard what sounded like the backfiring of a car, followed by the sirens of approaching ambulances and police cars. These sounds did not seem unusual for a large, teeming city like Istanbul. They continued with their meal, listening intently to a discourse by Professor Oguz on the building of the Blue Mosque by Sultan Ahmed I in the early seventeenth century on the site of the palace of the former Byzantine emperors.

When the waiter brought small cups of steaming black coffee, the conversation turned back to Dave's experience as a hostage of a Mexican drug cartel.

"That must have been a terrifying experience—locked up in that small motel room with your brother and Demir Ozmen, thinking that you could be killed at any moment," said Elizabeth sympathetically. "Do you still have nightmares about what happened?"

Dave shook his head. "No, not anymore. But I think about my experience from time to time. I have some bitter memories."

"About . . .?"

"An old friendship betrayed. I would rather not talk about it."

The weekend before his departure for Istanbul, he had received a letter from John Shafer. He had opened it reluctantly. It was an apologetic invitation from Shafer and his wife, Ellen, to Dave and Melanie, asking them to come for dinner at their home in Manhattan. This was nearly nine months after they had visited the Bigelow home. Was it a peace overture, an olive branch extended in an effort to dispel the mistrust that had grown up between them? Or was it another attempt to glean information about his brother, Bob, with whom he might have lost contact? Dave had felt the anger stirring within him over an old friendship renewed and then abused.

After several days, he was still uncertain about how he should respond. If he accepted, would he endanger a possible reconciliation with his younger brother? In all fairness, Bob was partly to blame for the events that had sucked Dave and him into the maelstrom of a murky war against drugs. Shafer's behavior had been devious, but in the end, he had not pressed criminal charges against Bob, for which Dave was grateful. That was the other side of the argument. Maybe he should put old grudges aside and accept the invitation. He would discuss it with Melanie when he returned home.

"Okay. Did you derive anything positive from that experience?" Elizabeth persisted. "Like bonding with your brother? The two of you should have war stories to swap about your captivity for many years." She laughed as she said it.

His face relaxed into a grin. "Funny that you should say that. I made a promise to my father to take care of my brother and—"

"And did you?"

"I think so, putting both my wealth and life at risk. But old attitudes die hard. My brother and I never bonded before our trauma, and our experience as prisoners of a Mexican drug gang did not change that. We saw each other only once after our rescue before he disappeared for seven months."

"No telephone calls, no emails. Nothing at all?"

"Nothing until yesterday, when I received an email from him inviting Melanie and me to his wedding in Vancouver. He also advised me to stay out of trouble because it might come looking for me." Dave laughed. "I wonder what he meant by that?"

"No idea, but this could be a turning point!" She chuckled, patting him on the arm.

They were interrupted by their excited waiter, who gestured in the direction of the Blue Mosque. "Come quickly! An important Turkish businessman has been shot!"

Everyone rushed to the side of the terrace to get a better view of the growing commotion in front of the Blue Mosque. A rising crescendo of police and ambulance sirens almost drowned out Professor Oguz's question: "Who was the victim?"

"Omer Tilki, the president of the Ottoman Trading Company. A Syrian refugee did it." The waiter's voice trembled with nationalist indignation. "These refugees show no gratitude for the hospitality that Turkey has extended to them. Think of it. There are millions of them in our country! We should expel them."

"Omer Tilki! Was anyone else hurt?" asked Professor Oguz anxiously, ignoring the waiter's xenophobic comment about Syrian refugees.

"There was a second casualty—Tilki's bodyguard. He was running after the killer. But then, Allah be praised, the police have trapped the assassin in a merchant's shop in the Grand Bazaar. Only a devil could escape. Soon he will be dead."

Dave felt like an accomplice in Tilki's death. He knew the identity of the killer, even the location of the shop where the killer had taken refuge before slipping through the door hidden behind carpets and down the stairs into the Basilica Cistern. But he would never share that information with the police. By the time the police discovered the door, it would be too late. Husayin Yilmaz would have escaped.

How had Yilmaz known where Tilki would be and at what time so that he could plan the assassination? He thought about Ahmet and knew with certainty that he was not the only accomplice in the murder. The information—which had been given to him casually by Elizabeth Waters and that he had passed on to Ahmet with equal nonchalance on Wednesday night—had proven deadly.

The guilty thought occurred to him that being a carrier of information with deadly consequences was becoming a habit. Divulging to Hayat that her cousin had been arrested by the Greek

Coast Guard had triggered a chain of events resulting in her death. Now Omer Tilki had died as well because of what he had told Ahmet.

Dave brushed away his moral qualms. Surely, he could not be held responsible for what others did with information he gave them with the best of intentions.

He looked at Professor Oguz. "Is this the Turkish justice for which you hoped for earlier?" he asked. It was a provocative question.

Oguz shook his head and then responded gravely, "This is not Turkish justice! This lawlessness is rather a symptom of how the Syrian civil war is infecting the body politic of my country, like a virus. Unless that war ends soon, I fear for Turkey's future."

"But are you not overlooking a second virus—the danger of political corruption in a government that is becoming more authoritarian and thwarting justice?" asked Dave, impatient with Oguz's evasion of what, to him, was obvious.

He immediately regretted asking the question. It was awkward, even presumptuous. What could an American visiting Turkey for only the third time tell the Turks about how to run their own country, especially when there was so much corruption at home?

Oguz avoided his gaze and did not respond. That puzzled Dave, who had talked enough with Oguz to know that he supported the goals of freedom and justice, which Hayat Yilmaz had pursued. He had called her the symbol of what he hoped Turkey would become.

When the professor finally looked up, his eyes flicked sideways in the direction of the waiter. Then Dave understood. Caution advised Oguz against speaking openly in front of the waiter, who represented what Turkey was becoming. The waiter might be a government sympathizer who could inform on him. He taught at a publicly funded university, where reprisals were possible. His job could be at risk. Even worse, he could be accused of treason and imprisoned. Oguz gestured toward the Blue Mosque, where attendants were lifting Omer Tilki's body into an ambulance.

And what was Tilki? Dave wondered. An enabler who had abetted the political ambitions of Turkey's authoritarian leader—without regard to the freedoms being crushed—in order to serve his own corrupt interests?

By instinct and by training, Dave recoiled from the manner in which Tilki had died. Even a drug kingpin and multiple murderer deserved a fair trial by jury. Yilmaz had usurped due process, acting as prosecutor, judge, jury, and executioner. Yet the likelihood of a fair verdict was slim in a country where an independent judiciary no longer existed and where Tilki could avail himself of the best defense counsel and powerful political connections. Dave was willing to concede that rough justice had been the best of the possible alternatives.

Then he thought about his own precarious situation. His orderly life as a New York lawyer had been turned upside down in a matter of months. What if an informer had observed him and Ahmet entering the shop Wednesday evening when he had first met the killer? Yilmaz would not have been seen by anyone outside the shop. Still, the Istanbul police might look for a connection, and he would be in trouble if they thought he was withholding information. He had met the killer, inadvertently provided him with the information that he needed to plot his revenge, and even knew how he planned to escape. Spending time in a Turkish prison did not appeal to him.

Hours later, Dave was on the first available flight back to New York.

J 975.2 C 40361
CARPENTER, ALLAN
MARYLAND

6.94

W9-CMD-557

DISCARD

U.S.POSTAGE
TENNESSEE-VOLUNTEER STATE
NEW MEXICO STATEHOOD
1912 U.S. POSTAGE 1962
U.S.POSTAGE
OREGON TERRITORY CENTENNIAL
JASON LEE
1912 ARIZONA 1962
U.S.POSTAGE 4¢
OHIO SESQUICENTENNIAL
UNITED STATES POSTAGE
U.S.POSTAGE
1636 1936
RHODE ISLAND
WASHINGTON
NATIONAL CAPITAL SESQUICENTENNIAL
1800-1950
Stone Mountain Memorial
VERMONT
150TH ANNIVERSARY OF STATEHOOD
5¢ UNITED STATES POSTAGE
SETTLEMENT OF FLORIDA 1565-1965
RASKA STATEHOOD
U.S.POSTAGE 5¢
JULY 4, 1960
U.S. POSTAGE
4¢
SAN JUAN, PUERTO RICO
U.S. 8
ILLINOIS 1818 1968
6¢ U.S.POSTAGE
INDIANA
1816 1966
5¢
U.S.POSTAGE
NEW HAMPSHIRE
LIVE FREE OR DIE
COLORADO
ANNIVERSARY OF STATEHOOD
WISCONSIN
1848 1948
CENTENNIAL
UNITED STATES
U.S.A.
300TH ANNIVERSARY OF NEW YORK CITY
ABAMA
1819 1969
UNITED STATES
THE LANDING OF CADILLAC AT DETROIT 1701-1951
THE LANDING OF THE PILGRIMS
U.S.POSTAGE 6 CENTS
STEPHEN WATTS KEARNY EXPEDITION
1846 ENTRY INTO SANTA FE 1946
WEST VIRGINIA
5¢
U.S.POSTAGE
WILDLIFE CONSERVATION
UNITED STATES 6¢
UNITED STATES POSTAGE
TEXAS CENTENNIAL
1836-1936
Missouri 1821-1971 United States 8c
UNITED STATES POSTAGE 3¢
THIS IS THE PLACE
1847 THE UTAH CENTENNIAL 1947
1880 1940
UNITED STATES POSTAGE
HAWAII STATEHOOD · 1959
U.S. AIR MAIL 7¢
N JERSEY
CENTENARY
ARKANSAS RIVER NAVIGATION
6¢
FORT TICONDEROGA
1755-1955
UNITED STATES POSTAGE
1812·1962
LOUISIANA
4¢
U.S.POSTAGE
3¢
THE MACKINAC BRIDGE
CHEROKEE STRIP
UNITED STATES POSTAGE 6¢
MAINE STATEHOOD
U.S. POSTAGE 6 CENTS
OREGON STATEHOOD
1859 1959
U.S. POSTAGE 4 CENTS
Carolina Charter
1663-1963
5 cents
U S postage
TEXAS
STATEHOOD
1845-1945
4¢
U.S. POSTAGE
KANSAS STATEHOOD · 1861 · 1961
CONNECTICUT
1635 1935
CALIFORNIA
1769 1969
United States 6 cents
ISSISSIPPI
1967
U.S. POSTAGE 5c
1815 UNITED STATES 5¢
BATTLE OF NEW ORLEANS
SEATTLE WORLD'S FAIR 1962
UNITED STATES POSTAGE
4¢
GREAT NORTHWEST
1820 FORT SNELLING 1970
US 6¢
SOUTH CAROLINA
1670 1970
U.S. POSTAGE
6¢
UNITED STATES POSTAGE
WASHINGTON SAVES HIS ARMY AT BROOKLYN
UNITED STATES
POSTAGE 3¢
1792 SESQUICENTENNIAL OF THE STATEHOOD OF KENTUCKY 1942
U.S. AIR MAIL 7¢
ALASKA STATEHOOD
TERRITORIAL CENTENNIAL
1838
U.S.POSTAGE
NEVADA
1864 1964
STATEHOOD

GARRETT
Oakland
ALLEGANY
Cumberland
WASHINGTON
Hagerstown
FREDERICK
Frederick
CARROLL
Westminster
BALTIMORE
Towson
BALTIMORE
HARFORD
Bel Air
CECIL
Elkton
HOWARD
Ellicott City
MONTGOMERY
Rockville
WASHINGTON D C
PRINCE GEORGES
Upper Marlboro
ANNE ARUNDEL
ANNAPOLIS
KENT
Chestertown
QUEEN ANNES
Centreville
CAROLINE
Denton
TALBOT
Easton
CALVERT
Prince Frederick
CHARLES
La Plata
ST MARYS
Leonardtown
DORCHESTER
Cambridge
WICOMICO
Salisbury
SOMERSET
Princess Anne
WORCESTER
Snow Hill

The New Enchantment of America

MARYLAND

By Allan Carpenter

CHILDRENS PRESS, CHICAGO

Pound Ridge, New York 10576

40361

ACKNOWLEDGMENTS

For assistance in the preparation of the revised edition, the author thanks:
MIANA S. JOPP, Division of Tourist Development, Department of Economic and Community Development.

American Airlines—Anne Vitaliano, Director of Public Relations; *Capitol Historical Society*, Washington, D. C. ; *Newberry Library*, Chicago, Dr. Lawrence Towner, Director; *Northwestern University Library*, Evanston, Illinois; *United Airlines*—John P. Grember, Manager of Special Promotions; Joseph P. Hopkins, Manager, News Bureau.

UNITED STATES GOVERNMENT AGENCIES: *Department of Agriculture*—Robert Hailstock, Jr., Photography Division, Office of Communication; Donald C. Schuhart, Information Division, Soil Conservation Service. *Army*—Doran Topolosky, Public Affairs Office, Chief of Engineers, Corps of Engineers. *Department of Interior*—Louis Churchville, Director of Communications; EROS Space Program—Phillis Wiepking, Community Affairs; Charles Withington, Geologist; Mrs. Ruth Herbert, Information Specialist; Bureau of Reclamation; National Park Service—Fred Bell and the individual sites; Fish and Wildlife Service—Bob Hines, Public Affairs Office. *Library of Congress*—Dr. Alan Fern, Director of the Department of Research; Sara Wallace, Director of Publications; Dr. Walter W. Ristow, Chief, Geography and Map Division; Herbert Sandborn, Exhibits Officer. *National Archives*—Dr. James B. Rhoads, Archivist of the United States; Albert Meisel, Assistant Archivist for Educational Programs; David Eggenberger, Publications Director; Bill Leary, Still Picture Reference; James Moore, Audio-Visual Archives. *United States Postal Service*—Herb Harris, Stamps Division.

For assistance in the preparation of the first edition, the author thanks:
Consultants Dorothy Davis Lloyd, Managing Editor, the *Maryland Teacher* and Jean R. Moser, Coordinator, Special Studies and Programs, Board of Education of Baltimore County; J. Millard Tawes, Governor; Maryland State Teachers Association; Department of Economic Development; and Baltimore Association of Commerce.

Illustrations on the preceding pages:
Cover photograph: Johns Hopkins Hospital, Trans World Airlines
Page 1: Commemorative stamps of historic interest
Pages 2-3: Sailing on Chesapeake Bay, Division of Tourist Development, Maryland Department of Economic and Community Development
Page 3: (Map) USDI Geological Survey
Pages 4-5: Baltimore area, EROS Space Photo, USDI Geological Survey, EROS Data Center

Revised Edition Copyright © 1978 by Regensteiner Publishing Enterprises, Inc.
Copyright © 1966, Childrens Press, Inc.
All rights reserved. Printed in the U.S.A.
Published simultaneously in Canada
2 3 4 5 6 7 8 9 10 11 12 R 85 84 83 82 81 80 79

Project Editor, Revised Edition:
Joan Downing
Assistant Editor, Revised Edition
Mary Reidy

Library of Congress Cataloging in Publication Data

Carpenter, John Allan, 1917-
Maryland.
(His The new enchantment of America)
SUMMARY: Presents the history, resources, famous citizens, and points of interest in the state nicknamed Old Line State.
1. Maryland—Juvenile literature.
[1. Maryland] I. Title. II. Series: Carpenter, John Allan, 1917- The new enchantment of America.
F181.3.C3 1978 975.2 78-14892
ISBN 0-516-04120-7

Contents

Many generations later, the great flag (as large as a tennis court) still flies "through the rocket's red glare."

A True Story to Set the Scene

"IN TRIUMPH DOTH WAVE"

The young lawyer from Frederick had not slept all night; the noise and tension and excitement were far too great. Whenever the frequent flashes of light burst on the scene, he peered through the dark and tried to see. Finally the sun rose, and at seven o'clock the firing ceased. The clouds of smoke rolled away. Yes, he could make it out plainly now; a great surge of thankfulness swept over him, and he sat down to write.

The words that he wrote and the circumstances that inspired them must rank among the most interesting and significant words not only of Maryland but also of the United States as well.

When it became clear toward the end of the War of 1812 that the British invaders would soon attack Baltimore, feverish preparations were made to defend the city. The preparations were so thorough they even included hiring Mrs. Mary Pickersgill to make a huge American flag to fly over the principal defense point of the city—Fort McHenry.

Before the invasion began, the young lawyer from Frederick, Francis Scott Key, had gone to the British under a flag of truce, attempting to ransom his friend Dr. William Beanes of Upper Marlboro, who had been captured.

When the battle began he was still on board the American truce ship in the harbor. All day September 13, on through the night, and into the dawn, the great British fleet blasted the fort with tons of shot. The spectacular new Congreve rockets were used for the first time, and as they streaked through the air the sky was filled with an eerie red glare. When dawn came and the bombardment ceased, Francis Key feared that the British must have captured Fort McHenry. In the flashes of the bombs he could see that a flag was flying, but could not tell which one.

Then he saw in the growing light of dawn that Mary Pickersgill's flag was still flying serenely from the fort. The American defenders had defeated the British all-out effort.

The delighted lawyer sees his country's flag still flying.

Francis Key had a surprising reaction to the wave of thankfulness he felt. He seemed compelled to write a poem about this great experience, and the words came tumbling out on his paper. "Oh say can you see," he penned in a firm angular hand. Then he wrote the word "through" and crossed it out, continuing with "by the dawn's early light—."

The events of that night had indeed "preserved us a nation," as Francis Scott Key claimed in the final portion of his writing. In addition, those events, combined with the genius of the young Maryland lawyer, had given the nation its national anthem—*The Star-Spangled Banner.*

Lay of the Land

The outline of Maryland looks as if someone had taken hold of it at both ends and was tugging with might and main to pull it apart. The western portion has been stretched away, leaving the middle like a tightened rubber band, and the eastern portion seems to be splitting in dozens of places.

It probably is safe to say that the shape of Maryland is the most unusual of all the states. The total width of the state in one spot between the Pennsylvania and West Virginia borders is so narrow that a person could easily walk across it without stopping to rest. In fact, it is at this point scarcely more than a mile (1.6 kilometers)—the narrowest width of any state.

A large part of the country's greatest inland arm of the ocean, Chesapeake Bay, lies within Maryland boundaries. This inland sea has been described as "a submerged meadow." When the waters of the ocean crept in to fill the bay, they also pushed up the many, many river and creek valleys, cutting the shoreline into dozens of drowned valleys, or estuaries. For this reason Maryland has far more navigable rivers than any other state.

The most mammoth of all the estuaries of Chesapeake Bay is that of the Potomac River. At Point Lookout the 10-mile (16-kilometer) wide Potomac rolls into the 30-mile (48-kilometer) wide Chesapeake Bay. An odd fact of Maryland geography is that the entire width of the Potomac as far north as the District of Columbia is entirely within Maryland's borders, and the state line hugs the Virginia shore. In most river boundaries, the line runs down the middle of the river.

The 1,726 square miles (4,470 square kilometers) of Chesapeake Bay and Potomac estuary in Maryland, added to the rest of the state's inland water, give Maryland more water within its borders than any other state in proportion to size. These waters are dotted with almost countless islands and multitudes of peninsulas.

Other inland arms of the ocean include Chincoteague Bay, Sinepuxent Bay, and Assawoman Bay, all sheltered within the thin sandy arm of the treeless coastal barrier reef.

Maryland boasts a total shoreline that seems incredible for its size—more than 3,200 miles (5,150 kilometers) of ocean front, tidal bays, and tidal rivers. To this must be added freshwater rivers, ponds, trout brooks, and mountain lakes.

The Susquehanna and Potomac are the only rivers of Maryland on the list of major rivers of the United States geological survey. The Potomac takes so many big loops that some parts of West Virginia are almost entirely surrounded by Maryland. Twice the river bends so far north that it almost touches the Pennsylvania line. The Choptank is the longest navigable river on the eastern Maryland shore. Other rivers include the Patuxent, Nanticoke, Elk, Patapsco, Sassafras, Magothy, South, Severn, Gunpowder, Bush, Miles, Chester, Northeast, Tred Avon, Wicomico, Pocomoke, Wye, and Great Bohemia.

All lakes of the state are artificial; they include Deep Creek Lake, Youghiogheny Reservoir, Liberty Reservoir, Triadelphia Reservoir, Loch Raven Reservoir, and Conowingo Lake.

Technically, Maryland is divided into three major regions. The Appalachian region is a rugged mountainous area of the west. Backbone Mountain, 3,360 feet (1,024 meters) high, in Garrett County, is the highest point in the state. The Piedmont Plateau region is mostly rich hilly agricultural land. This region comes to an end at what is known as the "fall line." Here the higher, harder rocks of the Piedmont meet the lower, softer rocks of the third major region—the Coastal Plain.

This fall line extends up and down the Atlantic Coast of the United States, giving an abrupt fall to the many rivers as they cross from the Piedmont to the Coastal Region. Along this fall line many of the great cities of the East have sprung up, due to the waterpower provided by the falls.

From the fall line the Coastal Plain gradually descends to sea level.

FROM EARLIEST TIMES

Much of Maryland, at several times in the past, was an ancient sea

The Narrows

Right: Fossil beds in Calvert Cliffs (below) have been visited by many scientists.

bed. The sands and mud have been hardened into many of the rocks of the present day. Even coral specimens from these ancient seas can be found. At other times the ancient Appalachian Mountains were thrust into the air far beyond their present heights, then were worn down by rain and wind over the eons, only to rise again and once more be cut by rivers and streams. The only effect of the glaciers in present-day Maryland was to change the shoreline as the waters rose or fell, due to the melting or freezing of the great ice sheets.

The fossil remains of ancient animals are plentiful in the region. They include sharks, rays, crocodiles, shellfish, dolphin, tapir, elephants, mastodons, the ancient horse, and many dinosaurs, among others.

Maryland has one of the finest locations of marine fossils in the world. This is the Calvert Cliffs, running for about 30 miles (48 kilometers) below Prince Frederick and rising at times to 100 feet (30 meters) in height. The cliffs are different from those found anywhere else. These famed fossil beds have attracted scientists from all over the world. The first American fossil ever brought to scientific attention was a shell from Calvert Cliffs, illustrated in the 1685 edition of Lister's book on shells. The cliffs contain three hundred varieties of shellfish alone. One of the notable finds in this tract of natural history was the complete fossil of a whale.

CLIMATE

The seasons change delightfully in Maryland, without the great temperature extremes found in other areas. In the northern part the temperatures may reach 0 degrees Fahrenheit (-17.8 degrees Celsius) not more than once every three years. The southern part is warmer, which means that summer heat is sometimes oppressive, but the beautiful springs and long mild autumns offer great compensations for any short periods of discomfort.

The annual precipitation is just under 42 inches (107 centimeters).

Most residents of the state would agree with an early observer who wrote, "The climate of the ayre (air) is very good."

The Cumberland Road, later known as the National Road, was authorized in 1807 and construction began in 1811. Many covered wagons traveled over the Burnside Bridge on the route to settlement in the West.

Footsteps on the Land

The history of Maryland is notable for the key part played by the state and its people in three decisive wars. Maryland troops saved American Revolutionary forces from a disastrous defeat that might have ended the war with a British victory. An unprepared group of Maryland fighters may well be said to have kept America free in the War of 1812, and except for a crucial battle on Maryland soil, the Civil War might have been turned into a Confederate victory.

Even more important, however, is the unusual part Maryland has played in things of the spirit, in human freedom and dignity.

PRIOR CLAIMS

Not much is known about the people who occupied the present-day region of Maryland in earliest times. Some of their disintegrated skeletons have been found and a few of their relics such as stone bowls, pottery, and weapons have turned up. Very old prehistoric villages such as Moyaone have been studied. This place is thought to have been occupied since the early Christian era.

The Algonquin Indians, who lived in the region when the first Europeans arrived, had a tradition that they came to the area about three hundred years before European settlement began. Where they came from or what happened to earlier groups may never be known.

Early Europeans found four major groups in Maryland. Three of these were Algonquin groups: Piscataway, Nanticoke, and Pocomoke-Assateague. The fourth major group was the Susquehannock, a part of the Iroquois nation that had invaded the region and greatly disturbed the Algonquin settlers. Each of the Algonquin groups had a leader who might be called a high chief. However, the settlers gave these chiefs the rather exaggerated title of emperors. The main spokesman for the Susquehannock group was their chief general counselor.

There is an early description of the Susquehannock by George

Alsop: "A people cast into the mold of a most large and warlike deportment, the men being for the most part seven foot (2.1 meters) high in latitude and in magnitude and bulk suitable to so high a pitch; their voice large and hollow, as ascending out of a cave, their gate strait and majestick." This also is considered to be an exaggeration.

Many of the Maryland Indians built huts or bark wigwams of the traditional type, fished and hunted, and gathered oysters and clams; the huge shell heaps they left are still seen in some parts, such as the one at Popes Creek.

They made log canoes that were developed later by the Europeans into what was called the Chesapeake log canoe. This was carved to shape from several logs fastened together.

Indian basket and mat weaving was highly developed. Lord Baltimore once ordered 350 yards (320 meters) of Indian matting to carpet his house in England.

It is interesting to note that for the most part Indian "emperors" had short lives. Often some leader who wanted to become emperor would find a means of poisoning the ruler and taking over the throne. The Emperor Kittamaquund, who was converted to Christianity, had reached the "throne" by poisoning the previous emperor, and it was not long afterward that he too went the way of his predecessor.

There was much battling among the various groups. The Piscataway were hounded by the Susquehannock, who in turn were harassed by the other Iroquois groups, first known as the Five Nations and later as the Six Nations.

TRADERS AND COLONISTS

Just when Europeans first touched present-day Maryland is uncertain. In 1524 explorer Giovanni de Verrazano described the shore of what is believed to be Chincoteague Bay. Undoubtedly fishermen, traders, and others sailed by in very early times. By 1556, the Spanish, from their settlements in Florida and the Caribbean, had mapped Chesapeake Bay and named it Santa Maria.

Famous Captain John Smith is the first European on record to have touched present-day Maryland. In 1608, he came up from the Virginia colony and explored the Chesapeake, pushing up the Susquehanna River until stopped by the rapids. He called the place "Smyth Fales" (falls), and wrote about the "abundance of fish, lying so thick with their heads above the water, as for want of nets (our barge driving amongst them) we attempted to catch them with a frying pan; but we found it a bad instrumente to catch fish with: neither better fish, more plentyous nor more varietie for small fish had any of us ever seen in any place, but they could not be catched with frying pans."

In the late 1620s William Claiborne, also from the Virginia colony, began to trade with the Indians in Maryland. In 1631, he established a headquarters on Kent Island in the Chesapeake opposite present-day Annapolis for his far-flung trading operations in the region. This became the first permanent settlement within Maryland. Edward Palmer earlier had attempted to establish a trading post in 1622 on Garrett Island in the mouth of the Susquehanna River, but this effort failed.

About this time one of the leading English merchants and politicians, George Calvert, who had become the first Lord Baltimore and secretary of state to the king, took an interest in obtaining a colony in the New World. He visited Newfoundland but left because of the climate. He also went to Jamestown in Virginia and took a liking to the peninsula between the ocean and Chesapeake Bay.

King Charles granted Lord Baltimore a charter for this land and land on the opposite shore in 1632, but Baltimore died before the papers were final. His oldest son, Cecilius (Cecil) Calvert, became the second Lord Baltimore, and a new charter was granted to him for a vast tract in the New World. In return, Baltimore owed the king only his loyalty and two Indian arrows a year. There were to be no royal taxes, and the freemen of the colony were to have a voice in their laws.

When Cecil asked the king to suggest a name for his colony, he proposed to honor his wife, Henrietta Maria, and so the name Maryland came about.

Lord Baltimore was a member of the Catholic church, but he took great pains to show that he did not intend to set up a Catholic empire in America. He selected well-qualified colonists of many faiths, and about two hundred of them sailed for America on November 22, 1633, under the leadership of Lord Baltimore's twenty-five-year-old brother, Leonard Calvert, as governor.

Their ships, the larger *Ark* and the smaller *Dove,* have taken their place among the famous colonizing vessels in American history. Following the long route by way of the Canary Islands and Barbados, they finally reached Virginia after almost four months of sailing. Then they sailed up the Potomac and first set foot on Maryland soil on an island which they called St. Clement, later named Blakistone.

On March 25, 1634, the colonists solemnly took possession of the soil of Maryland. Catholics in the party set up "a great cross hewn from a tree" and celebrated mass. The royal charter was read aloud as the official act of settlement.

Leonard Calvert hurried to Piscataway, capital of the Indian confederacy, to make friends with the Indians. He had with him Henry Fleete, a trader, who at that time probably knew more about the Indians than any other man in America. The arrangements for peace and friendship that Calvert made with the Indians helped in later days to keep Maryland free of the worst kinds of Indian troubles that plagued some of the other colonies.

He arranged to buy the Indian village of Yaocomico; and the people of the village were ready to move out anyway because of attacks by the Susquehannock. The villagers even sold their huts (made of grasses, bark, and saplings) to the settlers. When the colonists came to Yaocomico, they found a ready-made community waiting for them as their capital, and they called it St. Mary's.

Colonists who came at their own expense received 100 acres (40 hectares) of land, known as "headrights." Those who brought five settlers received 2,000 acres (809 hectares). The wealthy who brought many settlers received great tracts of land which became manors. Almost from the beginning the colony prospered. It did not suffer periods of famine and want as some of the bleaker northern colonies had. There was a small war with Trader Claiborne, who

George Calvert, the first Lord Baltimore.

would not recognize the new Maryland authorities, but he was finally put down.

The colony set up a general assembly, began to build houses and scatter out into the country to take up the many grants of land. A state publication says they made "spectacular progress. The land was fertile; the great bay and many rivers teemed with fish; there was an abundance of game, and the Indians were generally disposed to be friendly."

A GROWING COLONY

For many years most of the life of the colony developed around the manors rather than cities or towns. Sixty-one large manors were established in Maryland before the turn of the century. One of these manors came to be known as the "Thumb Grant" because Lord Baltimore gave as much land to Henry De Courcey as the tip of his thumb would cover on a certain map. Many of the owners of these great estates lived in lordly fashion with hordes of servants and slaves. They made stately social visits to their neighbors, sometimes traveling by elaborate barges, rowed by as many as a dozen slaves.

The first change in this manor system came in 1649 when a group of Puritans left Virginia because of the high taxes and because the Virginia settlers disliked them. They began a new community at the mouth of the Severn River where part of Annapolis is now.

That same year, 1649, was an important one in American history because the colonists of Maryland pioneered one of the real acts of progress. For the first time in the world's history they provided by law for religious freedom—introducing freedom of worship to the world. Jewish people were not included in this act, but there were not many in Maryland at the time.

When Charles the First was executed and Cromwell became the English leader, the change caused much difficulty in Maryland. Claiborne and others tried to overthrow the authority of Lord Baltimore, but, unexpectedly, Cromwell supported the Maryland proprietor, and in 1657 Lord Baltimore and the Puritans, who had taken over the Maryland government, reached an agreement.

Leonard Calvert had died in 1647; in 1660 Philip Calvert arrived in Maryland as governor, armed with orders from the new King Charles II restoring the authority of Lord Baltimore as the proprietor. This had been done previously by Cromwell.

Thirty years of peace and prosperity followed this move. Philip Calvert died after only two years as governor. Lord Baltimore's son Charles then became the governor, and when his father died in 1679, Charles became the first of the Lords Proprietors to govern Maryland in person.

At this time tobacco was the most important factor in Maryland life—as one man called it, "Our law, our religion, and always our curse." Tobacco was so important it was used as money. Old figures show the cost of building a house as being so many thousand pounds of tobacco.

The great plantations remained the center of life in the colony. However, in 1683 an act was passed calling for the establishment of 31 towns. This was in the hope of increasing trade and providing customs ports to handle that trade.

In 1692 the government was taken away from the Calverts and a royal governor was sent to take over; however, the Calvert property

rights were not affected. The Church of England became the official government church, and 40 pounds (18 kilograms) of tobacco per voter was assessed to support the church. In 1694 the capital was moved to the newly incorporated town of Annapolis. St. Mary's City, the old capital, was abandoned. In 1715 power was restored to the fifth Lord Baltimore.

It was not until 1729 that the town of Baltimore was created. Three years later part of the long-standing, stubborn dispute about the boundary between Pennsylvania and Maryland was settled.

TROUBLE WITH FRENCHMEN AND INDIANS

By the 1730s, settlement of the western part of the state was well under way despite occasional raids by the Indians. Western Maryland had only a small Indian population, and the Indians used that region mostly as a hunting ground. In eastern Maryland the once powerful Susquehannock had long been driven out by their brother Iroquois, and the Piscataway had taken refuge with the Iroquois.

The French through their government in Quebec, Canada, claimed all the regions west of the Allegheny Mountains, and when English settlers began to move to the west, the French set up forts in some western areas to keep them out. To offset this, Fort Mount Pleasant was started in 1754 and later called Fort Cumberland. The young man who began this fort was named George Washington.

The French encouraged the Indians to be hostile to the English, and some settlers in western Maryland suffered attacks. The story is told of Jan Frazier of the Cumberland area who was captured by Indians. When the Indians found she was expecting a child, they raided another settlement to get clothes for the baby's layette, but the baby died within a short time. Held captive for nearly a year, she finally escaped and after many hardships in a 300-mile (483 kilometers) walk, living on bark and herbs, she finally reached the house of friends who told her that her husband thought she was dead and had remarried.

"The next morning," she wrote, "they had about fifty men,

women and children and a couple of flags . . . and away we went as a surprise party, blowing horns . . . singing, and dogs barking. . . . Nearing the house my husband came out very frightened at the parade . . . then coming near he saw me and grabbed me off the horse shouting, 'The lost is found, the dead alive!' . . . The second wife being a woman of good sense took it all in good part, wishing me luck and said she would come some time and hear me tell about my captivity."

The English became alarmed at the growing danger of French and Indian attacks. In 1755 they sent a leading general, Edward Braddock, to drive the French back into Canada. General Braddock was completely ignorant of conditions on the frontier and of proper methods of Indian fighting. He expected to ride into battle in his coach, using formal battle lines in the woods; he did not give the volunteers long enough to assemble, and had utter disregard for the fighting abilities of the French and Indians. Benjamin Franklin hurried from Philadelphia to meet Braddock and explain the difficulties to him, but he refused to listen. He was, of course, defeated and killed in western Pennsylvania, and George Washington, who was assisting him, had to lead the difficult retreat.

There is a legend that a Maryland man named Fassit from Sinepuxent Neck shot General Braddock in the back. This, according to some sources, was in revenge for his brother who had been shot by the general for disregarding his orders against fighting in the frontier method by taking cover behind the trees.

General Braddock did make one contribution to the frontier. Following an old Indian trail, he built the first military highway in the United States, part of which later was developed to become the historic National Road.

After Braddock's defeat the pressure of the Indians on frontier Maryland became greater, and refugees from the war crowded into

Braddock's defeat near Fort Duquesne.

Fort Cumberland, where George Washington was in command. However, little damage was done in Maryland during the remainder of the war, and the French were finally defeated in 1783.

GATHERING STORM

As the years went by, England began to make more oppressive laws, imposing taxes and duties and attempting to limit the trade of the colonies. Maryland joined with other colonies in an attempt to break down these regulations by more or less peaceful means.

The first act of open rebellion in the colonies was claimed for Maryland through the actions of the County Court at Frederick when it declared in 1765 that one of these laws, the Stamp Act, was not in force in the county. This act required the purchase of revenue stamps for several important articles. The stamps and effigies representing the tax collector were publicly burned in Frederick, and this burning was copied throughout the state. Zachariah Hood, the British tax agent at Annapolis, was forced to resign and flee.

In 1769 Maryland joined with other colonies, agreeing to set up an embargo not to purchase certain items from England until the Townsend Acts should be repealed. Enforcement of this embargo was stricter in Maryland than any other colony. The Townsend Acts were repealed in 1770, but other misguided measures were put through the English Parliament.

Maryland agreed to a second boycott of English goods in 1774. The Marylanders agreed to boycott any other colony not cooperating and by forbidding lawyers to sue to recover debts owed to British merchants in Maryland. British merchants lost half a million pounds of business in Maryland in a single year due to the boycott.

Maryland's "tea party" was considerably more violent than those in other colonies. When a shipment of tea arrived at Annapolis on October 14, 1774, the owner, Anthony Stewart, was forced by the people of the city to burn the ship, the *Peggy Stewart,* and its cargo. Delegates were chosen for the Continental Congress, and a Maryland militia was organized.

Burning the Peggy Stewart, *painted by Frank B. Mayer.*

"PRECIOUS TO AMERICAN LIBERTY"

After fighting broke out between the northern colonies and troops of the mother country, Maryland began to raise troops for their defense; the Maryland delegates to the Continental Congress were authorized to vote for independence, and the Provincial Convention declared on July 3, 1776, "that the King of Great Britain has violated his compact with this people, and they owe no allegiance to him." Maryland had declared its independence.

A convention began meeting on August 14, 1776. It adopted a Declaration of Rights and approved a constitution for the new state of Maryland. This became the first state consitution to be adopted by any of the former colonies. Thomas Johnson began his term as first governor under this constitution on March 21, 1777.

Meanwhile, one of the most crucial actions of the war gave Maryland troops an immortal place in military history.

General George Washington's troops were hemmed in by British troops in the Battle of Long Island, August 27, 1776. His army was in grave danger of destruction. He assigned the Maryland soldiers,

known as the "Maryland Line," to cover his withdrawal to Manhattan Island. Only 404 of the Maryland troops under Major Mordecai Gist were available for the overwhelming job of holding back the British army. Three hundred eight (more than three-fourths) of these men died to save the infant Republic, and Washington's troops made their escape.

Without the brave defense of the Maryland Line, the war might have been lost before it was barely begun. That is why the 308 Maryland men who rest today on the soil of Long Island hold a special place in the hearts of their countrymen, and why General Washington sincerely called their action "more precious to American liberty than any other in its history." Ever since this time Maryland has been proud of the nickname "The Old Line State."

Maryland troops fought throughout the war and distinguished themselves in many other ways.

When the Continental Congress was forced to leave Philadelphia in December, 1776, they took up their meetings in Baltimore until it was safe to return north. One delegate impolitely wrote of his host city, "If you desire to keep out of the damnedest hole on earth come not here!" However, a delegate from New Hampshire wrote enthusiastically, "Congress is now doing business with more spirit than they have for some time past. I hope the air of this place, which is much finer than Philadelphia, will brace up the weak nerves."

Maryland did not suffer from battles during the war. Only once was Maryland soil invaded. On August 29, 1777, British General Viscount William Howe stopped at Elkton on his way to capture Philadelphia. He stayed in the same room General Washington had used only two nights before and was waited on by the same servant.

In 1778 Count Casimir Pulaski organized Pulaski's legion at Baltimore, and this became a renowned fighting force of the war.

Maryland made a great contribution to the war at sea. Two of the American Navy's first cruisers were outfitted in Baltimore by the Continental Marine Committee. The wife of the recruiting agent for one of these ships, the *Hornet,* describes the scene when the new American flag was first raised over the *Hornet:* "The heart-stirring sounds of the martial instruments . . . and the still novel sight of

the Rebel colors gracefully waving in the breeze, attracted crowds of all ranks . . . and before the setting of the same day's sun, the young recruiting-officer had enlisted a full crew of jolly 'rebels' for the *Hornet.*"

A Maryland navy successfully patrolled Chesapeake Bay. Some of the navy ships were only small barges with crews of six to twelve men, while others were cruisers carrying as many as twenty-two guns.

Private armed vessels, known as privateers, were authorized by Congress. This, according to one historian, "offered to the enterprise and patriotism of the citizens of Baltimore an opportunity of acquiring wealth, while defending their commerce and protecting the people from the depredations of the common enemy. Under this act privateering became a business as well of fortune as of patriotism."

Two hundred forty-eight privateer ships sailed out of Baltimore harbor and other Maryland ports. When one of those privateers captured a British ship, they would try to bring it to port with a skeleton crew; if this was impossible they took off everything of value they could and burned the prize at sea. They were so successful in this that for many years the British called Baltimore a "nest of pirates."

Not all Marylanders were in sympathy with the Revolution. Some Americans remained fiercely loyal to the crown. These "Tories" were often severely dealt with. Of seven prominent Tories held in the jail at Frederick, three were hanged, drawn, and quartered. Others frequently suffered the loss of their property and the esteem of their neighbors.

By contrast was the revolutionary loyalty of such men as General John Cadwalader of Galena, who was known as the "flaming patriot." When he learned of a plot, known as the "Conway Cabal," to relieve his friend General Washington of his command, Cadwalader challenged the plot's leader, General Thomas Conway, to a duel. General Cadwalader defeated and wounded Conway. After the duel, Conway wrote a letter of apology to General Washington.

When the war's fighting came to an end with Washington's victory over Cornwallis in Virginia, another close friend of Washington

from Maryland, Colonel Tench Tilghman, had the honor of carrying the news up through Maryland to inform the Continental Congress officially of the great victory which won the war for the colonies.

IN A GREAT STATE

Mob action in Philadelphia in 1783 caused the Congress to move to the new Capitol building at Annapolis. And so for eight months (from November 26, 1783, to August 13, 1784) Annapolis served as the capital of the United States. During this period, General George Washington came to the Capitol building and, with his task of freeing the colonies accomplished, resigned his commission as Commander-in-Chief of the Continental armies.

In the joint capital of Maryland and the United States, the Revolutionary War officially came to an end when the Congress ratified the treaty of peace in 1784; Annapolis thus became the first peacetime capital of the United States.

Maryland played a prominent part in the remodeling of the national government into the form we have today. In September of 1786 a convention met at Annapolis and voted to request a new convention at Philadelphia for the purpose of revising the nation's governing document—The Articles of Confederation. This was the first official act toward the forming of a new United States constitution.

During the many heated discussions over what form the new government should take, one of Maryland's most persistent points was that the states that claimed large tracts of western land because of their original charters should give these up. Maryland had no such claims and felt that the smaller states should be put on a more equal basis. At length, of course, all states with claims to western lands finally gave them up.

After the new constitution came into being, a Maryland state convention ratified it on April 28, 1788, and Maryland became the seventh of the original thirteen states, with Thomas Johnson as first governor of the state.

Fort McHenry National Monument and Historic Site.

Yesterday and Today

One of Maryland's early acts as a state, in 1791, was to make a gift to the new country—the land which later was to be the District of Columbia. This included about 70 square miles (181 square kilometers) of territory and $72 thousand for buildings in the new federal capital. Originally Virginia also gave land for the new capital, but later Virginia asked for its land back, so that all of Washington today is on land freely given by the people of Maryland.

In 1797 Baltimore was incorporated as a city, and also in 1797 Baltimore began its long running series of lotteries to raise funds for the city. In that same year the famous U.S. frigate *Constellation* was launched at Baltimore.

In 1801 Maryland extended its suffrage so that "every free white male citizen" of voting age received the franchise—one of the most liberal voting laws of the times. In 1808 Fort Severn was built to defend Annapolis and a year later Fort Washington was constructed as the earliest fort intended to defend Washington, D.C.

By 1810, Baltimore, only fourteen years old as a city, had become the third largest city in the United States, its population having quadrupled since 1790. The growth was due mostly to the tremendous amount of foreign commerce in the bustling port. Stately masted vessels, at home in Calcutta, Canton, Buenos Aires, or St. John, crowded the harbor.

"LAND OF THE FREE AND HOME OF THE BRAVE"

Trade and the prosperity of Baltimore and all Maryland became more and more threatened by the actions of the British, who began to capture American ships and shanghai American seamen. When the government placed an embargo on British products, the merchants and shippers of Maryland faced ruin.

As early as 1808 the people of Baltimore burned 720 gallons (2,725 liters) of gin because the owner paid a British duty. After the

War of 1812 was declared, a Baltimore mob attacked a Federalist newspaper, torturing the editor and some of his friends. One was killed, and "Light-Horse" Harry Lee, Robert E. Lee's father, was crippled for life.

For a time, mob rule prevailed in Baltimore, and a British leader called Baltimore "the great depository of the hostile spirit of the United States against England." Privateering was resumed. More privateers were built and commissioned in Baltimore than anywhere else during this war.

Throughout the war, Maryland communities, mostly shoreland cities, suffered attacks or threat of attack. In April, 1813, Admiral Cockburn attacked Elkton and was driven back, but in May, Havre de Grace was plundered and burned. St. Michaels was attacked in a night bombardment, but survived by a clever trick. The residents placed all the lights up high on their houses, and the British cannon overshot the town.

The people of Port Deposit hurriedly put up a small fort when the British entered the Susquehanna River, and the local residents were quite insulted when the enemy sailed by and failed even to notice it. On August 31, 1814, British troops landed near Tolchester, attacked twice and turned away defeated; they did not know that American forces had just run out of ammunition.

In late August word came that the British had captured Washington, D.C. Major General Samuel Smith, Revolutionary hero and U.S. senator, was appointed to defend Baltimore. Funds were raised by popular subscription; the militia was called up; even wheelbarrows, pickaxes, and shovels were conscripted. Elderly men hurried out to help dig new fortifications. Maximilian Godefroy, French engineer, supervised the plan of the entrenchments. Local newspaper ads urged men over military age to volunteer for actual combat.

New batteries of guns were hurriedly set up. Ships were sunk across the river approaches to the city to keep warships out. The breastworks at Patterson Park were manned by 12,000 volunteers.

Then on September 11, 1814, Baltimore's church bells began to toll the warning that the British fleet approached. The next day the enemy landed 5,000 troops at North Point and began to march

The U.S. frigate Constellation, *launched at Baltimore in 1797, can now be visited in Baltimore.*

toward Baltimore. British commander, General Robert Ross, had boasted that he was "going to eat dinner in Baltimore or in hell." Conspicuously riding a white horse, he was shot and killed by snipers early in the attack. The spirited American defense caused the attack to falter. Meanwhile the bombardment of Fort McHenry had begun from the sixteen ships of the British fleet. The invading land forces halted to see the result. The most advanced weapons of the British navy had rained their fire on the fort and still it held. One observer wrote that it was "terribly grand and magnificent." The British were attempting to land troops when hidden cannon on the south opened up on the landing boats, and took a fearful toll of British forces, many of whom were foundering in the water.

After the bombardment had ended, General Smith was able to write to the acting secretary of war: "Sir—I have the honor of informing you that the enemy, after an unsuccessful attempt both by land and water on this place appears to be retiring. We have a force hanging on their rear—I shall give you further particulars in the course of the day. . . . P.S. The enemy's vessels in the Patapsco are all under way going down the river. I have good reason to believe that General Ross is mortally wounded."

Before the Battle of Baltimore, the United States appeared to be a defeated nation, with its capital in ruins. After the volunteers of Baltimore had sent the British stealing away defeated, in what has come to be considered the decisive battle of the War of 1812, the tables seemed to be effectively turned.

As historian Dorothy Hoblitzell wrote, "By such small threads does fate hang! Baltimore did not fall. The Americans were in a stronger position at the negotiations at Ghent and the peace treaty bringing the war to a close was signed on December 24, 1814."

A TIME BETWEEN

The War of 1812 had greatly upset the commerce and industry of Maryland, but recovery was not long in coming after the close of the war. The state was at the beginning of a period of growth and new development that might be compared with present times in its almost incredible activity.

Almost daily progress was made in transportation, communication, manufacturing, farming, education, the arts, and other important fields.

However, there were disturbing events during this period, and most of these had to do with whether or not slavery should be continued or permitted to increase. Maryland found itself in the very heart of this terrible controversy.

Baltimore was a center of the slave trade, illegal after 1808. Fast Baltimore Clippers brought their human cargoes to the city, from where they were sent to many points in the South. Lucretia (Patty) Cannon became one of the country's most notorious women. She and her gang of terrorists specialized in kidnapping free blacks and selling them into slavery.

Yet strong voices in Maryland began early to denounce the inhuman practice of one human being "owning" another. William Lloyd Garrison published his *The Genius of Universal Emancipation* at Baltimore in the winter of 1829-30. One of Maryland's most courageous public figures was Governor John Thomas, who denounced the power of the slaveholding counties.

By 1860 Maryland had almost as many free blacks as slaves; the farmers of the Piedmont area and the industrial and commercial interests all opposed slavery.

A strange period in the state's history was the rule of the Know-

Nothing Party. This party had been started to fight political wrongdoing, but soon it turned to violence and fraud to keep its power. Voters who tried to cast an opposition ballot might be beaten; there was even a battle using cannon and small arms between Know-Nothing supporters and Democrats. Stranger still, a group of Know-Nothing men from Baltimore attacked Washington, D.C. and were only put down with difficulty. Finally the state authorities were able to break the Know-Nothing Party's hold.

GATEWAY TO THE SOUTH

When the Civil War came, the sympathies of the people of Maryland were divided. On April 19, 1861, mobs attacked Union troops as they were transferred from one railroad station to another in Baltimore on their way to defend the nation's capital. Many people say the first bloodshed of the Civil War came in this brief riot. Firebrands were heard shouting "Capture Fort McHenry!" The fort had only a small garrison. However, the defenders used a clever ruse; they spread the word that a ship had brought 800 troops, and pitched tents in the fort's courtyard for these imaginary reinforcements. Rebel supporters did not attack, and some authorities say that this hoax may have kept Maryland from joining the Confederacy.

Because of its key position surrounding the national capital, keeping Maryland for the Union was essential to the federal government. The state was placed under military rule by Lincoln. Federal troops occupied Federal Hill and turned fifty cannon toward the city of Baltimore.

The first Civil War skirmish in Maryland occurred in May, 1861, when a Confederate party tried to capture the ferryboat near Clearspring. Cumberland suffered a slight raid on June 16, 1862. Troops of General Robert E. Lee invaded Maryland in September of 1862. They were delayed at the fierce Battle of South Mountain. The roar of the battle was heard in Frederick and the women of Frederick cared for hundreds of wounded. One of the wounded was a future president of the United States, Rutherford B. Hayes.

On September 17, three days after the Battle of South Mountain, the opposing forces met at Antietam Creek near Sharpsburg. This has been called the bloodiest single day's battle in United States history. More than 23,000 men from both sides were killed or wounded in this slaughter, which has been considered a northern victory, because once more the Confederates went south of the Potomac.

Confederate troops were in Maryland before and after the Battle of Gettysburg, and General J.E.B. Stuart fought an all-day battle with federal troops at Boonsboro on July 8, 1863.

The third major invasion of Maryland came in July, 1864, when Confederate General Jubal Early's army crossed into the state. At Monocacy Junction, General Lew Wallace, with fewer than 6,000 men, attempted to hold off 15,000 Confederate invaders. After a desperate struggle the Union troops were defeated, but the Confederate forces were delayed so long that Washington's defenses were strengthened, and this battle of Monocacy is considered to have saved the national capital from capture.

After the battle of Monocacy, Frederick was captured and forced to pay $200,000 ransom. Confederate troops swept on and southern sympathizers in Baltimore thought the city was going to be "liberated." However, the invaders turned toward Washington. They were delayed further, giving General Grant enough time to send additional troops to defend the capital. As a result the southern forces were turned back at Silver Spring.

Altogether, more than 70,000 Maryland men served on both sides in the Civil War—50,000 for the Union and 20,000 for the Confederacy.

A MODERN STATE

Maryland enjoyed ten years of fairly general prosperity following the Civil War. In 1867 Maryland approved its fourth state constitution, the one still in use today. The state grew and changed in many ways.

Antietam Bridge

In 1872 one of the several national political conventions that have taken place in Maryland was held in Baltimore. The Radical Republican Party chose Horace Greeley as its candidate. In 1889 the Johns Hopkins Hospital was opened in Baltimore, and ten years later Maryland boasted of having the first county-wide rural mail service in the country—in Carroll County.

Baltimore was swept by a tragic fire in 1904. Fire companies from as far away as New York City and Richmond, Virginia, helped the local fire fighters, but the blaze caused $125,000,000 in damage, with only $50,000,000 covered by insurance.

Another national convention, that of the Democrats, was held in Baltimore in 1912. This convention was to be especially significant in American history because the successful candidate nominated there was Woodrow Wilson.

During World War I, 62,568 Marylanders were members of the armed services.

Maryland created a unique record in 1927 by establishing the country's first permanent interracial commission. In 1934 Maryland celebrated the 300th anniversary of its founding. As a part of this celebration a handsome reconstruction of the old State House at St. Mary's was built almost on the original site.

In World War II, 6,454 of the state's people died, and a total of 250,787 Marylanders were in the armed services during that conflict, including 3,500 women.

Fort McHenry was appropriately the scene in 1959 and 1960 when the official flags of the 49th and 50th states were raised after Alaska and Hawaii reached statehood. Baltimore completed its $14,000,000 Civic Center in 1962, and held a Star-Spangled Banner Festival in 1964 to commemorate the 150th anniversary of the National Anthem. The ladies of Maryland made a replica of the historic banner, 42 feet (13 meters) long and 30 feet (9 meters) wide, to be hung at the Maryland exhibit in the New York World's Fair. Yarn for this flag was made at the old Dickeyville Woolen Mill of fiber that duplicated the original exactly; 35 members of the Baltimore Weavers Guild wove this into cloth on hand looms at home. The sewing was done as nearly as possible like the original.

The rapid growth of Maryland in modern times is illustrated by the new, planned city of Columbia, and the vast expansion around the District of Columbia and Baltimore.

THE PEOPLE OF MARYLAND

Maryland has been said to have a "distinctive genius of its own." This must certainly be due to its people, who, among other qualities, have been described as "magnificent in emergencies."

Although the state is still largely English in heritage, the original English settlers were followed by Germans, Irish, Italians, Ukranians, Acadian exiles from Nova Scotia, Czechs, Lithuanians, Polish, and other peoples. Descendants of some of the early Indian converts still live in Maryland.

The more than 500,000 blacks of Maryland have made notable contributions.

On the quiet islands of the Chesapeake, life goes on with many of the same customs of more than 300 years ago.

The description of a theater opening gives an interesting account of early Baltimore social life: "Grave matrons and stirring damsels moving erect in stately transit . . . arrayed in gorgeous brocade and taffeta, luxuriantly displayed over hoops . . . and faces so rosy, so spirited and sharp."

LAND OF SANCTUARY

Because of the principle of freedom of conscience laid down by the first Lord Baltimore, and followed, with interruptions, by his successors, Maryland came to be known as a land of sanctuary, where men might worship as and if they pleased. Even on the *Ark* and the *Dove* as the first colonists came to Maryland, religious disputes were forbidden.

At the time of its founding, Maryland was the only colony in America where Catholics were tolerated. Maryland was so significant in the Catholic faith that it became the administrative headquarters of the Catholic church in America. As late as 1806, more than half of the Catholics in the United States lived in Maryland. The first Catholic bishop in the United States, John Carroll, was nominated at Whitemarsh. Baltimore had the first Catholic cathedral in the United States, the first chapter of the Sisters of Charity, and the first national Catholic shrine.

With this record of religious freedom it is not surprising that Maryland has nurtured many religions and faiths before they took root elsewhere in the country.

Old Bohemia Church in Cecil County.

The Wye Oak

The Reverend Francis Makemie, founder of Presbyterianism in the United States, came to Maryland in 1683. The Rehobeth Presbyterian Church, 1705, is the oldest of its denomination in the United States. The church, never locked, is still in use.

The Sam's Creek meetinghouse near New Windsor is considered to be the first Methodist church in the United States. The Methodist church in this country was formally organized at Baltimore in 1784, and Francis Asbury was elected first superintendent of the United Methodists.

The name Protestant Episcopal Church of America was adopted in Chestertown, and Thomas John Claggett, born near Marlboro, was the first Episcopal bishop to be consecrated in the United States.

Still another ecclesiastical beginning occurred in 1819 when William Channing, at Baltimore, preached the sermon that established the Unitarian faith.

Today, whatever their beliefs, Marylanders can look back with pride on the traditions of true liberalism that are their heritage.

A fisherman proudly displays crabs from Chesapeake Bay.

Natural Treasures

Maryland has a distinction in the animal field not matched by any other state. The sturdy Chesapeake Bay retriever was developed from Newfoundland, otter hound, and other setter types into the only pure strain of dog ever created in the United States.

One of Maryland's most unusual "living" novelties is the Cranesville sub-Arctic swamp. In this natural history landmark are growing things normally found only near the Arctic Circle.

The Pocomoke River runs through the northernmost cypress swamp in the United States. The state tree is the white oak, and Maryland is especially proud of the enormous Wye Oak, the largest of this species in the United States and considered to be 400 years old. Maryland has a mixture of northern and southern types of plants. Most of the state lies in the eastern belt of hardwood forests, but it touches the northern and southern zones. Holly, magnolia, and sweet gum help to give a southern touch.

Many Marylanders would consider the fox the most important animal of their state. This is because of the popularity of fox hunts—any number of them still conducted in the formal manner of past days. Large animals are seldom seen in Maryland. Black bears are quite rare, and found only in the mountains. Bobcats are fairly common in the wilder parts of Garrett County. Virginia deer, rabbits, raccoon, opossum, and mink are found throughout the state.

Maryland is noted for one of the world's greatest concentrations of waterfowl. The Atlantic flyway brings Canada geese in such numbers that they can be heard for miles. Hooper Island has such an unbelievable number of wild ducks that many buildings need iron bars on the windows to keep the fowl from flying through them. The Blackwater Wildlife Refuge is one of the country's most notable.

The variety of birds runs from shore birds through the mountain types, including herons, plovers, sandpipers, rails, bald eagles, turkey buzzards, ruby-throated hummingbirds, Baltimore orioles (the state bird, bearing the colors of the House of Calvert), thrushes, finches, warblers, rosebreasted grosbeak, Wilson's thrush, and even possibly the snowbird.

Hunting is a popular sport in Maryland.

Maryland is noted for its supremacy in seafood. The diamond-back terrapin, growing increasingly rare, is considered the rarest and one of the most expensive of all marine delicacies—the favorite of epicures worldwide. Also world famous is the soft-shelled Chesapeake crab. As one Maryland resident said, "Our hard crabs are good, too."

Chesapeake Bay oysters are another renowned seafood. Chesapeake Bay striped bass are said to be "to Maryland what lobsters are to Maine." Cobia is a favorite Chesapeake Bay sport fish. The striped bass, or rock fish, is the single biggest species in Chesapeake Bay. Ocean City is famed for its white marlin and other big game fishing. Solomon's Island is another sport fishing center.

People Use Their Treasures

TRANSPORTATION AND COMMUNICATION

The barrels of 69 muskrat guns were used for tubing in its boilers, it took ten minutes longer on its first run than a horse did, and it wasn't much to look at, but it marked the beginning of a complete transformation of the American way of life. This was Peter Cooper's *Tom Thumb,* America's first railway locomotive. Until this time horses had been used to pull the few railway cars that operated in this country.

An 1835 school book carried the following passage: ". . . the most curious thing about Baltimore is the railroad. This consists of iron bars laid along the ground and made fast. One horse will be able to draw as much as ten horses on a common road. A part of this railroad is done. If you choose to take a ride . . . you will mount a car, something like a stage, and then you will be drawn along by two horses at the rate of twelve miles (19 kilometers) an hour."

On August 28, 1830, Cooper took his locomotive on its first trial run from Baltimore to Ellicott's Mills. The trip took an hour and fifteen minutes out, but only sixty-one minutes on the downhill return trip. The day of the "iron horse" had arrived.

At the urging of Philip E. Thomas, the Baltimore and Ohio Railroad had been chartered in 1827. Thomas persuaded the people of Baltimore that if they did not have a quick freight route to the west they might lose most of their trade to New York, with its popular Erie Canal. The first section of track was laid in 1829; the Mount Clare Station at Baltimore became the first passenger station in the United States. Later, when the Camden Station was built in 1852, it was called the largest in the world at that time. The first train rolled into Cumberland in 1842.

Maryland's highway system began with the buffalo. The Indians followed the buffalo trails, and the principal Indian trails were well known long before the time of the settlers. The Warrior's Path, the main route between North and South, was one of these. When Europeans came they marked routes through the woods by notching

Three Boy Scouts take a canoe trip down the old Chesapeake and Ohio Canal. The use of railroads for transportation diminished the importance of canals.

trees—for example, three equidistant notches on a tree meant a road to a ferry. A regular post route from the Potomac River to Philadelphia was set up as early as 1695. This became, roughly, U.S. Highway 1. In 1807 the Cumberland Road was authorized, and work began in 1811. This later became known as the National Road.

Passing through the Cumberland Narrows, it was a vital gateway between east and west, and at the time was the busiest thoroughfare in the United States, swarming with stagecoaches, lumbering Conestoga freight wagons, carriages, horsemen, and drovers. A freighter of the mid-nineteenth century wrote that he spent his usual night on the road stretched out on the floor of an inn's public room, with dozens of other travelers lying around. At the inn were 36 six-horse teams, a hundred Kentucky mules, a thousand hogs and a thousand fat Illinois cattle—all following the buffalo trail that had become America's first federal highway.

Today's superhighways crisscross Maryland like a spider web. Eastern and western shores were linked for the first time in 1952 with a 7¼ mile (11.7 kilometers) long engineering marvel—the Chesapeake Bay Bridge. The Bay Tunnel-Bridge near the entrance of Chesapeake Bay, although not in Maryland, placed the Delmarva Peninsula (Delaware, Maryland, and Virginia) on the main route between east and west.

Maryland's early growth was speeded by the fact that so many places could be reached by water. The kind of sailing ship developed in Maryland that was known as the Baltimore Clipper took the sailing leadership toward the close of the clipper era, from 1820 to 1850. Shipbuilding is still important in the state.

The first steamboat appeared on Chesapeake Bay in 1813. The many ferries crossing the bay and the wide river mouths have been a part of the Maryland tradition almost from the very beginning. The oldest non-cable ferry in the country crosses the Tred-Avon River at Oxford. This was begun in 1760. Local freight was carried between Chesapeake Bay ports in a fleet of sailing boats known as "Bugeyes."

Today the port of Baltimore handles a large tonnage of foreign freight.

Another avenue of trade has been through Maryland canals. The old Chesapeake and Ohio Canal was defeated, almost before it was finished, by the coming of railroads. However, the Chesapeake and Delaware Canal, opened in 1829, has remained valuable to the present day because it cuts as much as 286 miles (460 kilometers) from the water route between Philadelphia and other Delaware River and Chesapeake Bay ports. It is still an important link in the Intercoastal Waterway.

Maryland ranks as a communication pioneer because the fragile connections of the world's first telegraph line were strung across the state; the first official telegraph message was sent from the Capitol building at Washington and received in Mount Clare Station at Baltimore in 1844. The first newspaper published in the South was the Maryland *Gazette,* started in 1727 at Annapolis. It was the sixth newspaper to be founded in the American colonies. Today the Baltimore *Sun* must be ranked among the country's best-known newspapers. It has been responsible for many newspaper innovations.

Town and Country Almanack, published at Hagerstown beginning in 1797, has been one of the best-known publications of its type. It boasts that its predictions have been 60 percent accurate.

MANUFACTURING AND AGRICULTURE

Maryland manufacturers produce over five billion dollars worth of products each year. Maryland industries includes one of the world's largest steel mills, spice processors, the world leader in aluminum snow ski production, and the largest producers of tin cans, bottle caps, electric hand tools, high-tension insulators, and gas equipment.

The streams on the fall line and elsewhere provided water power for early manufacture in Maryland. Linchester Mill, near Preston, is the oldest grist mill in operation in the United States today. Its wheel began turning in the 1600s. By 1825 Baltimore had become one of the great milling centers of the United States, with sixty mills in operation.

One of the notable early manufacturers of Maryland was John

Chesapeake Bay Bridge

Frederick Amlung, who established his factory near Frederick and produced glassware of fine quality. One of his pieces is ranked with the most valuable glass art today.

Maryland took an early lead in the manufacture of pianos and organs. Best known of several Baltimore piano makers was William Knabe, who opened his plant in 1839. Matthias Peter Moler began a business at Hagerstown which became the world's largest organ manufacturing company.

One of the state's earliest industries, surprisingly, was the making of umbrellas. These were introduced from India as a novelty, and a Baltimore firm began to manufacture them in 1772. Before long there was a well-known umbrella slogan: "Born in Baltimore—Raised Everywhere."

Notable recent industrial developments include the astonishing growth of electronic and science-based industries. Maryland now claims to be one of the nation's principal science industry centers.

Probably more government research agencies are located in Maryland than anywhere else. These include the NASA-Goddard Space Flight Center, National Bureau of Standards, Edgewood Arsenal, Army Chemical Center, Atomic Energy Commission, and Agricultural Experiment Station at Beltsville. Another notable government installation, not in the research field, is the tremendous National Social Security headquarters in Baltimore County.

Although Maryland is one of the smaller states and has a comparatively small agricultural acreage, farm products still bring nearly three quarters of a billion dollars per year to the state.

Because of the 24 different major types of Maryland soil, many kinds of crops can be grown successfully. Major crops today are corn, hay, tobacco, tomatoes, and soybeans. Tobacco is Maryland's most historic crop. For many years tobacco was used for money, and for some reason Maryland soil grows tobacco that is lowest in natural nicotine content, making it much sought after at the colorful tobacco auctions in various parts of the state.

Due partly to the fact that tobacco quickly exhausted the soil, Maryland early took a lead in methods of restoring the soil by fertilizers. Guano fertilizers from Peru were first brought to this country through the Port of Baltimore in 1824. In the 1850s the chemical fertilizer industry developed at Baltimore.

Another traditional rural occupation of Maryland is the raising of fine horses. Governor Samuel Ogle brought to his Belair estate, near Bowie Race Track, two famous thoroughbred horses—Queen Mab and Spark. From these, many thoroughbreds have descended. The Glen Riddle Farm near Berlin was the home of War Admiral and other prominent horses. Naturally, of course, the state is also known for developing horses for its popular steeplechases.

FROM OCEANS, MARSHES, AND LILYPONS

Chesapeake Bay is noted as one of the world's greatest producers of seafood. Probably no other area of similar size yields such quantity and variety of sea delicacies.

Woodstock Farm in Baltimore County.

Baltimore became the chief oyster packing center of the world in 1880. Then the oyster beds began to be depleted. Today the industry is growing again. This time, however, oysters are cultivated in their beds much the same as other "crops." Maryland's skipjack fleet still sails and is known as the only remaining oyster sailing fleet in the nation.

Crisfield is the self-styled "Seafood Capital of the World." Many men of the shore area make their living solely from the water, oystering in winter, crabbing in summer, and fishing and clamming the year round.

One of the country's most unusual aquatic industries was the albino frog farm of C.C. Moler near Mapleville. These frogs were in demand by biologists and other experimenters.

Another unique enterprise is that of the Three Springs Fisheries at Lilypons (bearing the name of the singer Lily Pons). It is considered to be the world's largest grower of goldfish, water lilies, and other floating plants.

The flower filled marshes of Maryland have for centuries supported a flourishing trapping industry and continue to do so to this day (mostly muskrats).

Mary Pickersgill lived in Flag House in Baltimore.
In this house, built in 1793, she made the flag that
inspired Francis Scott Key to compose "The Star-Spangled Banner."

Human Treasures

FIRST "PRESIDENT" AND OTHER PUBLIC FIGURES

There is much to be said for the argument that a Maryland man, John Hanson, was the first president of the United States. In any event, he was the first man to bear that title. When the Articles of Confederation were adopted (Maryland was the last state to adopt them), the first of the articles stated, "The stile of this confederacy shall be the United States of America." The governing body was a congress, and this was to be presided over by a president.

In November, 1781, the Congress selected one of their members, John Hanson, as first "President of the United States in Congress Assembled." Because this was a different government and the president was not elected by the people, the presidents under the Articles of Confederation are not usually considered in the same line as presidents under the Constitution. However, if a visitor should wonder for whom the fine John Hanson Memorial Expressway was named and if he should turn off the highway to inquire, a Marylander might well reply with a twinkle in his eye, "Oh, he was the country's first president.

John Hanson was born near Port Tobacco in 1715. He later served as one of Maryland's first two United States senators, and he lived to the age of ninety-seven.

Four Maryland men signed the Declaration of Independence. These were Samuel Chase, William Paca, Thomas Stone, and Charles Carroll. There were several Charles Carrolls, so the signer, born in Annapolis in 1737, was usually identified as "Charles Carroll of Carrollton." Later he became the other of Maryland's first two United States senators. He was much opposed to slavery and was active in the early efforts to found the Republic of Liberia.

Charles Carroll of Carrollton lived to the age of ninety-five, and was the last surviving signer of the Declaration of Independence. During his long life he was noted for his many activities on behalf of both state and national governments. He was particularly influential in the fight for freedom of religion and government separation from

religion, and was the author of the Maryland Declaration of Rights. He turned the first shovel of earth on the B & O Railroad. When he died, he was considered to be the wealthiest man in the United States.

Roger Brooke Taney, born in Calvert County, became Chief Justice of the United States. He is known primarily because he wrote the Dred Scott decision, which many believe helped to bring on the Civil War.

Arthur P. Gorman was one of the most influential men in state politics from 1869 to 1895, becoming a United States senator in 1881. In 1892 he almost became the Democratic nominee for president of the United States.

A Maryland Revolutionary leader was well known for his unusual name: Daniel of St. Thomas Jenifer. He was president of the wartime Maryland Council of Safety and was particulary important in raising Maryland supplies to feed and clothe the Revolutionary armies.

CREATIVE MARYLANDERS

One of America's most distinguished literary figures was first recognized while living in Baltimore, and his life came to its tragic close there. This was poet, originator of the detective story, and critic Edgar Allan Poe. His *Manuscript Found in a Bottle* won a Baltimore literary prize, giving him his first recognition as a writer. His death in 1849 in Baltimore was mysterious. Some say that he was kidnapped by hoodlums during an election. They were said to have forced him from one polling place to another as a "repeater" voter until he collapsed and died. Poe was so little known at the time of his death that only one carriage of mourners followed his body to the grave in Baltimore's Westminster Churchyard.

Baltimore erected a monument to Poe and placed a quotation from his *The Raven* in raised stone letters on the monument. It reads "Dreaming Dreams no Mortals Ever Dared to Dream Before." A Poe admirer, Edmund Fontaine, said Poe wrote the word "mortal," not "mortals." In the dark of night he slipped up to the monument

and chipped off the offending letter "s." He was arrested but later released.

The state's official anthem was inspired by the riots in Baltimore at the beginning of the Civil War. Soon after James Ryder Randall wrote the poem *Maryland, My Maryland,* it had appeared in almost every journal of the South. Set to the tune *Tannenbaum,* it became a kind of unofficial anthem of the South.

Francis Scott Key, author of our national anthem, practiced law in Washington, D.C., was a prominent Episcopal layman, and was a United States district attorney under President Jackson. His *Star-Spangled Banner* was first published in the Baltimore *Patriot* on September 20, 1814. It was set to the tune of *Anacreon in Heaven,* as Scott noted in one of the early copies. It became popular throughout the country but was not declared the official anthem by Congress until March 3, 1931. As someone has said, "few songs have had such dramatic birth." Key also wrote the hymn *Lord, With Glowing Heart I Praise Thee,* but his only real claim to fame is the inspired verse that was wrung from his excited being on that fateful night in 1814.

H.L. Mencken, editor, author, and critic, has been called "Maryland's most important modern literary figure." He was born in Baltimore, and made important contributions in the development and study of the American language. He was the founder and editor of the *American Mercury* magazine, and he is also known as "the Sage of Baltimore."

Poet Sidney Lanier was a prisoner-of-war at Point Lookout in Baltimore. After the war he continued his literary career as a lecturer at Johns Hopkins University. A less well-known Maryland poet was Amelia Welby of St. Michaels, whose work was highly praised by Edgar Allan Poe. Another prominent early Maryland poet was Edward Coote Pinkney. His brother, Frederick P., was also a well-known writer.

Being written about in a poem made a Maryland woman famous. This was Barbara Fritchie of Frederick, the heroine of Whittier's poem of the same name. According to the legend, she was a sharp-tongued lady in her late nineties who flew the American flag from

her upper window and defied the invading forces of General Stonewall Jackson. The Whittier line about her, "Shoot if you must this old grey head, but spare our country's flag, she said," has been a favorite almost since it was written and made Barbara Fritchie a beloved even though somewhat dubious heroine.

Another almost legendary figure was Mason Locke (Parson) Weems who began his ministry at All Hallows Church near Annapolis. When he could not support himself as a pastor, he took to the road, selling books from a wagon and playing the violin. He collected stories and wrote many of these down in book form. His *History of the Life and Death, Virtues and Exploits of General George Washington* was his best-known work. In this he invented the still popular story of Washington and the cherry tree. The book has been published in almost eighty editions and still sells.

Other literary figures of Maryland include Sophie Kerr, Fulton Oursler, Evelyn Harris, William Eddie, and Martha Farquharson Finley, creator of *Elsie Dinsmore.*

In the field of art, Maryland showed early promise. The first record of a commission for a work of art for a public building in America is that of the St. Barnabas Church in Queen Anne Parish. Gustavus Hesselius was commissioned to "draw ye history of our Blessed Saviour and ye Twelve Apostles at ye last supper . . . Proportioned to ye space over the Altar piece."

Charles Willson Peale is considered one of the outstanding artists of early America. He was born in Queen Anne County. Frank A.

John Paul Jones *by Charles Wilson Peale. With great ceremony the almost perfectly preserved body of America's naval hero of the Revolution was removed from its Paris grave and buried in a crypt of the chapel of the Naval Academy in Annapolis.*

Warren received renown as a muralist. Maryland sculptors Emily Clayton Bishop and William Buckland are also well known.

In the field of music, Henry Dielman was the first musician in the country to receive the degree of Doctor of Music. This was granted to him at Georgetown University. At one time his compositions received considerable attention. David Creame of Baltimore purchased all of the available poems of John Wesley and created the *Methodist Hymnology* in 1849. Rose and Ottilie Sutro were the best-known duo pianists of their day.

BLACK LEADERS

One of America's most unusual careers is that of Benjamin Banneker. His father had been born a slave but bought his freedom and a 100-acre (40-hectare) farm near the Ellicott mill on the Patapsco River. Benjamin learned to read and write in a country school. His determination to learn all that he could may well be compared to that of Abraham Lincoln.

In the time he could take from the hard farm work, Benjamin Banneker taught himself mathematics, astronomy, and many related skills. He watched the skies for hours and worked out the most complicated calculations. The most remarkable achievement of this extraordinary man was his publication of a highly regarded almanac. This contained helpful information on phases of the moon, tides, and other materials requiring the most skilled kind of calculation.

Banneker became widely known in Europe and was respectfully called the "African Astronomer." Benjamin Banneker became the first black to receive a presidential appointment. This was to assist in the survey of the new District of Columbia under his friend Andrew Ellicott, surveyor-general of the United States. Another of Banneker's interesting accomplishments was whittling a wooden clock that proved to be the first clock work made in Maryland.

After years of harsh and insensitive treatment as a slave, Frederick Douglass, born in Talbot County on the eastern shore, escaped to New England in 1838 and became one of the most effective voices

against slavery. He lectured in England and became widely admired there. Returning to America, he published the abolitionist paper *The North Star,* became a member of the governing board of the District of Columbia, and later was a United States marshal, recorder of deeds in the district, and minister to Haiti.

Harriet Tubman has been called the "Moses of her people." After escaping into Pennsylvania, she managed to return and help members of her family to escape. Later she became so effective in leading other slaves to freedom that a reward of $40,000 was placed on her capture by wrathful slaveholders. She is said to have led as many as 400 people out of slavery. She became a Union nurse and also undertook dangerous assignments as a spy for her country.

Baltimore native Frances E. Watkins Harper was a prominent poetess, novelist, and lecturer. The life story of Josiah Henson is supposed to have been the inspiration for Harriet Beecher Stowe's novel *Uncle Tom's Cabin.* Cab Calloway, one of the most highly regarded of all popular musicians, was also a native of Baltimore.

OTHER MEN AND WOMEN OF DISTINCTION

One of the great contributions to education and world understanding of all time was made by a Baltimore man, Ottmar Merganthaler. With the help of Julien Friez, Merganthaler invented the Linotype. Setting type by hand had been very tedious. After this invention, books, newspapers, magazines, and other printed matter could be put out in tremendous volume at much lower cost.

At the Antietam Iron Works, inventor James Rumsey built many of the parts for the first steam propelled boat ever to run upstream. Fayette Gibson is considered by many at Tunis Mills, where he lived, to have been the inventor of the reaper, but his machines and models were destroyed in a fire.

One of America's most far-seeing and neglected inventors and experimenters was Robert Hutchings Goddard, now known as the "father" of the modern rocket. For many years Dr. Goddard tried to interest American leaders in rocket power, which he predicted would

become very important in later years. Many people considered him ridiculous for holding such beliefs. As early as 1926 he successfully fired the first liquid fuel rocket. He received some support for his efforts in Maryland and died in Baltimore in 1945. If more attention and support had been given to Dr. Goddard, it is probable that the United States would have been far ahead in the space race today. His name is honored in the Goddard Space Flight Center at Greenbelt.

America's naval hero, Stephen Decatur, was born near Berlin, Maryland. He won fame in the Tripoli War when he recaptured the American ship *Philadelphia* and later compelled the Barbary pirates to stop holding Americans for ransom. His bravery during the War of 1812 was legendary, but he is probably best known for his toast: "Our country! In her intercourse with foreign nations may she always be in the right; but our country, right or wrong." He was killed in 1820 in a duel with James Barron.

One of the most influential of all Catholic educators was Elizabeth Ann Seton, founder of the Daughters of Charity in America. She opened the first Catholic free school at Emmitsburg and founded St. Joseph's College for women, and became the first American-born saint.

A painting of Commodore Stephen Decatur by Rembrandt Peale.

The Reverend Joshua Thomas gained fame as "Parson of the Islands," as he went about among the islands of Tangier Sound in the little log canoe he called *The Methodist.* He was among the most successful of early evangelists in America. Parson Thomas is still remembered for his daring sermon delivered to British troops during the Revolution in which he predicted that they would lose the war.

No account of Maryland would be complete without further mention of the great American who, among a legion of titles, is known as America's most famous overnight guest. George Washington began at the age of sixteen a lifelong habit of visiting in many parts of Maryland. In his diary he carefully kept a record of the inns and other establishments where he ate and slept. Many a Maryland establishment is still profiting because they can use that familiar phrase: "George Washington slept here."

SUCH INTERESTING PEOPLE

One of the nation's least recognized and most remarkable women was another of the famed Carroll family—Anna Ella Carroll, often called the "unofficial member of Lincoln's Cabinet." She was born in luxurious Kingston Hall, where 150 slaves in green and gold uniforms ministered to every need. As Anna Carroll grew she became very skillful in writing letters and tracts and in influencing people. She believed fiercely in the preservation of the United States, and freed her slaves at great financial sacrifice because she saw clearly that slavery was the issue that might divide the country.

When it appeared that Maryland might secede, she wrote and distributed 50,000 copies of a pamphlet skillfully designed to oppose the Confederate government. Through her uncle, General Winfield Scott, she learned military strategy and was introduced to leaders in high places. It is thought that it was she who influenced Lincoln to suspend the right of habeas corpus in Maryland.

President Lincoln sent Anna Carroll to St. Louis to study the war situation along the Mississippi River. She concluded that the southern river fortresses were too strong to attack. However, she

conceived the idea of attacking the South through the Tennessee Valley and wrote to Lincoln and his advisers about it. Assistant Secretary of War Thomas A. Scott later revealed that he was instructed to put into operation the "plan presented by Miss Carroll in Nov. 1861 for a campaign upon the Tennessee River and thence South." When it appeared that Vicksburg could not be captured, Anna Carroll devised a plan to take it in a land campaign.

The influence of this remarkable lady was not revealed to the generals, who might have resented following the plans of a woman, no matter how brilliant. Lincoln often consulted with her. On one occasion he is supposed to have remarked, "This Anna Carroll is the top of the Carroll race. When the history of this war is written, she will stand a good bit taller than ever old Charles Carroll did." However, the prophecy never came true and the government could not give her either the salary or credit she deserved.

In the famous painting of Lincoln reading the Emancipation Proclamation to his Cabinet, there is an empty chair. It is thought that this may have been artist Francis B. Carpenter's way of giving credit to Anna Carroll by implying that the empty chair in the Cabinet should have been hers.

During President Garfield's time a bill was drawn up to provide for her "the pay . . . of a major general in the United States army . . . as a partial measure of recognition of her services to the nation." But her friend President Garfield was also assassinated, as was President Lincoln. The bill was never passed, and the tremendously valuable papers and writings on all of her amazing experiences disappeared. She became ill and spent the rest of her life as an invalid.

Today few outside of Maryland remember the Civil War "Assistant President" of the United States, a situation which surely should be remedied.

Another remarkable Maryland woman was Margaret Brent, born in England in 1601. On coming to America she soon became the first woman owner of an estate in America, accumulating hundreds of acres. She became the executrix of Governor Leonard Calvert upon his death, and is noted as the country's first woman lawyer. She is

also considered to be the first American woman to work systematically for women's rights.

Still another Maryland woman of unusual influence is Wallis Warfield, who grew up in Baltimore. Her courtship by the king of England and their later marriage, when he gave up his throne, as he said, for her love, has been called the "world's greatest modern romance." Wallis Warfield was presented to Baltimore society in 1914 at the Bachelors' Cotillion, and was married in Baltimore to her first husband, Earl Winfield Spencer.

In an earlier time another Maryland woman had married a famous royal personage. Elizabeth Patterson met the nineteen-year-old Jerome Bonaparte, youngest brother of Emperor Napoleon, and they were married in Baltimore in 1803. Napoleon persuaded his brother to give up his "commoner" wife, but their son, Jerome Napoleon Bonaparte, was born in 1805 in England. The Pope would not annul the marriage, but Elizabeth's family persuaded the Maryland General Assembly to have it annulled.

Elizabeth Patterson Bonaparte lived on in Baltimore to the age of ninety-four, always in the hope that her descendants might some day take the throne of France. It is interesting to note that her grandson, Joseph Bonaparte, became the secretary of the navy under President Theodore Roosevelt.

Thomas Cresap defied the people of Pennsylvania in a border dispute that would have taken away his land. When they captured him he was so strong that, even though in shackles, no one could handle him, and he became known as the "Maryland Monster."

After his return to Maryland he became one of the most prominent figures of the West. The Indians fondly called him "Big Spoon" because he ladled food to them most hospitably. Thomas Cresap made a trip to England at the age of seventy, married at the age of eighty, visited Nova Scotia at the age of one hundred and did not die till his one-hundred-sixth year.

Another vigorous frontiersman was Meschach Browning, author of *Forty-four Years of the Life of a Hunter.* When hunting became dull, he is said to have wrestled with a buck deer or boxed with a bear. He claimed a kill of nearly 2,000 deer, almost 400 bears, and 50

panthers. He was mourned by 122 descendants, and his favorite rifle is preserved in the Smithsonian Institution.

George Alfred Townsend gained fame as a Civil War correspondent and novelist. He built a weird house at Burkittsville on which he spent half a million dollars. It is said to have been a combination of a Moorish arch and a firehouse tower, both of which he admired. He also built a memorial to war correspondents which is the only one ever constructed for members of that profession.

A.J. Creswell, of near Elkton, is credited with introducing the use of the penny postcard while he was U.S. Postmaster General. Dr. John Archer of Aberdeen is remembered for receiving the first medical diploma issued in America. Another noted medical man was Dr. Philip Synge Physick, who performed a complicated operation successfully on Chief Justice John Marshall who was then seventy-three years old. Thomas Kennedy, among other distinctions, was one of the most noted advocates of Jewish rights in America, although he himself was not Jewish.

John Stewart Crossey and John Hart were among the noted comedians of their day. Each weighed over 300 pounds (136 kilograms) and they were famed for their parties in their Denton home, attended by prominent people from all walks of life.

Jacob Tome arrived penniless at Port Deposit, floating in on a raft in 1833. To get an education, after working all day, he rode on horseback to Perryville, took the train to Philadelphia for night school, returned by train, picked up his horse and arrived just in time to go to work. During all the time he went to school the only period he had for sleep and study was on the train. When he died, he left an estate of $3,500,000. He had already given $1,650,000 to the Jacob Tome Institute at Port Deposit.

One of the world's most famous athletes was a Baltimore native—George Herman (Babe) Ruth. He was known as the Home Run King, and the Sultan of Swat, and had a remarkable career in sports.

Above: Bancroft Hall at the United States Naval Academy, Annapolis. Below: Gilman Hall, John Hopkins.

Teaching and Learning

One of the world's distinguished universities is a pride of Maryland. Johns Hopkins was born in Millersville. He became a wealthy Baltimore merchant, and on his death he left $4,000,000 to be divided equally between a university and a hospital to be operated by the medical college of the university. Johns Hopkins University was incorporated at Baltimore in 1867 and opened for classes in 1876. It claims to be the first institution of higher education in the United States to adopt the true university form.

The medical school was begun in 1893. With the hospital, it has come to be regarded as one of the world's finest schools of medicine and as a center of medical research is generally considered not to have a superior. Principal figures in the growth of the medical school were Doctors William Osler, William S. Halsted, Howard A. Kelly, and William H. Welch—often fondly known as "The Big Four."

Distinguished research has been carried out in other fields at Johns Hopkins. Harry A. Rowland, first professor of physics, perfected a method of ruling diffraction gratings with as many as 50,000 lines per inch (2.5 centimeters). Ira Remsen began the research which led to another's discovery of saccharin. Remsen's Law, regarding certain chemical processes, was also a discovery of Dr. Remsen.

One of Johns Hopkins most notable and controversial students was the writer Gertrude Stein.

Another institution with a unique history is St. John's College at Annapolis. It was founded as King William's School in 1696 and is ranked as the third college to be founded in the United States. In recent years, St. John's made educational history and stirred much controversy by changing its course. The work at St. John's is now based on what is called the "Great Books" system of education.

St. John's was a men's college until recently. One of its presidents at one time suggested that young ladies might be admitted, and he was immediately dismissed from his position. On St. John's campus is Maryland's Hall of Records, repository for the state's priceless historical documents, including the ancient volumes of 1695 that

formed the basis of America's first circulating library. Francis Scott Key is one of St. John's distinguished alumni.

Another of the world's leading institutions of higher learning is the United States Naval Academy at Annapolis, founded in 1845 at what had been old Fort Severn. Franklin Buchanan, native of Baltimore, was the first superintendent. He later became the principal naval officer of the Confederate States.

Today's academy prepares future Navy men for a complex and unexpected world of rapidly changing scientific and military situations. They become familiar with such modern problems as the orbits of satellites and interceptor missiles, nuclear power plants, and missile submarines, as well as navigation and gunnery.

Those who are eligible for appointment may be nominated in a number of ways. Those who do not quite meet the physical requirements have been very ingenious in many cases. The story is told that one applicant, slightly too short, had a friend hit him on the head, and when the bump raised he was just tall enough. Other stories are told of applicants' drinking enormous quantities of water to bring their weight to the required level, and of other efforts.

Bancroft Hall is the heart of the student's life. This vast dormitory has everything from a post office to a dental office, including bookstore, tailor shop, soda fountain, a great galley, and an enormous mess hall that seats the whole brigade at one time.

In 1899 the old buildings of the academy were destroyed to make way for new buildings, and many historians were saddened at the removal of some very historic structures. A modernization program was completed in 1976, the year women were admitted.

In 1808 Dr. John B. Davidge was the leading figure in opening a College of Medicine of Maryland at Baltimore, financed by a public lottery. By 1812 this had become the University of Maryland. The university's schools of medicine and law are still in Baltimore. The world's first school of dental surgery was founded by Dr. Horace H. Hayden in Baltimore in 1840 and is now a part of the university. Headquarters of the university is at College Park. This was the home of the Maryland Agricultural College, which merged with the university in 1920, and the two institutions became one state university.

The educational leadership of Baltimore is illustrated by the fact that there are twenty-five colleges and universities in the metropolitan area. One of these is the Peabody Conservatory of Music. George Peabody, who made his home in Baltimore while a young man, provided $1,400,000 from his vast fortune to establish a school of music in Baltimore; over the years this has become one of the nation's foremost centers of music study and performance. Established in 1868, this was the first endowed school of music in the United States.

One of the many denominational colleges in Maryland was Cokesbury College, founded at Abingdon in 1785 and named for its founders, Thomas Coke and Francis Asbury. It was notable for the fact that it was the first Methodist college in the Western Hemisphere. It burned ten years after its founding.

Washington College, a small institution still operating at Chestertown, is notable as the first college honoring George Washington and as the only one which ever received his personal permission to use his name. It was founded in 1782.

The first free school in Maryland was opened in Annapolis in 1693, and some general provisions were made for public education in Maryland in the next year, when the Assembly passed an act for "the encouragement of learning." By 1723 schools had been authorized in all twelve counties, but there was a lack of qualified teachers.

Unusual distinction came to Maryland in the 1740s when the first Catholic school in the British colonies opened, in connection with Old Bohemia Church at Warwick. America's first Roman Catholic bishop, John Carroll, was a student there.

An act to establish public schools was passed as early as 1826, but only moderate progress was made until 1864 when the post of state superintendent was established and a state board of education was set up. In 1902 Maryland was one of the first two states in the country to pass a compulsory school attendance law.

It is interesting to note that the country's first choir school for boys was organized in 1870 at St. Paul's Protestant Episcopal Church in Baltimore by the Reverend John Sebastian Bach Hodges.

The Constellation *dominates Baltimore Harbor.*

Enchantment of Maryland

Maryland has been called "America in Miniature." This is because, while only a small state, it offers a large part of the variety of attractions found in the United States as a whole. Particularly interesting is the contrast of old and new. Much of the historical graciousness has been preserved. Among its greatest treasures are the fine old houses, found in numbers hardly duplicated elsewhere. Contrasted with these are such ultra-modern advances as the Goddard Rocket Center. In Maryland, advanced and modern as it is, visitors may still take a rumbling ride through one of its covered bridges and marvel at the colors of autumn's glory. Most visitors would agree with that first visitor—Captain John Smith—who called it "a delightsome land!"

Maryland is especially notable for its interest in sports, particularly some of the more unusual ones. It is the only state that has an official state sport (adopted in 1962). This is jousting. The state championship tournament is held in October at different locations from year to year. At tournaments the "knight" is mounted and armed with a lance. From his madly running horse, he must spear dangling rings with his lance. It is sometimes called tilting at the ring. Earnest jousters often pay very high prices for their skilled horses.

Horsemanship of many kinds is admired in Maryland. The first fox hunt held in America took place in Maryland in 1650. Riding to the hounds is still widely practiced, along with point to point races. There are four famous race tracks within the state, probably more than in any similar area. Pimlico at Baltimore is one of the nation's major tracks, where the Preakness is held, "the middle jewel of racing's triple crown." In 1877 even Congress adjourned to come to Baltimore to see a Pimlico race between horses of the East and the West.

Hunting and fishing are other favorite sports in Maryland, which is the only state with an official state dog—the Chesapeake Bay retriever. This is the only breed of dog native to the United States.

Maryland's northern and eastern boundary is possibly the most historic in the United States. It follows the famous route laid out by

the surveyors Mason and Dixon—the traditional line between North and South. The first marker of the Mason-Dixon Line may be seen where Maryland Route 467 crosses the border. Most of the original Mason-Dixon markers are still in place.

MONUMENTAL CITY: BALTIMORE

Baltimore, the seventh largest city in the United States, is proud of a number of "firsts": first national commercial railroad, first telegraph line, America's first architectural museum, first umbrella factory, first large monument to George Washington, and many industrial firsts—including the largest producers of tin cans, Venetian blinds, paint brushes, weather instruments, superphosphates, the largest processors of copper and bichromate, and straw hats.

Baltimore is sometimes known as the "Monumental City." The first major monument ever made to honor George Washington was begun at Baltimore in 1815 and finished in 1829. Today it is the most notable feature of the Mount Vernon Place area, said by many to rank among the most beautiful city squares of the world. Sculptor Henrico Causici created the enormous statue of Washington.

Another Baltimore monument is Battle Monument, built to honor those who died in 1814 during the Battle of Baltimore and the defense of Fort McHenry. Heroes of World War I are remembered in the two-block square World War Memorial Plaza.

The French war hero Lafayette is honored by a monument in Washington Place. Baltimore's renowned statue of Edgar Allan Poe was created by sculptor Moses J. Ezekiel. The only monument to Queen Victoria in the United States is the one at the Baltimore suburb of Pikesville. Among the unusual sights in Baltimore is the Repeal Statue, thought to be the only one ever erected in honor of the repeal of the 18th Amendment to the Constitution.

The Peale Museum is one of America's oldest. It was begun in 1814 by Rembrandt Peale to house his collections. It is now a municipal museum. The first practical use of gas for illumination was made at the museum in 1816.

The skyline of Baltimore.

The Baltimore Museum of Art, in Wyman Park, has a wide variety of masterpieces. An important part of its collection is the group of masterpieces donated by Baltimore philanthropist and art collector, Jacob Epstein. The works of Goya, Titian, Rembrandt, Reynolds, Hals, Gainsborough, and Jacob Epstein, the sculptor, are housed in it.

Another city-owned art museum is the Walters Art Gallery. Henry Walters, son of William, said at one time to have been the wealthiest man in the South, bought a million dollar collection of art abroad. He hired an entire ship to bring his treasures back to America and

built a fine structure to house his collection. He left the museum to the city of Baltimore.

The Enoch Pratt Free Library has often been ranked as one of the oustanding public library systems in the country.

There is a museum in the base of the Washington Monument in Mount Vernon Place, and not far away is the Maryland Historical Society, with its museum displaying one of the most interesting manuscripts of the nation. This is the original copy of the *Star-Spangled Banner,* written by Francis Scott Key. Other museums are the Maryland Academy of Science and Planetarium and the Natural History Society of Maryland.

At the Johns Hopkins Medical Center may be seen the famous painting "The Four Doctors" by John Singer Sargent. This shows the four Maryland medical men who were in part responsible for the growth of Baltimore as one of the world's leading medical centers. The center also displays a priceless collection of items illustrating the history of medicine.

The Baltimore zoo, a collection of more than 1,000 animals, is located in Druid Hill Park; it has a new children's zoo.

Fort McHenry was made a National Monument in 1925. Here visitors may see the flag site, the guardhouse, overlook, cannon, and soldiers' quarters, much as they were when Francis Scott Key strained his eyes during the night to see what was happening at this historic five-pointed structure with its 20-foot (6-meter) thick walls.

Mary Young Pickersgill's home has become a National Historic Site. Here at this Star-Spangled Banner Flag House the seamstress began to make the huge flag to be flown over Fort McHenry. She found there was not room in her house to finish the 42 by 29 foot (13 by 9 meter) flag, and she had to move the work to a nearby brewery to complete it.

Another much-visited home is that of Edgar Allan Poe. The tragic poet is buried in Westminster Churchyard. Green Mount Cemetery contains the graves of many prominent people, including Betsy Patterson Bonaparte, Johns Hopkins, four-time Maryland Governor Albert Cabell Ritchie, and poet Sidney Lanier. There, in an unmarked grave, is buried Lincoln's assassin, John Wilkes Booth.

The oldest house in Baltimore is the Mount Clare Mansion, town home of Charles Carroll of Carrollton. Not far from Baltimore is the main Carroll estate, Doughoregan Manor, near Ellicott City. This has long been one of America's most elegant estates.

There is much of interest for visitors on Baltimore's 25-mile (40-kilometer) long waterfront. Seamen from all over the world, speaking almost every language, add to the bustle and color of the dock area. Here also is one of the nation's most famous ships—the United States frigate *Constellation,* launched at Baltimore in 1797, now at rest from much warfare at sea. Visitors who step aboard to see the displays may feel a sense of awe at treading the decks of what is said to be the world's oldest ship still afloat.

Much remains in Baltimore of the city's early leadership of the Catholic faith. Baltimore, in fact, remains the Primatial See of the Catholic church in the United States. The first Roman Catholic cathedral in the United States was the Basilica of the Assumption of the Blessed Virgin Mary. Bishop John Carroll, first Catholic bishop

Stained glass depicting Saint Elizabeth Seton, canonized in 1975.

of the country, laid the cornerstone in 1806, and it was dedicated in 1821. Pope Pius XI bestowed the rank of minor basilica on the cathedral, indicating its historic importance to the faith.

As a center of culture, Baltimore has a unique history. Its social leaders have gained recognition throughout the world. The Peabody Conservatory of Music has long provided top musical education and performance. An example of this is the 1924 visit to Baltimore of Siegfried Wagner, whose father Richard Wagner had composed his *Siegfried Idyll* in honor of his young son. In his Baltimore appearance Siegfried Wagner conducted the Baltimore Symphony in music of both his father and of his grandfather, Franz Liszt.

The symphony itself has provided music for Baltimore and the state since its founding in 1916.

Memorial Stadium holds 50,000 sports fans who root for local teams. The Baltimore Orioles, a baseball team, and the Baltimore Colts, a football team, rank consistently high in their leagues. The Baltimore Civic Center seats 13,000 for major league basketball and hockey and other programs.

Oliver Wendell Holmes once described Baltimore as "the gastronomic capital of the Union." Most visitors are apt to agree with him. The fine cooking and restaurants of the city, especially for Chesapeake Bay's unique seafood, are internationally famous.

The city today might still be described as a writer in the 1780s wrote of it: "so bustling and debonnaire, growing up like a saucy, chubby boy, with his dumpling cheeks and short, grinning face, fat and mischievous, and bursting out of his clothes in spite of all allowance."

A modern writer from England spoke of the city as "more like London than any other city in the world."

LAND OF TRADITION: THE EAST

Maryland's portion of the Delmarva Peninsula, especially the region known as the "Eastern Shore" of the Chesapeake, is a land of tradition, showing the influence of its centuries of pleasant, quiet liv-

The Preakness Stakes, a horse race, is run every May at Pimlico.

ing. This tradition is remembered all over the area in many ways, such as is done at Chestertown in the annual celebration called the Chestertown Tea Party, when town and country houses are open to the public.

Old Trinity Episcopal Church near Cambridge is considered the oldest denominational church in the country still in use. It was built in 1674. Here is the grave of Anna E. Carroll.

Fairlee is noted for another of the oldest churches in Maryland used continuously as a place of worship. This is St. Paul's Church, built in 1713. Its pews were once rented for the payment of a stated number of pounds of tobacco. The Third Haven Meeting House, built at Easton in 1682, is one of the oldest frame churches in the United States, but services are no longer held there.

Bethlehem slumbers quietly most of the year, but experiences a rush at Christmas time when people want to have their mail stamped with a Bethlehem postmark. The Wye region has much of interest for visitors. The Wye House is the home of nine generations of the Wye family. Here is the huge white oak, largest in the nation, that gave Maryland its state tree.

The town of Delmar is divided by the Maryland-Delaware state line, which runs down the main street. Salisbury is noted as home of the National Chicken Festival. The principal fame of Berlin is that it was the birthplace of naval hero Stephen Decatur.

Maryland's main seaside resort is Ocean City, often called one of the finest resorts on the Atlantic coast. It has a broad, clean, sandy beach, magnificent surf, and 3 miles (5 kilometers) of public boardwalk. Ocean City claims the title of White Marlin Capital of the world. Frontier Town has a commercial amusement park patterned after the "old West."

Among the leading natural attractions of the state is Assateague Island, where the picturesque wild ponies still make their home. This is to be the Assateague Island National Seashore—one of the last remaining natural seashore expanses on the Atlantic.

Among the best-known annual festivals is Olde Princess Anne Days, featuring the noted old homes and buildings of the town. The elaborate mansion known as Beverly was the center of a plot to liberate Napoleon from his exile on St. Helena Island and bring him in hiding to Princess Anne. The former emperor died before the plan could be carried out.

Smith Island (named for Captain John Smith) is in Maryland's most remote archipelago, with its people living much as they did in the seventeenth century. The ferry from Crisfield brings only passengers—no cars—to this charming 300-year-old community.

THE WEST

Almost totally different from the Chesapeake Bay area is Maryland's most westerly county—Garrett. Here is Deep Creek Lake, with its 60-mile (97-kilometer) shoreline, heart of the state's mountain recreation area. Garrett County gained fame as the location of the summer camp where Henry Ford, Thomas Edison, and Harvey Firestone vacationed together to restore their energies in a natural setting. Presidents Grant, Benjamin Harrison, and Cleveland also preferred Garrett County for their vacations, and Oakland boasts of

A wild pony of Assateague Island.

the Church of the Presidents, where the chief executives worshipped. Camp David is in Frederick County near Thurmont. It was used by President F.D. Roosevelt and named "Shangri-La" by him. President Eisenhower called it Camp David, in honor of his grandson. It has also been used by succeeding presidents.

Wisp ski area, near Deep Creek Lake, is one of the few snow skiing areas south of the Mason-Dixon Line. Casselman River Bridge, part of the old National Road, has been named a National Historic Landmark. Built in 1813, it was the longest single-arch stone bridge in America.

Wisp ski area

Historic Cumberland occupies more than half the width of the state, where it is poised between Pennsylvania and West Virginia. Here is the first military headquarters ever administered by George Washington.

Hagerstown is noted for its progressive spirit. It is thought that the "traveling library" plan originated there when a two-horse wagon with outside bookshelves carried books to out-of-town readers. Also originating at Hagerstown was the "honor system" now used in many penitentiaries. This was first tried at the nearby State Penal Farm.

The Washington County Museum of Fine Arts, Hager House and Museum (showing articles of early frontier life), and the Hagerstown Symphony are other attractions of the city. Remnants of the old C and O Canal near Hagerstown are interesting to visitors.

The entire area of the most bloody battle of the Civil War is accessible by road, winding through the well-kept farms and beautiful, rocky countryside near Antietam Creek and Sharpsburg, almost unchanged since 1862. Here the American Red Cross had its beginnings. Nearby South Mountain was the scene of another Civil War battle. At Gathland State Park is the world's only existing monument to the Freedom of the Press, erected by George Townsend in 1896 in memory of the war correspondents who served in such Civil War engagements as South Mountain.

Other memories of the Civil War period are preserved at Monocacy National Military Park and Sandy Hook, where John Brown stored his supplies before the raid on Harper's Ferry.

When the citizens of Boonsboro decided to erect a monument to George Washington, they all pitched in, and the crude but interesting structure was completed in one day's work on July 4, 1827. It is noted as the first monument ever completed in Washington's memory and may still be seen there.

Fort Frederick, erected in the 1750s during the French and Indian Wars, is a classic fort of the period, beautifully preserved in a state park. The massive stone walls provided protection for hundreds of settlers who came there in terror of the Indians. A museum on the grounds displays relics found on the site.

Above: Grass strips are left on steep slopes to minimize winter and spring erosion. Below: Paca house and gardens in Annapolis.

Chesapeake Bay retriever

After Braddock was defeated, the elders of Frederick were disturbed because the young men of the town put on Indian costumes to show their displeasure with Braddock. This struggle between old and young has a familiar ring in modern times.

Two famous graves are located at Frederick. Peppery Barbara Fritchie is buried in Mt. Olivet Cemetery. In the same cemetery lies Francis Scott Key. In tribute to the man who gave his country the *Star-Spangled Banner,* the United States flag flies over his grave twenty-four hours a day in perpetual recognition of that other flag that flew both night and day and became visible in the dawn's early light.

CENTRAL MARYLAND

The first Maryland colony established under the charter granted to Lord Baltimore was St. Mary's City. The imposing simple building, erected as the first Maryland capitol, has been reconstructed as near to the original as possible, without disturbing the old graves. Parts of the original foundation may still be seen. This building has been called one of the few really oustanding structures of the seventeenth century in America.

Bricks of the original building were used to build nearby Trinity Church. In the churchyard is a monument to the first governor, Leonard Calvert, on the exact location where the colonists assembled to establish their first government. Another monument is the Freedom of Conscience Monument, commemorating that internationally historic event when Maryland gave to the world government recognition for freedom of religion.

At St. Inigoes is Cross Manor, the oldest brick structure remaining in Maryland. It was built in 1643. Another noted house is Hard Bargain. Tradition says that Gwynn and Tom Harris both wanted to marry Kitty Root. When she married Gwynn, he offered to build his brother a house if he would kiss the bride. They named the house Hard Bargain, and no one is quite certain which one of the brothers thought he received a hard bargain.

A replica of the old statehouse in St. Marys City.

Fort Washington is one of the most interesting of the older military centers in Maryland. It was designed for the defense of Washington, D.C., by Charles L'Enfant, who also designed the nation's Capitol.

South-central Maryland has several places associated with the plot to kill Abraham Lincoln. The plot is said to have been hatched in Surratt Tavern at Clinton. John Wilkes Booth hid near Bel Alton after killing the president, and Beantown was the home of Dr. Samuel Mudd, who attended to the assassin's broken leg and who was imprisoned for the help he gave.

One of the natural wonders of the region is the Great Falls of the Potomac, where the river narrows its flood and crashes down in a series of roaring cascades. Only a few minutes from Washington is the Calvert Mansion at Riverdale, built in 1802. Bladensburg, a Washington suburb, was the scene of many notorious duels. Naval hero Stephen Decatur was shot and killed there in a duel with James Barron.

Another Washington suburb, Bethesda, is home of the Naval Hospital and the National Institutes of Health, where public health research is conducted. At College Park, the buildings of the University of Maryland stretch along Highway 1. Of particular interest to visitors on the campus is the Herbert T. Shannon collection of antique tools in the Patterson Building.

Upper Marlboro is the leading tobacco center in an area where tobacco has been grown for over 300 years. Here was born John Carroll, first Catholic bishop of America, and his brother Daniel, one of the framers of the United States Constitution.

The Baltimore suburb of Towson is noted for one of the finest of old houses, now known as Hampton National Historic Site, showing fully the elegance of the age which created it. This has been called possibly the finest early house in Maryland. This was built in 1783-90 and was for 162 years the house of the Ridgelys.

Hereford is noted as the home of the Grand National Steeplechase. At New Windsor is the famed International Gift Shop. This is operated for the benefit of the Church World Service. Fabulous gifts from all over the world are sold at relatively low prices, for charity.

Detour is remembered principally as the birthplace of Francis Scott Key. At Union Mills is the grist mill (1796) and home which the Shriver family occupied for 150 years. It is now a museum of Americana. Frederick and Carroll counties are famed for the unique brick end barns found there and nowhere else. The bricks in these barns have been set in interesting and unusual designs.

At Emmitsburg is a shrine of Mother Seton, who was canonized by the Catholic church in 1975. The original buildings of her school, dating from 1809, are now part of St. Joseph's College.

Central Maryland is dotted with federal government installations. The United States Army Proving Ground at Aberdeen is one of the most important in the country. It has a fine ordnance museum. Fort George G. Meade, Andrews Air Force Base, and Patuxent Naval Air Test Center are other federal establishments.

THREE CENTURIES OF BEAUTY: ANNAPOLIS

Historical Annapolis has been labeled the genuine colonial city because it still possesses one of the largest collections of colonial homes—more eighteenth century buildings than any other city of its size. As someone has said, the city, founded in 1649, represents

three centuries of beautiful architecture. This heritage is guarded by an organization called Historic Annapolis.

Maryland is proud of its historic Statehouse, oldest in daily legislative use. Previous capitols were built in 1697 and 1706. The present structure was begun in 1772, and was the only colonial capitol designed to be the seat of government. The newer portion of the building was erected in 1902. A bronze plaque in the building shows where George Washington resigned his commission as Revolutionary commander-in-chief. In the Statehouse, also, Thomas Jefferson became the first ambassador to be appointed by the United States.

The dome, made without nails and held together with wooden pegs, is the largest wooden dome of such construction in the United States. One of the principal exhibits inside the Statehouse is the only official American flag known to have been carried in the Revolutionary War.

The Statehouse is the only one which has served as the national Capitol and in which Congress has met. In 1960 it was designated as a National Historic Landmark.

Visitors find much of interest on the shaded grounds, among the impressive buildings of the Naval Academy. The dress parade of the corps is a thrilling sight. In a crypt beneath the great dome of the academy chapel is buried one of America's outstanding naval heroes—John Paul Jones. His burial in Paris had been almost forgotten. Then Horace Porter became interested and found the body by a six-year study of old records. The body was brought to America through his influence.

Commencement time at the academy is most interesting. Sweethearts and parents are on hand in numbers. The familiar sight of the white hats of the graduating class being tossed in the air is always memorable.

It was during commencement, or June Week, at the academy that one of America's famous songs was born. Each year bandmaster Lieutenant Charles A. Zimmerman composed a new song for graduation week. In 1907, working with Midshipman Alfred H. Miles, he created *Anchors Aweigh,* the beloved anthem of both the academy and the Navy as a whole.

Maryland's Statehouse

Annapolis harbor

At St. John's College are many of Maryland's priceless documents. On the campus is the Liberty Tree, an enormous tulip poplar, considered to be 600 years old. Here the original settlers signed a treaty of peace with the Susquehannock Indians in 1652.

Another registered National Landmark is Hammond-Harwood House, a handsome Georgian home of fine woodwork and superb antiques. Matthias Hammond, who built the house, took such an interest in it that his fiancee broke their engagement because she said he thought more of the house than of her.

Culture and fine living have long been a tradition of Annapolis. The first circulating library in America began there in 1699. One critic complained that the city's first theater was much bigger than the church. The ending of a poem he wrote on the subject reads, "Here in Annapolis alone / God has the meanest house in town."

The Maryland Jockey Club is world famous, and the South River Club near Annapolis is the oldest social club in the United States. From the beginning, its members have been forbidden to discuss religion or politics on the property.

TERRESTRIAL PARADISE

In summing up the beauty and merit of their state, most Marylanders probably would agree with George Alsop, who wrote in 1666, "They need not look for any other Terrestrial Paradise to suspend or tyre their curiosity upon."

Handy Reference Section

Instant Facts

Became the 7th state April 28, 1788
Capital—Annapolis, founded 1649
Nickname—The Old Line State
State motto—*Scuto Bonae Voluntatis Tuae Coronasti Nos* (With the Shield of Thy Good Will Thou Has Covered Us)
State bird—Baltimore oriole
State animal—Chesapeake Bay retriever
State flower—Black-eyed Susan
State tree—White oak (Wye oak, Wye Mills)
State sport—Jousting (only state with an official sport)
State song—"Maryland, My Maryland," by James Ryder Randall
Area—10,588 square miles (27,394 square kilometers), including 686 square miles (1,777 square kilometers) of inland water but excluding 1,726 square miles (4,470 square kilometers) of Chesapeake Bay
Rank in nation—42nd
Greatest length (north to south)—125.5 miles (202 kilometers)
Greatest width (east to west)—198.6 miles (319.6 kilometers)
Highest point—3,360 feet (1,024 meters), Backbone Mountain
Lowest point—Sea level
Geographic center—Prince Georges, 4.5 miles (7.2 kilometers) northwest of Davidsonville
Number of counties—23
Population—4,782,000 (1980 projection)
Rank in nation—18th
Population density—371 persons per square mile (143 persons per square kilometer), 1970 census

Principal cities—

City	Population (1970 census)
Baltimore	905,787
Dundalk	85,377
Towson	77,768
Silver Spring	77,411
Bethesda	71,621
Wheaton	66,280
Rockville	41,821
Glen Burnie	38,608
Essex	28,193
Hagerstown	35,862

You Have a Date with History

1608—Captain John Smith explores
1632—Lord Baltimore granted a charter
1634—Colonists arrive on *Ark* and *Dove*
1649—Religious toleration act passed, Annapolis founded
1694—Capital moved to Annapolis
1696—King Williams School (St. John's College) founded
1729—Baltimore Town established
1754—Fort Mount Pleasant (Cumberland) established
1763—Mason-Dixon survey begins
1774—Brig *Peggy Stewart* "Tea Party"
1776—First Maryland constitution adopted
1783—Annapolis made temporary national capital
1788—Statehood
1791—Maryland gives District of Columbia to United States
1797—*Constellation* built at Baltimore
1814—Baltimore successfully defended, *Star-Spangled Banner* written
1821—America's first cathedral consecrated, Baltimore
1828—America's first railroad begun
1844—World's first telegraph line reaches Baltimore
1845—United States Naval Academy founded
1862—Battle of Antietam (Sharpsburg)
1864—Delay at Monocacy saves national capital
1867—Present state constitution adopted
1876—Johns Hopkins University opens
1889—Johns Hopkins Hospital opened at Baltimore
1904—Fire destroys property at Baltimore valued at $125,000,000
1918—62,562 Marylanders served in World War I
1927—First interracial council established
1934—300th anniversary of founding of Maryland
1946—264,000 Marylanders served in World War II
1952—Chesapeake Bay Bridge dedicated
1960—Maryland Statehouse becomes National Historic Landmark
1962—Civic Center completed at Baltimore
1964—150th anniversary celebration of *Star-Spangled Banner*
1969—Governor Spiro T. Agnew becomes vice-president of the United States
1975—Elizabeth Ann Seton becomes first American-born saint

Thinkers, Doers, Fighters

People of renown who have been associated with Maryland

Amlung, John Frederick
Asbury, Francis
Bonaparte, Elizabeth Patterson
Banneker, Benjamin
Brent, Margaret
Cadwalader, John
Calloway, Cab
Calvert, Leonard
Carroll, Anna Ella
Carroll, Charles (of Carrollton)
Carroll, John
Chase, Samuel
Decatur, Stephen
Finley, Martha F.
Fritchie, Barbara
Gist, Mordecai
Goddard, Robert Hutchings
Halsted, William S.
Hanson, John
Harper, Frances Watkins
Hopkins, Johns
Howard, John Eager
Kelly, Howard A.
Kerr, Sophie
Key, Francis Scott
Lanier, Sidney
Mencken, H.L.
Merganthaler, Ottmar
Molder, Matthias Peter
Osler, William
Oursler, Fulton
Paca, William
Peabody, George
Peale, Charles Willson
Peale, Rembrandt
Poe, Edgar Allan
Pratt, Enoch
Randall, James Ryder
Remsen, Ira
Rowland, Harry A.
Ruth, George Herman (Babe)
Seton, Elizabeth Ann (Saint)
Shriver, Sargent
Sinclair, Upton
Smith, Samuel
Stone, Thomas
Taney, Roger Brooke
Tilgham, Tench
Tubman, Harriet
Washington, George
Welch, William
Windsor, Wallis Warfield Simpson

Governors of Maryland

Thomas Johnson 1777-1779
Thomas Sim Lee 1779-1782
William Paca 1782-1785
William Smallwood 1785-1788
John Eager Howard 1788-1791
George Plater 1791-1792
James Brice 1792
Thomas Sim Lee 1792-1794
John H. Stone 1794-1797
John Henry 1797-1798
Benjamin Ogle 1798-1801
John Francis Mercer 1801-1803
Robert Bowie 1803-1806
Robert Wright 1806-1809
James Butcher 1809
Edward Lloyd 1809-1811
Robert Bowie 1811-1812
Levin Winder 1812-1816
Charles Ridgely 1816-1819
Charles Goldsborough 1819
Samuel Sprigg 1819-1822
Samuel Stevens Jr. 1822-1826
Joseph Kent 1826-1829
Daniel Martin 1829-1830
Thomas King Carroll 1830-1831
Daniel Martin 1831
George Howard 1831-1833
James Thomas 1833-1836
Thomas W. Veazey 1836-1839
William Grason 1839-1842
Francis Thomas 1842-1845
Thomas G. Pratt 1845-1848
Philip F. Thomas 1848-1851
E. Louis Lowe 1851-1854
T. Watkins Ligon 1854-1858
Thomas Holliday Hicks 1858-1862
Augustus W. Bradford 1862-1865
Thomas Swann 1865-1868
Ogden Bowie 1868-1872
William Pinkney White 1872-1874
James Black Groome 1874-1876
John Lee Carroll 1876-1880
William T. Hamilton 1880-1884
Robert M. McLane 1884-1885
Henry Lloyd 1885-1888
Elihu E. Jackson 1888-1892
Frank Brown 1892-1896
Lloyd Lowndes 1896-1900
John Walter Smith 1900-1904
Edwin Warfield 1904-1908
Austin L. Crothers 1908-1917
Phillips L. Goldsborough 1912-1916
Emerson C. Harrington 1916-1920
Albert C. Ritchie 1920-1935
Harry W. Nice 1935-1939
Herbert R. O'Conor 1939-1947
William Preston Lane Jr. 1947-1951
Theodore R. McKeldin 1951-1958
J. Millard Tawes 1958-1967
Spiro T. Agnew 1967-1969
Marvin Mandel 1969-1979
Harry Hughes 1979-

Index

Page numbers in bold type indicate illustrations

PICTURE CREDITS

Color photographs courtesy of the following: Division of Tourist Development, Maryland Department of Economic and Community Development, pages 9, 13, 15, 26, 37, 40, 41, 42, 44, 49, 51, 64 (top), 68, 71, 73, 75, 77, 78, 80 (bottom), 81, 83, 86 and 87; USDI, National Park Service, 10; USDI, NPS, Antietam National Battlefield Site, 16; American Airlines, Inc., 30, 33, and 52; USDI, NPS, C & O Canal National Historical Park, 46; USDI, NPS, Independence National Historic Park, 56; New York Historical Society, 59; John Hopkins University, 64 (bottom); and USDA, Soil Conservation Service, Branstead, 80 (top).

Illustrations on pages 21, 24, and back cover by Len W. Meents.

ABOUT THE AUTHOR

With the publication of his first book for school use when he was twenty, **Allan Carpenter** began a career as an author that has spanned more than 135 books. After teaching in the public schools of Des Moines, Mr. Carpenter began his career as an educational publisher at the age of twenty-one when he founded the magazine *Teachers Digest.* In the field of educational periodicals, he was responsible for many innovations. During his many years in publishing, he has perfected a highly organized approach to handling large volumes of factual material: after extensive traveling and having collected all possible materials, he systematically reviews and organizes everything. From his apartment high in Chicago's John Hancock Building, Allan recalls, "My collection and assimilation of materials on the states and countries began before the publication of my first book." Allan is the founder of Carpenter Publishing House and of Infordata International, Inc., publishers of *Issues in Education* and *Index to U. S. Government Periodicals.* When he is not writing or traveling, his principal avocation is music. He has been the principal bassist of many symphonies, and he managed the country's leading non-professional symphony for twenty-five years.